With warmest regards
Wesley L. Gould

AF677622

International Law and the Social Sciences

International Law and the Social Sciences

By Wesley L. Gould and Michael Barkun

Princeton University Press, Princeton, N.J. 1970

Copyright © 1970 by Princeton University Press
ALL RIGHTS RESERVED
Library of Congress Card: 77-90948
ISBN 0-691-07530-1

This book has been composed in Linotype Granjon

Printed in the United States of America
by Princeton University Press

To Richard C. Snyder

Table of Contents

Table of Contents

Preface

Is INTERNATIONAL law insignificant, secondary, impotent? Is it merely a product of the relations between states and, therefore, an instrument of no value in efforts to produce a more orderly, less violent world? Is there no feedback from international legal norms that can so assist a transition away from international entropy or chaos that the law itself becomes one cause of order and one indispensable instrument for the nonviolent management of conflict? Is law so tied up with individual cases that it cannot contribute to an upgrading of aggregative justice for nations and their aspiring millions? Are power, threat, deterrence, shrewd bargaining, propaganda, organization, and political manipulation sufficient routes to self-realization and avoidance of frustration in international affairs?

To those writers—and they are many—who give affirmative answers to such questions, we respond that their arguments must have been heard frequently during the Dark Ages even while the evolving law of the land was spreading over wider areas among then diverse peoples. But, unlike the scholars of the Dark Ages who may have despaired about the utility of law, today's intellectuals have both historical records and a variety of analytical tools and concepts with which to identify and evaluate the functions of law in societal development. Unfortunately, much still needs to be done to combine the knowledge of legal procedures, legal norms, and lawmaking processes with the tools and concepts of modern social science. Not only is there need for individual scholars to develop the capability of interrelating the concepts and findings of different disciplines, but there is also need for university teaching and structures within the university to organize research and to facilitate cooperative work by scholars possessing complementary skills.

As they proceed from an introductory overview to increasingly specific problems, the paragraphs and chapters that follow provide suggestions for integrating approaches to law and social science in ways that can probe closer to the core of the contemporary international system than does the traditional legal literature. As one political scientist says, "International law has been both more eulogized and derided than studied."* We prefer that future expenditure of energy be upon study.

IN OUR dedication we have expressed our appreciation to Richard C. Snyder who made it possible for us to get together to produce this study. For similar reasons we are especially indebted to Victor G. Rosenblum for his continuing and invaluable support. Particular thanks are due to the American Society of International Law for its sponsorship of this undertaking and to its Executive Directors, H. C. L. Merillat and Stephen M. Schwebel, and its Assistant Director, Richard W. Edwards, Jr., for the many things that they have done to facilitate this project. For reading the manuscript and providing useful suggestions we are grateful to Brunson MacChesney, who also had a role in the initiation of the project, William D. Coplin, Percy E. Corbett, Harold D. Lasswell, Myres S. McDougal, John R. Raser, Oscar Schachter, and Donald A. Strickland. Our typists were Harriet Kay of Evanston, who prepared the basic draft, and Patricia Anne Woodruff of Detroit, who prepared the final version. Far more people than can be listed provided us with information concern-

* Frederick H. Hartmann, *The Relations of Nations*, 2nd edn. (New York: Macmillan, 1962), p. 111.

ing their work in progress, and we hope that in our text we have taken account of their assistance in some appropriate measure. To our wives, Jean and Janet, we can say only that there is no way of saying adequately how much has depended on them.

Wesley L. Gould
Michael Barkun

Introduction

THE CURRENT radical transformation in legal studies has reached the field of international law, and there is no doubt that this admirable presentation by Professors Gould and Barkun will provide both a guide and an incentive to teachers, researchers, and practitioners who are sensitive to the changing climate of opinion and judgment. For years we have been told that the legalistic approach to the legal process is unnecessarily sterile and that a new birth of relevance calls for full account to be taken of the findings and procedures of the rapidly expanding social and behavioral sciences. Proclamations of the importance of this development are not rare. It has, nevertheless, been unusual for monographs, treatises, or textbooks to execute a sample project. Professors Gould and Barkun, sponsored by the appropriate instrument of The American Society of International Law, have prepared a study that stands somewhere between an innovating treatise and a textbook. Their eyes have swept the range of international law and dealt with selected topics in sufficient detail to furnish a sound basis for the choice of questions likely to yield useful answers if re-examined in a richer factual context. The book lends itself to surveys of the legal component of the international decision process and is a welcome addition to the otherwise sparsely populated shelf of professional tools helpful to beginners and veterans alike.

The principal opportunity open to any integrator of international law and the social sciences is to find conceptual and terminological devices that help to elucidate how they are inescapably connected in the world community. The fundamental point is the crucial fact of social process, which is the fact of *interaction*. An interaction is much more than physical confrontation. The actors do not usually bump into one another like billiard balls; rather, they modify behavior by affecting one another's perspectives of past, present, and future events. Since thought, communication, and collaboration are component elements of an interaction, and since legal patterns combine the same elements, it is obvious why any useful conception of international law implies the use of complex indicators of each dimension.

As Gould and Barkun show, the legal component of world social process is accessible to empirical study by the use of indices of the types common to all the social and behavioral sciences. The indicators include words, as when it is alleged that a multilateral treaty has been ratified and that it provides evidence of prevailing expectations about which norms are to be accepted and applied in contingent circumstances. Words, however, are not enough to establish the presence of a legal pattern; we know that "articulated norms" are unreliable predictors of overt acts. Actual deeds must be observed in order to establish the degree of concurrence between words and deeds that is essential to warrant the use of the term "law." The significant point is not to obtain general agreement about the specific frequencies to be insisted upon in "law." All that is needed is simple precision of reference, since this permits definitions to be translated into one another. It is also important to recognize the uselessness of attempting to limit the "law" to "articulated norms" on the one hand or to "overt acts" on the other.

The authors effectively mobilize data from primitive societies to show that many gradations are to be found in the institutional patterns of effective norms. Hence they make it obvious that many traditional arguments about the presence or absence of law, especially in the world arena, rest on "either–or" assumptions that impede clarity. Effective norms do *not* necessarily depend on the declarations of a centralized and specialized body acting as a "legislature," or on the activities of a centralized and specialized "police force" responsible for putting norms into effect. Neither among tribes nor among nation states do effective norms necessarily depend on such institutions. To imagine that these structures must exist in a legal system is to ignore the formative phases of what, under some circumstances, may become a fully centralized decision-making process. Such a view condemns one's approach to international law to futility.

And it is not necessary to postpone the investigation of legal institutions until a comprehensive corpus of authoritative and controlling prescription is enforced throughout the entire world arena. The facts of life allow varying degrees of comprehensiveness at different universal and regional levels.

Gould and Barkun are properly insistent on the point that the interactionist approach of the social sciences is contextual. To process contextually is to search for a theoretical formulation that identifies international law within a comprehensive, hence systematic, map of the world social process. It gives prominence to models that depict the flow of authoritative and controlling decisions. Since the traditional study of international law has been neglectful of this viewpoint, the authors have wisely selected "bridge topics" to demonstrate why a contextual technique is important to practitioners as well as teachers and researchers. Anyone who fails to perceive the factors that limit his traditional tools is less than a master of his instruments and is almost certain to overlook novel possibilities that would occur to him if his assumptions were less culture-bound.

The international lawyer of today is functioning in the midst of a crisis situation where much more is expected of him than of most lawyers. His position has much in common with that of a lawyer in an ex-colonial or a developing nation where, since pressing problems are constitutive, the body politic needs to develop an allocation of authority and control that succeeds in mobilizing the motives, behaviors, and physical resources required to consolidate and maintain a functioning system of public order. In many cases the legal arrangements of the former imperial master—British, French, or what not—no longer correspond to the dominant realities of power. The new coalition of effective forces may be composed of the elites of nomadic or sedentary tribes, the landlords and peasants of a feudal structure of society, or the new commercial, manufacturing, scientific, and educational groups who have partially incorporated the routines of the universalizing civilization of science-based technology. A legal counsellor must look after particular clients while contributing where possible to the growth of an inclusive system of public order. Acting on behalf of clients he must walk a tight rope between public presentations and private negotiations. The "third-party tribunal" composed of authorized decision-makers for the community may not make the decisions that stick. The effective decision-makers must be dealt with by negotiation. In many ways the role of the counsellor in such circumstances is parallel to the part that is regularly played by counsel in many transnational controversies in which governmental and non-governmental parties make important decisions according to complex expectations about the net advantages of maintaining a less than comprehensive system of public order. At the same time there is widespread recognition of the disastrous perils of an inadequate system of public order, and a demand that all who have expert knowledge of the world situation, including international lawyers, initiate more action to improve the institutions of authoritative and controlling decision.

The authors call attention to several pioneering studies that connect legal processes with factors of culture, class, interest, personality, and crisis level in the world community. Once traditional blinders concerning useful ways of thinking about law have been removed, an extraordinarily rich terrain is visible for cultivation. It is pertinent, for instance, to examine the norms proclaimed in the treaties of a given period and to discover how many articulated prescriptions are actually put into effect in the appropriate contingencies. Relevant indicators—often quantitative—refer to the texts of bilateral and multilateral treaties, the judgments and opinions of international or nation-state tribunals confronted by controversies that involve transnational prescriptions, the content analysis of statements made in national or transnational forums, and so on.

No informed person can examine the researches mentioned in the present book without recognizing how scanty are the studies that summarize the significant trends of decision that comprise the distinctive frame of reference of international law. Equally evident is the paucity of inquiries that are directly responsive to the scientific questions involved, namely, the constellation of factors that account for the flow of decision or that provide a critical projection of future developments, policy alternatives, or postulated goals for the world community.

In view of the magnitude of their task, it would be too much to expect Gould and Barkun to give attention to the future organization of university, professional, and official activity in forms adequate to the challenge. We have, as yet, made little progress toward providing for a continuing set of public and private operations adequate to the performance of the intelligence and appraisal functions that, when properly conceived, are components of the total decision process of any legal system—universal, general, or local. The concluding chapter, when systematically worked out, provides a clue to the value-institution sectors of the world community that invite professional effort. For lack of continuing application of a contextual and problem-oriented view of law, a number of urgent issues have hitherto received a modicum of attention.

The panels of The Board of Review and Development of The American Society of International Law, together with some university centers of research and policy, are pointing in the right direction. Gould and Barkun's book is a giant signpost and an indispensable roadmap. The presentation is as valuable to social scientists as it is bound to be to law teachers, students, researchers, and practitioners who concern themselves with the institution-building tasks of public and civic order.

Harold D. Lasswell

International Law and the Social Sciences

Chapter I: The Significance of the Social Sciences for International Law

In a number of his discussions of the evolution of mathematics, John Von Neumann noted a recurrent process of renewal of creativity:[1] when a particular segment of mathematics had drawn to itself the efforts of many mathematicians whose use of an essentially common approach or methodology had produced a thorough exploration of the nooks and crannies of that segment, a condition was arrived at in which technical proficiency abounded but no significant new contributions to knowledge were made. For a discipline to reach such a condition is not of itself a misfortune. For it is the purpose of scientific effort to render itself obsolete or at least to render commonplace the intellectual manipulations that were once pioneering.[2] Only continuation of the condition of sterility is to be regretted, less because it may lead to intellectual passivity than because keen minds may encounter frustration. At this stage, according to Von Neumann, those mathematicians who step back from their specialty to survey the field as a whole and to develop new combinations of ideas restore creativity and perhaps even develop a new subfield of mathematics.

To an important degree this has been happening in the social sciences. Today's pioneering entails an examination of both the social and the natural sciences to seek and to find ap-

[1] John Von Neumann, "The Mathematician," in R. B. Heywood (ed.), *The Works of the Mind* (Chicago: University of Chicago Press, 1947), p. 196; von D. Hilbert, "Mathematische Probleme," in Richard Bellman (ed.), *A Collection of Mathematical Classics* (New York: Dover, 1961); Alvin M. Weinberg, "But is the Teacher Also a Citizen?," in Boyd R. Keenan (ed.), *Science and the University* (New York and London: Columbia University Press, 1966), pp. 162-78.

[2] Thomas Kuhn, *The Structure of Scientific Revolutions* (Chicago and London: University of Chicago Press, 1962), chaps. VII, VIII, IX.

proaches, points of view, methods, and data that will broaden and deepen our knowledge of man and of human society. Joint appointments in two or three departments and the creation of interdisciplinary research institutes as well as teaching departments—e.g., Communications, International Relations—are symptomatic. Speculation, even though not garbed in the language of traditional political and social theorists, is an important feature of today's intellectual effort in the social sciences. "Model building" is, perhaps, a preferable term, but whether one uses the more modern terminology or the older word, "speculation," one process of learning about the unknown and the unexplained is necessarily the construction of a mental image of what to look for and of where to store bits of information, subject to subsequent correction or revision, in order to facilitate explanatory recall. As the speculation of an earlier day borrowed from religion, ethics, and philosophy, today's model building in the social sciences blends the methods of other disciplines, for example, mathematics to add logical rigor, statistics to measure and to provide tests of relationships among variables, and biology, electronics, sociology, psychology, economics, etc., for both data and methods of collecting or generating data.

Far from encompassing the universe, undertaking a reexamination of man and his social relations has a particular focus, namely, human interaction. Some ventures that probe within the individual are, of course, characteristic of psychology's concern with cognitive structure and other attributes of personality. But even in such areas much data lies in the realm where inferred and measurable structures and processes are primarily those that entail interaction (at the least between tester and subject even when through the medium of a printed questionnaire or similar intervening instrument). One must not, of course, underestimate the importance of the accumulated knowledge of physiological processes that permits explorations by neuropsychologists, e.g., the exploration of maximum channel capacity of information processing systems ranging from neurons in the frog's sciatic nerve through increasingly complex systems to a small social institution.[3] But it is that which is manifested externally, which can be observed with available instruments including the observer's senses, and which can be represented as structured or patterned that commands the attention of social scientists. This same realm of human behavior—of identifiable action, reaction, and interaction—is the enduring area of interest of legal practitioners and legal scientists.

It may seem paradoxical that in a day characterized by a flood of information and resultant specialization the route to a renewed creativity in law, more specifically in international law, should require a broad survey of man and of nonlegal ways of studying his behavior. Or is it paradoxical? Doesn't the lawyer's pride in applying his refined methodology to those human interactions brought within his professional purview have its roots in the breadth of life?

The technique of the lawyer, marked by the extension of the law into more and more new fields of action, appears similar to that which Von Neumann attributed to mathematicians. The rubrics of the original *Code Napoléon* hardly embrace the extensions of the law to newer areas of activity without examination of the nonlegal facets of the railway rate problem, the air safety problem, the public health problem, etc. We would not argue that all lawyers or even many lawyers in history have succeeded in viewing man without the distortion of writs and other technical impedimenta that amused W. S. Gilbert. But that some do so and by doing so have led the law into new paths is symbolized by the Brandeis brief. Perhaps the proper criticism is that too few lawyers, and they quite late in the day, emerge from day-to-day concern

[3] James G. Miller, "The Individual as an Information Processing System," in William S. Fields and Walter Abbott (eds.), *Information Storage and Neural Control* (Springfield, Illinois: Charles C. Thomas, 1963), pp. 301-28.

with technicalities to take a new look at man and society in their nonlegal complexities.

In an early 20th-century sociological approach to international law[4] Max Huber argued that the nature of the law includes a tendency to separate itself from the social reality that gave rise to the law and to which the law in turn tries to give order and form. Perhaps the existence of the Inns of Court and of separate Colleges and Faculties of Law are representative of the separation, particularly at those universities at which joint appointments in law and social science have been resisted or in those countries in which the law is treated as a closed, technical, apolitical system.

However that may be, Huber himself did not regard the duality of law and social reality to be equally pronounced in all legal realms. His position was not based upon the manner of teaching or upon intellectual walls built on the foundations of professional pride or jealousy. It rested on the nature of the law itself and the nearness of different forms of law to governmental policy-making processes. On the basis of a sort of intuitive distance-scale Huber viewed the separation of law and social reality to be greatest in private law. The two are much closer together in relations affected by administrative law where government brings about constant readjustments, while the gap is least where international law is concerned because, in Huber's view, the objective legal order rests immediately upon the will of the subjects—a conclusion inadvertently supported by critics who hold legal argument in international affairs to be but a façade for policy.

Perhaps Huber's statement requires refinement. It could be argued that in some subfields of international as well as private

[4] Max Huber, "Beiträge zur Kenntnis der Sociologischen Grundlagen des Völkerrechts und der Staatengesellschaft," *Jahrbuch des öffentlichen Rechts der Gegenwart* 4 (1910); reprinted as *Die Soziologischen Grundlagen des Völkerrechts* (Berlin-Grunewald: W. Rothschild, 1928).

law the assumption that matters are at least sufficiently settled that courts and similar agencies can handle the problem serves to place those subfields in the hands of technicians. In contrast, other, less settled subfields or subfields that have become areas of political controversy after having appeared to be settled and noncontroversial—e.g., the limits of territorial waters—are open to nontechnical influences. Since a more refined placement of legal subfields along a scale of distance from the policy processes cannot be attempted here, Huber's generalization, even though essentially speculative, will serve to support this point that by fits and starts, by broad area or by subfield, technical proficiency and creativity alternate as dominant approaches (but in cycles that differ from one subfield to another).

It may be, as Maxwell Cohen has suggested in a manner not unrelated to Huber's assessment, that the process of legal evolution is characterized by time-lags between changes in community values and changes in legal rules, which Cohen saw as widest for private law, small for American constitutional law, and very narrow for international law.[5] Since Cohen did not restrict his comment to the formal legislative process—he could hardly have done so and still seen a small time gap for American constitutional law—we can assume that the extent of the time-lag is related to the capacity of attorneys, judges, and scholars to step away from law and established methodology, to reexamine man and society with nonlegal tools, and then either to lead an established subfield in new directions or to introduce a new subfield, perhaps by recombining earlier approaches, findings, or theories about social units ranging from individuals to nations.

An argument could be made that public international law acquired its 17th-century prominence as a result of just such a recombination. Grotius fused the specialized work of his

[5] Maxwell Cohen, "'Basic Principles' of International Law—A Revaluation," *Canadian Bar Review* 42 (1964): 449-62.

predecessors, adapted the Scholastic tradition of the *ius gentium*, and secularized the law-of-nature doctrine—all prompted by a quite nonlegalistic reaction to the horrors of the Thirty Years' War that symbolized the depth of Europe's religious and political division. More recently, Hans Kelsen's extended debate with sociologists and his eventual relaxation of the rigor of his legalism are representative of the capacity of international lawyers to accord attention to other disciplines.

In terms of attention to nonlegal studies, perhaps the most interesting of Kelsen's many publications is the seldom-mentioned *Society and Nature* (1943) that rests an explanation of the emergence of the idea of causality on anthropological as well as historical data. Kelsen provided an excellent assemblage of data on the nature of retribution as well as the views of a number of anthropologists. Moreover, the debate about Kelsen's theory of international law was debate about a theory that rests the legal nature of that law on an international equivalent of political retribution. Yet, apart from some passing references to the primitive state of the international community and to decentralization, it was more than twenty years before theory-building outside the Kelsen framework and tradition drew inferences from the fields of anthropology, social psychology, jurisprudence, and international law and began to blend them into a theoretical system accommodating diverse forms of decentralized law.[6] In other words, the many

[6] Michael Barkun, *Law Without Sanctions: Order in Primitive Societies and the World Community* (New Haven: Yale University Press, 1968). For an account of the relationship between anthropology and history and how both suffer from polarization, see E. E. Evans-Pritchard, "Anthropology and History," in *Social Anthropology and Other Essays* (Glencoe: Free Press, 1962), pp. 172-91. For another discussion of the two as well as sociology with respect to the problem of analytical cuts in space and time, see Johan Galtung, "The Social Sciences: An Essay on Polarization and Integration," in Klaus Knorr and James N. Rosenau (eds.), *Contending Approaches to International Politics* (Princeton: Princeton University Press, 1969), pp. 243-85. For an example of the potential that lies in a synthesis of anthropological and

anticipations that anthropologists provided were not seized and systematically developed even when embraced by a controversial theorist of international law.

Actually, the invitation to amalgamate disciplines to advance comprehension of international law may be said to have been issued earlier in Sir Henry Sumner Maine's expressed interest in both ancient and international law and in Sir Paul Vinogradoff's discussion of similarities between intertribal law and international law.[7] However, allowing time for an accumulation of anthropological data and for the orderly accumulation of international law materials, it would not be amiss to treat 1943 as marking the time that opportunity for innovation was present for scholars in the social sciences and not just for international law specialists. Not only had one renowned theorist of international law displayed his interest in anthropology but another had just the year before published *A Study of War*, and our comment on that international law specialist's work is fully made by the dedication of a recent behavioralist book: "To Quincy Wright, who showed us the way."[8]

Given the Wright and Kelsen indicators, among others,[9] of

---

historical data, in this case by an anthropologist turned historian, see I. M. Lewis, *The Modern History of Somaliland: From Nation to State* (New York: Praeger, 1965). For an argument that United States law would be better analyzed by use of the methods of students of primitive law, see David Riesman, "Toward an Anthropological Science of Law and the Legal Profession," *American Journal of Sociology* 57 (1951): 121-35.

[7] Sir Henry Sumner Maine, *Ancient Law: Its Connections with the Early History of Society, and Its Relation to Modern Ideas* (London: J. Murray, 1861), and *International Law* (London: J. Murray, 1888); Sir Paul Vinogradoff, *Outlines of Historical Jurisprudence*, 2 vols. (London and New York: Oxford University Press, 1920), 1: 351, 353.

[8] J. David Singer (ed.), *Human Behavior and International Politics: Contributions from the Social-Psychological Sciences* (Chicago: Rand McNally, 1965).

[9] For suggestions of the potential of a sociological approach and for an attempt to relate domestic politics and international law, see

directions for innovation, it is an ironic commentary that at a political science conference in the spring of 1966 international law could be properly characterized as twenty years behind the other social sciences. Certainly international law specialists, among whom are a number of political scientists, are relatively infrequent contributors to the *Journal of Conflict Resolution*. But it also may be that the characterization indicates that the other social scientists, not just the international law specialists, have paid insufficient attention to the potential indicated by the scholars mentioned and, at the beginning of the postwar period, by the applications of psychology by Ranyard West and Paul Therre, the former unfortunately a captive of the Austinian concept of international law.[10] Ignoring the possibility of bringing other disciplines to bear upon the study of international law and going even farther to exclude international law from consideration when studying international relations may result from a combination of preoccupation with war and the resultant disdain for legal prescriptions that alone do not prevent war,[11] hasty rejection of the old in the eagerness to embrace a new approach, overly specialized training, and, for at least some individuals, unhappy experiences with

---

Dietrich Schindler, "Contribution à l'étude des facteurs sociologiques et psychologiques du droit international," *Académie de Droit International: Recueil des cours* 46 (1933): 233-325; Maurice Bourquin, "Stabilité et mouvement dans l'ordre juridique international," *ibid.* 64 (1938): 351-475; Joseph-Barthélemy, "Politique intérieure et droit international," *ibid.* 59 (1937): 429-520.

[10] Ranyard West, *Conscience and Society: A Study of the Psychological Prerequisites of Law and Order* (New York: Emerson Books, 1945); Paul Therre, *La psychologie individuelle et collective dans l'efficacité du droit international public* (Paris: Pedone, 1946).

[11] On disillusion with prescriptive international law among scholars of the interwar period, see Ronald Rogowski, "International Politics: The Past as Science," *International Studies Quarterly* 12 (1968): 400-407.

legalistically oriented international law courses offered by political science departments.[12]

The best known and certainly the most productive incorporation of a nonlegal approach with the substance of international law has been Myres S. McDougal's application of Harold D. Lasswell's analytical framework.[13] Indeed, the Lasswell-McDougal collaboration, joining political scientist and lawyer, represents the teamwork over an extended time span that Julius Stone held to be essential to bring about marked advances in international law.[14] On a smaller scale but quite venturesome are William D. Coplin's efforts to identify the functions of international law and to treat international adjudication as a part of the international bargaining process, Ib Martin Jarvad's employment of rank analysis to examine the International Court of Justice and the behavior of nations toward it, and Robert L. Friedheim's factor analysis of data from the records of the Geneva Law of the Sea Conferences.[15] For his re-

[12] American Society of International Law–American Political Science Association, *A Survey of the Teaching of International Law in Political Science Departments* (Washington, 1963), pp. 59-63; Wesley L. Gould, "Some Influences Upon the Place of International Law in Political Science Curricula: A Review of a Survey," *American Journal of International Law* 58 (1964): 979.

[13] For a concise exposition of the framework, see Myres S. McDougal, "Some Basic Theoretical Concepts about International Law: A Policy-Oriented Framework of Inquiry," *Journal of Conflict Resolution* 4 (1960): 337-54.

[14] Julius Stone, "Of Sociological Inquiries Concerning International Law," in D. S. Constantopoulos, C. Th. Eustathiades, and C. N. Fragistas (eds.), *Grundprobleme des internationalen Rechts—Festschrift für Jean Spiropoulos* (Bonn: Schimmelbusch, 1957), pp. 412-13. See also Georg Schwarzenberger, "The Interdisciplinary Treatment of International Law," *ibid.*, pp. 401-10; Michael Barkun, "Bringing the Insights of Behavioral Science to International Rules," *Western Reserve Law Review* 18 (1967): 1639-60.

[15] William D. Coplin, *Functions of International Law* (Chicago: Rand McNally, 1966); and "The World Court in the International Bargaining Process," in Robert W. Gregg and Michael Barkun (eds.),

cent Ph.D. dissertation Irvin L. White employed a computer variance reduction routine to make a comparative study of international legal decision-making in certain problem areas related to the sea and airspace and then make a projection for outer space.[16] More comprehensive, even though often including treatment in depth of specific problems of international law such as nationalization and the act of state doctrine, are Kenneth S. Carlston's examination of the fundamentals of international law and organization and Richard A. Falk's undertakings to analyze international law in terms of the structure of the society of states and to find rules of international law that are supported by a consensus.[17] Adding the interest-provoking Kaplan-Katzenbach collaboration, Roger Fisher's venture into the social sciences, to date best represented by his contribution to and editing of a symposium on international conflict and behavioral science, Jan Triska's studies of Soviet treaty patterns, and Peter Rohn's efforts to develop

---

The United Nations System and Its Functions: Selected Readings (Princeton: D. Van Nostrand, 1968), pp. 317-31; Ib Martin Jarvad, "Power versus Equality: An Attempt at a Systematic Analysis of the Role and Function of the International Court of Justice, 1945 to 1966," Paper presented at the Second General Conference of the International Peace Research Association (IPRA), revised, mimeographed (Copenhagen: Institute for Peace and Conflict Research, 1967); Robert L. Friedheim, "Factor Analysis as a Tool in Studying the Law of the Sea," in Lewis M. Alexander (ed.), *The Law of the Sea: Offshore Boundaries and Zones* (Columbus: Ohio State University Press, 1967), pp. 47-70.

[16] Irvin L. White, *Decision-Making for Space* (Lafayette, Indiana: Purdue University Studies, 1970).

[17] Kenneth S. Carlston, *Law and Organization in World Society* (Urbana: University of Illinois Press, 1962), and "World Order and International Law," *Journal of Legal Education* 20 (1968): 127-45; Richard A. Falk, "International Jurisdiction: Horizontal and Vertical Conceptions of Legal Order," *Temple Law Quarterly* 32 (1959): 295-320; and *The Role of Domestic Courts in the International Legal Order* (Syracuse: Syracuse University Press, 1964), esp. pp. 10, 18, 128, 170-73.

treaty profiles of nations[18] virtually exhausts the list of efforts to blend disciplines for the direct advance of the field of international law toward the stage reached by other social sciences. The numbers are few compared with the many researchers dealing with the several aspects of psychology, sociology, anthropology, economics, and political science—to list only the traditional disciplines. But it is our belief that, although the number of innovators are few to date, their efforts indicate the potential for rapid gains in international law research, provided that advantage is taken of the methodological advances and the accumulation of findings made available by the other social sciences. We trust that neither quantity nor the resultant chaotic state of the many undertakings in these other fields, of which only a fraction are included in our inventory, will prove discouraging.

Tools and Concepts: Disorder and Progress

IF THE appearance of chaos is any indicator of progress, then the social sciences are well off indeed. As a matter of fact, the present disordered state of the social sciences may well be far more fruitful than a more tidy arrangement. The impression of disorder derives largely from a quantum jump in the num-

[18] Morton A. Kaplan and Nicholas de B. Katzenbach, *The Political Foundations of International Law* (New York: Wiley, 1961); Roger Fisher (ed.), *International Conflict and Behavioral Science: The Craigville Papers* (New York: Basic Books, 1964), esp. pp. 91-109; Jan F. Triska and Robert M. Slusser, *The Theory, Law, and Policy of Soviet Treaties* (Stanford: Stanford University Press, 1962); Triska, "Soviet Treaty Law: A Quantitative Analysis," in Hans W. Baade (ed.), *The Soviet Impact on International Law* (Dobbs Ferry: Oceana, 1965), pp. 52-65; Peter H. Rohn, "Institutionalism in the Law of Treaties: A Case of Combining Teaching and Research," *Proceedings, American Society of International Law, 1965*, pp. 93-98; "Treaty Profiles" (bound computer printout of treaty patterns from United Nations Treaty Series, vols. 1-503; copies at University of Washington, American Society of International Law, Harvard and Michigan Law Libraries, Health Law Center of the University of Pittsburgh, and University of Paris Law School; 1967).

ber of methods for studying the same phenomena; and, predictably, as the number of methods has increased, new subjects of study have suddenly appeared to match the increased variety of tools. Since, with the social sciences, nearly everyone's house is in an equal state of disarray, both substantive and methodological hallmarks that once identified a particular discipline must now be shared with a number of fields of study.

Disarray—bringing with it a breakdown of the boundaries that once appeared to neatly segregate sociologists, economists, psychologists, political scientists, philosophers, linguists, geographers, biologists, and other natural scientists—may be a compelling force. True, the forces that created boundaries still exist. A combination of established institutional structure, protection of hierarchy and status, disciplinary loyalties, and jurisdictional disputes has extended these boundaries into the present period of the emergence of such areas of study as decision-making, organization behavior, communications and information, ecology, and bargaining. New fields of study, incapable of being confined within the boundaries of traditional disciplines and traditional teaching departments, are a sign of the reexamination of social units and social processes. As we discovered when we attempted to include classifications of literature both by "traditional discipline" and by "new discipline," individual scholars, teams of scholars, and often particular publications do not fit single categories definable by method or subject matter. Men are brought together and ideas are exchanged in ways that break down old barriers. Hopefully, this intermingling will survive the impact of physical separation in university plants exponentially expanded to accommodate the growing student mass. The all-encompassing mind of the 17th and 18th centuries may no longer be possible, but it can be hoped that the collective minds and complementary skills of communities of scholars will not be forced into a collectivized intellectual compartmentalism. Current chaos and disarray present a wealth of ideas and findings demanding the order brought by synthesis, not that of a new segregation.

There is within the social sciences a kind of tacit agreement to keep open as many roads of inquiry as possible, a feeling that this is not the time to close off options. This pragmatic orientation requires the multiplication of methods, theories, and problem-formulations, with the hope that out of a competitive situation certain roads will emerge as superior to others. There is a phrase that one encounters frequently in social science literature, "premature closure," which we can broadly define as a tendency to cut off an avenue of research before it has yielded its maximum dividends. All avenues begin on a level of parity, only to continue through a rigorous sifting and sorting process through which—hopefully—the trivial is discarded and the significant retained.

Numerous extrinsic institutional factors have developed to impose, often indirectly, some measure of structure on the behavioral sciences. Yet in large measure they remain stubbornly laissez faire. The assumption remains widespread that the scientific community has its own version of the "invisible hand" through whose operation maximum competition may produce maximum gain.[19]

The Search for General Theory

The attempt to digest and make sense of this flood of research is, by virtue of the sheer volume involved, very nearly doomed before it starts. Nevertheless, data and low-level generalizations are next to useless by themselves. It is the function of theory to turn the appearance of chaos into the reality of order. And yet the attempts thus far made to order data and generalizations through their incorporation into general

[19] Michael Polanyi, *Science, Faith, and Society* (Chicago: University of Chicago Press, 1960).

theories of behavior have largely failed. Harold Lasswell's and Talcott Parsons' attempts[20] have their partisans, but in no sense has either received the general acceptance of the behavioral science community.

One can only look back with awe to the time when a single man like Giambattista Vico could encompass what Europeans knew about the entire developmental cycle of human societies within a single theoretical framework. In the first half of the 18th century there was probably little reason to suspect that the days of manageable information were coming to an end. Yet even during Vico's life (1668-1744) the sources of data had begun to spread not only backward through time but eastward in space to include the non-Western world.

It is, however, significant that when Maine's *Ancient Law* was published in 1861, 136 years after Vico's *Scienze nuova,* there was still relatively little recognition in many quarters of the amount of data that was becoming available. Historical and archeological research had been bringing and would continue to bring to light new information concerning ancient ways of life. The steamboat had begun to carry to Africa, the Far East, and Oceania an increasing number of travellers, scholars, and government agents to report on the Maori and other peoples whose cultures had grown in separation from Europe. Even the data on more recent European times was expanding. For positivists it may have seemed a sufficiently large task simply to take account of the increment of treaties published in the Hertslett and Martens series, the decided cases being more thoroughly reported in increasing number, and other documents.

Still, increases in primary materials notwithstanding, at-

[20] Harold D. Lasswell, *The Analysis of Political Behavior: An Empirical Approach* (London: K. Paul, Trench, Trubner, 1948); Lasswell and Abraham Kaplan, *Power and Society: A Framework of Political Inquiry* (New Haven: Yale University Press, 1950); Talcott Parsons and Edward A. Shils (eds.), *Toward A General Theory of Action* (Cambridge: Harvard University Press, 1951), pp. 47-109.

tempts to produce general theories, whether they fell under the rubric *Allgemeine Staatslehre, Rechtswissenschaft* (the theoretical science of law), or *Allgemeine Rechtslehre* (the practical science of law in which juristic technique looms large), persisted. Even today, a common Anglo-Saxon criticism of Continental works including those not claiming the character of general theory is that too little attention is paid to data, legal or nonlegal. In addition, traditional Continental efforts to construct general theory are open to the criticism that they rest on the experiences and theoretical categories of municipal law and thereby fail to meet Charles Boasson's demand for functional adaptations to basic differences between municipal and international situations.[21] Meanwhile, the Anglo-Saxon finds himself hard put to cast aside Austinianism despite a hundred years or so of both logical argument and evidence of its inadequacies for societies not characterized by the constitutional supremacy of a parliament or other sovereign.[22] The search or, at least, the felt need for general theory with categories into which to deposit new information, to store it, and from which to retrieve it—in other words, the felt need for an adequate, comprehensive program for the human memory—remains. Discomfiture induced by confrontation with the mass of data observed and now generated as well neither completely drives out the patterns of thought acquired from what once passed for general theory nor prevents search at a less ambitious level of analysis for partial theory as a step, taken in hope, toward eventual general theory.

Data sources, methods, institutional bases from which re-

[21] Charles Boasson, "The Place of International Law in Peace Research," *Journal of Peace Research* 5 (1968): 28-43. See also C.A.W. Manning's distinction between the study of government and the study of international relations, *The Nature of International Society* (London: G. Bell, 1962), pp. 182-84.

[22] It is significant that Roger Fisher recently felt it necessary to revive the case against Austinianism. See his "Bringing Law to Bear on Governments," *Harvard Law Review* 74 (1961): 1130-40.

search can be launched—all are factors which combine in various ways to determine the design of research and the thrust of theory. As each factor increased in volume, so, too, did the potential for differing combinations of factors increase. Indeed, we are faced with the paradox that the more necessary general theory seems to be and the more intense the striving for it, the more difficult it is to attain.

The Accessibility of Data

IF THE GROWTH of general theory seems to have fallen short of expectations, the same surely can not be said of data. The social sciences have reached the point where the way in which data is collected and stored becomes a crucial factor in determining the uses to which it can be put. Law long ago reached this point; the breadth and sophistication of legal indexing systems is proof of that. The movement in social science, where the point of data saturation has coincided with the computer age, has been toward the electronic storage of statistical information. This electronic transmutation avoids the space problems confronting conventional libraries, while at the same time it makes the data available for almost instant recall. Some notion of the mass of data that must be handled is given by the information on opinion surveys alone. In 1963, interviewers in the United States and Europe recorded 8 million individual interviews, most containing multiple questions.[23] To this must be added as a matter of course national, state, and local election figures and census statistics.[24] In the foreign affairs

[23] Charles L. Ruttenberg, "Report on Data Archives in the Social Sciences," *American Behavioral Scientist* 8 (April, 1965): 33-34; Ralph L. Bisco, "Social Science Data Archives: A Review of Developments," *American Political Science Review* 60 (1966): 93-109. More recent information is obtainable from the Council of Social Science Data Archives (Bureau of Applied Social Research, Columbia University, or Institute for Social Research, University of Michigan).

[24] Warren E. Miller, "The Study of Man: Political Science Partnership," *Trans-action* 2 (Sept.-Oct., 1965): 37-38.

field there are legally imposed delays before analysts outside government face such source materials as the 551 thousand telegrams exchanged between the Department of State and its overseas missions in 1966, to say nothing of airgrams and other documents.[25]

From this perceived need for the rational storage of data on human behavior arose the concept of the "data bank" or "data library," some central repository to which data would be sent as collected and to which scholars from many disciplines might come. A number of such centers have already been established, notably the Roper Center at Williams College, holding about 8 million punched cards of public opinion data in 1965, the Data Library at Berkeley, and the Inter-University Consortium for Political Research based at the Survey Research Center of the University of Michigan and holding about 2 million data cards. The Consortium draws on the resources of the Survey Research Center, but is funded by fifty American and foreign universities.[26] Outside the United States, cooperation between UNESCO and the International Social Science Council assisted the first steps to bring social and political data centers into being in Paris, Cologne, Amsterdam, and Buenos Aires and the consideration of other possible centers in Latin America and Asia.

It seems only natural that the legal profession, with its long-standing practical interest in easing research burdens, would eventually be drawn to new methods of arranging its data.

[25] Curtis L. Fritz, et al., *A Modern Information System for the Department of State (Preliminary Design)* (Washington: Department of State, 1967), p. 4; E. Raymond Platig, "Research and Analysis," *Annals of the American Academy of Political and Social Science* 380 (November, 1968): 54.

[26] Platig, *loc. cit.*; Warren E. Miller and Philip E. Converse, "The Interuniversity Consortium for Political Science," *International Social Science Journal* 16 (1964): 70-76. Information on other data banks is to be found in the same issue of the journal, which should also be consulted for reports on the establishment of centers overseas.

Pilot studies of computer applications, however, met some strong resistance, centering around the objection that computerization would lead to an inflexible, mechanical form of decision-making. Such misgivings often stem from a failure to appreciate the very real limitations of computers and the genuine ties between computerized and conventional methodologies. Much the same objection, with as little merit, might be directed against *Shepard's Citations*.

The techniques already exist for making bibliographies and legal materials available by means of computer retrieval.[27] Such groups as the Special Committee on Jurimetrics of the Association of American Law Schools and the Special Committee on Electronic Data Retrieval of the American Bar Association have done much to demonstrate the potentialities of computer technology to the legal profession. In short, the reordering of disciplinary boundaries discussed earlier has been matched by novel and exciting means of treating the raw material of research.

The Significance of Topic Selection

It is commonplace to observe that the appropriateness of a research method (assuming adequate funds and facilities) is a function of the interrelationship of the subject chosen for investigation, questions asked about that subject, and the type of data that is needed and can be collected. Scholarly undertakings raise no need to borrow the techniques of other disciplines when the topic investigated, the questions asked, and the

[27] Richard W. Edwards, Jr., "Electronic Data-Processing and International Law Documentation," *American Journal of International Law* 61 (1967): 87-92; Kenneth Janda, *Information Retrieval: Applications to Political Science* (Indianapolis and New York: Bobbs-Merrill, 1968). A service, ABC POL SCI (Advance Bibliography of Contents: Political Science and Government), now provides tables of contents for more than 260 journals in advance of publication and accepts orders for single articles in those journals (Santa Barbara: American Bibliographical Center, Clio Press). Sixty-one of the periodicals are law journals including eight specifically devoted to international law.

data available and required lie within the limits of a single discipline's established boundaries. For example, a simple exposition of the course of Supreme Court decisions interpreting the supremacy clause of the United States Constitution would require only the lawyer's tools for reading decisions, relating decision to text and to related cases, understanding the uses of precedent, noting distinctions, etc., together with narrative skill. But if the topic extends beyond simple narration to explanation of why particular decisions were handed down at particular times, questions arise that would render data from one or more Justices' personal papers relevant. The investigator must then resort to the historian's craft in using and determining the relevance of private papers. He may also need the political scientist's skills to study legislative, party, and pressure politics or the content analyst's skill in handling news stories, editorials, and the motifs in the opinions themselves. Since the selection of topic, in this example the supremacy clause, includes determination of the relevant historical moment or period, it may also introduce the problem of whether a comparability requirement exists to suggest restricting collection of data for the period after the introduction of public opinion polls and structured interviews to the types of information available for earlier periods. Of course, there may not be so strong a need for comparison that the use of more types of data for a later period would render the additional information, together with related analytical techniques, superfluous. The point is that the selection of topic, refined by questions asked about the topic, may be expected to determine the type of data needed and thus the methods to collect and analyze it. Reciprocally, lack of certain data or of methods to collect and analyze it may modify or even exclude a particular topic.

When either the term "interdisciplinary" or "multidisciplinary" is employed to suggest the use of differing skills, it is not always adequate to think of methodology alone. Methodological bridges are important, but we suggest that a stronger bridge between disciplines would also be substantive in nature. Bridge topics, connecting two fields of action such as politics and law,[28] as well as the disciplines that specialize in the study of each, probably represent the areas of investigation drawing the least attention because they are difficult to identify in the concrete. Or, when identified, the implications of the identification are not seen. Lawyer and behavioral scientist may each attack the problem of treaty negotiations. The one may concentrate upon the powers of negotiators, the other upon the strategies and tactics of negotiations. Both may fail to produce a bridging product.[29] Their outputs are then discrete items of scholarship that leave unformulated questions and problems for future discovery. To miss an opportunity for topical bridging of disciplines is to miss a rich vein for scholarly mining. Missed opportunities of this sort may be a reason why some scholars fail to find compelling evidence of advantages in interdisciplinary collaboration.[30] Advantages exist only when questions not answerable by a single discipline's concepts and techniques are asked.

Possibilities for developing bridge topics have certainly been implicit, sometimes explicit, in writings on the sociology of law.[31] A number of our chapters try to suggest bridge topics.

[28] No dichotomy is intended merely because man can create analytical categories such as "politics" and "law" and can make distinctions based on scholars' methodologies. At the same time, we do not imply identity. To say that A is not B does not necessarily imply that they are not interrelated. The argument for formulation and investigation of bridge topics implies interrelationships.

[29] See Wesley L. Gould, "Laboratory, Law, and Anecdote: Negotiations and the Integration of Data," *World Politics* 18 (1965): 92-104.

[30] For a comment that a search among behavioral studies for light on administrative decision-making proved virtually fruitless and that "writers who get close to it seem to fade out," see Kenneth Culp Davis, "Behavioral Science and Administrative Law," *Journal of Legal Education* 17 (1965): 142. Perhaps the topics covered by the behavioral scientists referred to did not permit a convincing demonstration of the relevance of the methods of specialists on administrative behavior.

[31] E.g., Joseph Thomas Delos, *Le Problème de civilisation—la*

Negotiation has already been mentioned as a broad area not yet exploited for bridges. Legal advice to Foreign Offices, virtually untouched even through an historical approach, is an open field calling for at least the techniques of specialists in law, decision-making, and organizational behavior. The list can be extended, but for the moment it suffices to note the significance of bridge topics.

Whenever a bridge topic can be identified, a new group of questions demands answers. Indeed, merely to identify a bridge topic is usually to ask a question about a portion of human interaction about which we know little or nothing, although often the needed data is on hand in separate collections. Broadly, to ask questions about the links between economics and law is to ask about relationships between two traditionally demarcated spheres of human activity, or, differently phrased, between two types of behavior. It is asking one set of questions about the place of law in human affairs. Adequate answers, as complete as the data allows, require discipline-bridging research procedures. What this suggests is that more effort be spent to identify and work on bridge topics to permit methodological bridges to be built more freely. Even more, it suggests that what has already been done to bridge disciplines, as in the communications and decision-making areas, indicates that the bridge topic has a "logic of its own."

The Utility of Social Science Methods

Resort to social science methods for the investigation of legal phenomena and bridge topics signifies not just an undertaking to improve methodology but also a striving for richer conceptual schemes and the unification of theorists' thinking beyond what formal theories of law and formal theories of politics permit. At the same time, since adoption of a partic-

---

nation, 2 vols. (Montreal: Editions de l'Arbre, 1944), which presents a sociological analysis of the nation and of the relationship between nationalism and the legal order.

ular method or set of methods imposes limits on what can be done, it is possible to take a step toward the elimination of ambiguities. Experiment by simulation, for example, imposes the requirement of rigorous conceptualization.[32] Indeed, forcing oneself to use the tools of an alien area of investigation prevents dismissal of the unfamiliar as irrelevant, brief exposition of ambiguous, imprecise generalities acquired from secondary sources, or reliance on a remembered general theory of the past.[33]

Structural-functional analysis, not exactly a new approach to those who recall the efforts of E. L. Shoup and certain other political scientists to provide new approaches to the study of American Government and of foreign governments, has been given promising new thrusts in the 1950's and 1960's. Perhaps the most intriguing is that of Gabriel Almond's application of Marion J. Levy's structural-functional requisite analysis.[34]

[32] On the experience of converting assumptions about processes of international politics into arithmetical statements on the choices and compromises that a group at Northwestern University had to make in the early stages of research, see Harold Guetzkow, "Some Uses of Mathematics in Simulation of International Relations," in John M. Claunch (ed.), *Mathematical Applications in Political Science* (Dallas: The Arnold Foundation, Southern Methodist University, 1965), pp. 21-40. See also William D. Coplin, "Inter-Nation Simulation and Contemporary Theories of International Relations," *American Political Science Review* 60 (1966): 562-78.

[33] For an example of a brief excursion into law, employing a common but restrictive association with the state apparatus, followed by brief reference to legislative assemblies as a means of resolving some conflicts that are not resolved by appeal to existing law, see Kenneth E. Boulding, *Conflict and Defense: A General Theory* (New York: Harper & Row, 1962), pp. 320-22.

[34] Marion J. Levy, Jr., *The Structure of Society* (Princeton: Princeton University Press, 1952); Gabriel A. Almond and James S. Coleman (eds.), *The Politics of the Developing Areas* (Princeton: Princeton University Press, 1960), pp. 3-64; Almond, "A Developmental Approach to Political Systems," *World Politics* 17 (1965): 183-214; Almond and G. Bingham Powell, Jr., *Comparative Politics: A Developmental Approach* (Boston: Little, Brown, 1966).

Almond's effort, based upon the treatment of social structures as performers of functions, embraces a measure of systems theory. It also includes a systematic examination of comparative history in the effort to construct a theory of political development. Functional categories, which include rule-making, application of rules, and adjudication among the conversion functions, along with aggregation, articulation of interests, and information, are intended to permit comparisons of complex political systems with each other and with simpler systems. As is evident, the method at least provides approaches by which to bridge law and economic systems and, indeed, much more. International law would enter the picture through treatment of the interaction of political units with the international environment. What Almond called "an international accommodative capability"[35] can be viewed as an invitation to tie studies of the relations between international and municipal law closely to the functional analysis of national political systems.

Systems theory represents an advance over the organic theory of the state that provided the 19th century and the first decades of the 20th century with a method for studying the static and dynamic relations of parts to each other and to the whole. The term "general system theory" was introduced by a biologist, Ludwig von Bertalanffy, in 1932 and began to receive general recognition two decades later. This attempt to abandon metaphor by resort to generalization has helped to inhibit the reification promoted by the organic theory's implied and sometimes express analogy to biological organisms—e.g., Rousseau in the *Discourse on Political Economy* (1755). Von Bertalanffy's version is applicable to more than biological systems or their analogues.[36]

[35] Gabriel A. Almond, "Political Systems and Political Change," *American Behavioral Scientist* 6 (June, 1963): 7.

[36] The Rousseau example can be found in the Everyman edition of *The Social Contract and Discourses*, pp. 236-37. Ludwig Von Berta-

An interesting byproduct of generalization is the opportunity to employ inanimate systems, particularly the electronic and the mechanical, as analogues. Doing so both introduces an additional useable control on the tendency to reify and leads into the study of homeostasis or self-regulation by conjuring images of such familiar regulators as thermostats. The electronic analogy is particularly evident in the early sections of Morton Kaplan's path-breaking study of *System and Process in International Politics*, of which only an elementary portion has been given expression in the Kaplan-Katzenbach collaboration in an exposition of the elements of international law.

General systems theory provides, we think, the most promising approach to date for integrating more specialized studies into a general theory. Richard N. Rosecrance's *Action and Reaction in World Politics,* although suffering from the use of only a limited number of secondary historical sources, indicates the potential for the application of general systems theory and of the concept of homeostasis to historical data. Another direction of potential integration is that of cybernetics. Karl Deutsch's *The Nerves of Government* is one demonstration of the possibilities for use of the electronic analogue for more than mere literary illustration. Ecology, provided that it heeds the warning of the Sprouts to avoid attributing human characteristics to environments,[37] is linked with systems theory. The

lanffy, "General System Theory," *General Systems Yearbook* 1 (1956): 1-10; "General System Theory—A Critical Evaluation," *ibid.* 7 (1962): 1-20. For perhaps the most important exposition of general systems theory in relation to living systems, see the three articles by James G. Miller, "Living Systems: Basic Concepts," "Living Systems: Structure and Process," and "Living Systems: Cross-Level Hypotheses," in *Behavioral Science* 10 (1965): 193-237, 337-79, and 380-411.

[37] Harold and Margaret Sprout, *The Ecological Perspective on Human Affairs with Special Reference to International Politics* (Princeton: Princeton University Press, 1965), pp. 34-38.

interplay of a system with its environment is also an interaction of systems.[38]

Given the frequency with which the terms "legal system" and "legal order" have been used in formal theories of law, systems theory should find a ready welcome among international lawyers. There have been many guesses, usually uninformed in some vital aspect, concerning the place of international law in human affairs. That place has been both overemphasized and underemphasized, chiefly in harmony with successive popular fashions. A more accurate assessment than that of fashion would be welcome. So, too, would be a use of system theory that would not impose an a priori hierarchical structure upon legal norms. Neither an overly neat logic of monism, whether it accords supremacy to the national or the international legal order, nor an a priori dualism has demonstrated satisfactory explanatory power. Certainly, neither is descriptive. A more accurate portrayal might result from a systems approach that accepts the course of history, its accidents, and its unevenness in producing normative hierarchies. Not a closed system but one open to interaction with nonlegal systems is needed. Perhaps a systems approach accommodating historical unevenness is too difficult and the subsumption of all under an a priori hierarchical or dualistic scheme avoids potential confusion by classification without distinction among the real, the hoped for, and the passé. But then what is one to do with deviant empirical research findings?

Comparison is in a sense an inevitable research tool. Employment of a point of reference, use of a framework for analysis, determination of the relationship of A to B—all introduce comparison. Usually, at least in political science and in comparative law, we refer to cross-national comparisons, although

[38] James G. Miller, "Living Systems: Basic Concepts," p. 218, defines the environment as the suprasystem (or next higher system) minus the system itself plus all higher level systems that contain it.

a broadening to include the major social units on which social anthropology focuses might suggest use of the term "cross-societal" or, perhaps, "cross-cultural." In any case, the comparative approach, when it is not merely parallel description, may include research taking such forms as attribute surveys, trend analyses, cross-unit testing of behavior hypotheses including the testing by simulation that has now begun,[39] and other cross-national uses of now common behavioral techniques. Even though it may render more difficult the problems of data quality, comparison may also be across time, as in comparisons of the earlier undertaking of the West to industrialize with the present efforts of industrializing countries.[40] Hopefully, intertemporal comparisons will be facilitated by quantitative historical analyses such as Douglass North and the trio of Lance Davis, Jonathan Hughes, and Duncan McDougall have employed in respect to the development of the American national economy and Phyllis Deane and W. A. Cole to British economic growth between 1688 and 1959.[41] It makes a great deal of difference, for example,

[39] Wayman J. Crow and John R. Raser, "A Cross-Cultural Simulation Study," A Report to Project Michelson, U.S. Naval Ordnance Test Station, China Lake, California (LaJolla: Western Behavioral Sciences Institute, November 20, 1964).

[40] Discussion of the problems of intertemporal studies may be found in a report on a study of deterrence in various parts of the world during decades a century apart from 376-67 B.C. to 1776-85 A.D. Raoul Naroll, "Method of Study: Northridge Deterrence Project, Report No. 34," Report to Project Michelson, NOTS, China Lake, California (June 15, 1964).

[41] Douglass C. North, *The Economic Growth of the United States, 1790-1860* (New York: Prentice-Hall, 1961; Norton paperback edition, 1966); Lance E. Davis, Jonathan R. T. Hughes, and Duncan M. McDougall, *American Economic History: The Development of the National Economy* (Homewood, Illinois: Richard D. Irwin, 1961); Phyllis Deane and W. A. Cole, *British Economic Growth, 1688-1959: Trends and Structure* (New York: Cambridge University Press, 1962). See also Robert F. Berkhofer, *A Behavioral Approach to Historical Analysis* (New York: Free Press, 1969); N. Rashevsky, *Looking at History Through Mathematics* (Cambridge: M.I.T. Press, 1968); Wil-

whether the doctrine of freedom of the seas is a product of laissez-faire economic thought or a function of the size of commercial and fishing fleets.[42]

Uses of mathematics, even simple counting, may be more revealing than verbalizations, although not necessarily. Counting is a first step toward determining the propensity of states to abide by treaties. But counting is not always useful. Jurimetrics that does little more than count judges' votes either to try to predict their future decisions in particular types of cases or to find blocs may accomplish no more than is possible verbally with less effort. And, of course, poor concepts are not helped by making substitutions for verbal symbols.

There are, however, circumstances in which mathematical techniques are helpful. Rudolph J. Rummel argues for mathematization of theory on the ground that although classification of patterns and relations is essential as a precursor to scientific theory, theory that is only verbalized too often stagnates by not passing beyond the stage of classification.[43] Whether Rummel's argument may not be somewhat too sweeping is subject to debate. At the minimum, however, an assertion can be made that occasions occur when, in order to rise above a stagnant situation or to overcome a particular obstacle or set of obstacles to scientific progress, mathematical models may

---

liam O. Aydelotte, "Quantification in History," *American Historical Review* 71 (1966): 803-25. See also the employment of a probabilistic model to analyze the capacity of the German "Risk fleet" to threaten England in 1899-1914, James H. McRandle and James P. Quirk, "An Interpretation of the German 'Risk Fleet' Concept" (Paper delivered at the Econometric Society meetings, December 30, 1960); abstracted in *Econometrica* 29 (1961): 475-76.

42 This point was made in Wesley L. Gould, *An Introduction to International Law* (New York: Harper, 1957), pp. 475-79, and more recently, with respect to the Soviet position at the Geneva Conferences on the Law of the Sea, by Friedheim, "Factor Analysis," pp. 57, 60, 61.

43 Rudolph J. Rummel, "A Field Theory of Social Action with Application to Conflict Within Nations," *General Systems Yearbook* 10 (1965): 183-211.

be needed. The same may be said about statistical analyses, although on other grounds such as the susceptibility of data to particular manipulations.

On the theoretical level, the problem of comparability may impel a researcher to develop a model accounting for two differently conceived political or economic phenomena. Edward Ames, attacking the problem of the comparability of West European economic integration based on the concept of the market and East European collaboration based on a productivity concept, found resort to a mathematical derivation to be a means of obtaining a bridging model.[44] There seems to be no good reason why properly equipped scholars could not mathematize models of international legal systems, either their own or preexisting models of verbal legal theory, in an effort to provide more satisfactory reference points derived from essential similarities of structure, function, or process. As reference points, such models could serve to highlight divergences.

Factor analysis serves to produce clusterings of variables into "factors" or "dimensions" to reduce the disorderliness of an excess of variables. Raymond B. Cattell and his associates have employed factor analysis in an attempt to identify cultural configurations among nations. Whether such configurations are more useful than linguistic maps, together with an overlay of political boundaries, depends upon whether one's purpose is to discover "national" groupings of states or to examine nationalistic or tribalistic territorial issues and problems of nation-building.

A certain danger in the use of factor analysis lies in premature selection of names for the factors that emerge after either orthogonal or oblique rotation, probably the result of overanxiety to interpret. The problem can be seen if we take an empathetic look at the progress of a portion of a study which is available to us at two stages of its development, namely,

[44] Edward Ames, "Economic Integration in the European Soviet Bloc?," *American Economic Review* 49 (1959): 113-24.

Bruce M. Russett's excellent examination of several types of relationships in an effort to delineate international regions. One of Russett's efforts to make such delineations on the basis of socio-cultural dimensions may not determine regions at all and perhaps not even cultural groups. Certainly it was a surprise to read an early tentative version and find Puerto Rico, Lebanon, and Greece emerging as Western European; China as Eastern European; Haiti and Jamaica as Asian; Iceland, Finland, Sweden, and Norway as Anglo-Saxon, and the United Kingdom ranking higher on Western European than on Anglo-Saxon dimensions.[45] Russett could not and did not settle for the early alignments. Aware of the difficulties encountered in his earlier efforts to group nations by socio-cultural dimensions, Russett not only employed a different procedure but also relabeled the resultant "regions."[46] Although not eliminating all difficulties—most of which derive from connotations of spatial proximity, if not necessarily contiguity, associated with the term "region"—the later analysis provided defensible results.

It has been suggested that a difficulty lay in the variables selected for factoring, which themselves produced factors labeled (1) economic development, (2) communism, (3) size

[45] Bruce M. Russett, "Delineating International Regions," Carnegie-IDRC Joint Study Group on Measurement Problems, mimeographed (Bloomington: Indiana University, 1965).

[46] Asia was extended to become Afro-Asia (excluding Africa south of the Sahara which was in neither version); Western Europe and Anglo-Saxon became Western Community; Latin America was divided to add a group of "Semi-Developed Latins." Haiti (earlier Asian), Jamaica (Asian), and China (East European) became unclassifiable. From the earlier unclassifiable group, Egypt became Afro-Asian and the Philippines, Latin American. Argentina, Trinidad and Tobago, Cyprus, Israel, and Japan became Western. Other countries appeared in expected groupings. Bruce M. Russett, "Delineating International Regions," in J. David Singer (ed.), *Quantitative International Politics: Insights and Evidence* (New York: Free Press, 1968), pp. 317-52; and *International Regions and the International Systems: A Study in Political Ecology* (Chicago: Rand McNally, 1967), chap. 2.

(discarded), (4) Catholic culture, and (5) intensive agriculture. Banks and Gregg, on the ground that the Yale Political Data Program had provided Russett with socioeconomic rather than political variables, employed variables taken primarily from Banks and Textor, *A Cross-Polity Survey*, to produce different groupings of nations to which they applied labels descriptive of internal political systems.[47] The Banks-Gregg criticism obviously relates to investigation rather than to interpretation of what has been investigated. In regard to the latter, while the choice of variables is important in that it provides the substance to be interpreted, it still leaves the problem of interpretive labeling. Unsatisfying as it may seem to settle for "Factor A," "Factor B," etc., it may be that the effectiveness of the promising factor analysis route to mapping may only require the patience to withhold conclusions or labels expressive of judgment until additional projects have been designed and executed. One purpose of factor analysis is to avoid prejudgment, and prejudgment then ought not to be inserted through the choice of names for factors at a time when relatively little work of this sort has been done.

Both Rummel and Raymond Tanter have resorted to factor analysis to try to ascertain the clusters of variables to which internal conflict and external conflict are related and also to look for relations between internal and external conflict during the periods 1955-57 and 1958-60.[48] Rummel and Tanter do not emerge with the same number of factors for internal conflict, a circumstance not to be regarded as a flaw but as a stimulus to questions for subsequent investigation. However, despite extensions by Rummel to other years, limits on the

[47] Phillip M. Gregg and Arthur S. Banks, "Dimensions of Political Systems: Factor Analysis of A Cross-Polity Survey," *American Political Science Review* 59 (1965): 603, note 12.

[48] Rudolph J. Rummel, "Dimensions of Conflict Behavior Within and Between Nations," *General Systems Yearbook* 8 (1963): 1-50; Raymond Tanter, "Dimensions of Conflict Behavior Within and Between Nations, 1958-1960," *Journal of Conflict Resolution* 10 (1966): 41-64.

number of years that could be covered to date require that the studies be carefully handled to avoid unwarranted generalizations.

To our knowledge, there is no factor-analysis study attempting to delineate either regional or cultural legal affinities. Law is included as one variable among many socio-cultural or political variables. Certain formal governmental arrangements are generally counted as political rather than legal variables. What is done to classify legal systems is essentially no better grounded than Wigmore's identifications. It would appear that there is room for the employment of factor analysis provided that key legal provisions, including judicial decisions concerning property, contracts, and the like could be employed as variables to be factored. But the task may be as difficult as the attempt to verbally identify principles of law common to independent nations. Above all, there are traps into which a factor analyst unversed in law can fall. Rummel's use of acceptance of the Optional Clause, wrongly labeled as subscribing to the Statute of the International Court of Justice, as the lone indicator of states' acceptance of international law was an elementary error that drew proper criticism from Don C. Piper.[49]

Communication research permits the development of models serving organizing, heuristic, predictive, and measuring functions. Such models can assist in the mapping of international systems. More importantly, communication models are directly relevant to law, particularly in decentralized systems that rely primarily upon self-interpretation and self-help as modified by bargaining and negotiation. For laws are communications from a formulator, whether legislator, law-making judge, rule-making administrator, treaty-maker, or

[49] Rudolph J. Rummel, "Understanding Factor Analysis," *Journal of Conflict Resolution* 11 (1967): 466, Table I, note f; Don C. Piper, "Communication: Determining State Adherence to International Law," *Journal of Conflict Resolution* 12 (1968): 398-401.

custom-producing community action. Laws are addressed to a public, general or particular, the latter including judges and administrators. Inviting responses, some immediately, some at later dates, such requirements as promulgation, publication, or registration are introduced to assure at least a minimum effort to perform the act of communication with those who are expected to respond by behaving or by not behaving in certain ways. Indeed, a traditional section of international law texts identifies normative communications and authoritative communicators including, in the case of custom, judges, arbitrators, and publicists.

Law is stored in memories—enough is in the minds of the general public to keep most people out of trouble. More is stored in the minds of experts who serve as agents of those in conflict or potential conflict and of those simply seeking to conform to legal technicalities of which they lack knowledge, as well as in the minds of experts who serve as third parties in conflict situations. Still more enters collections of statutes, treaties, executive orders or decrees, and judicial decisions. Storage on magnetic tape is now coming into being. The laws thus stored are signs that represent people's aspirations and attitudes, among other things. How well they communicate what they were intended to represent is not only a subject for inquiry but also a reason why law is something more than a collection of messages or rules.

Formulating and storing a legal communication provides no guarantee that recall on an appropriate occasion will occur or that what is brought forth from memory will not be modified or distorted by a bargainer, a disputant, or a mediating third party.[50] Part of legal analysis consists in seeking out the reasons

[50] For a parliamentary draftsman's complaint, see Sir Granville Ram, "The Improvement of the Statute Book," *Journal of the Society of Public Teachers of Law*, 1951, p. 442. For complaints about unintelligible drafting, see the remarks of Lord Buckmaster in *G. W. Ry. Co.* v. *Bator* (1922) 2 A.C. 1 at 11, and of Lord Goddard in *Bebb* v. *Frank* (1939) 1 K.B. at 568.

for particular distortions, modifications, or interpretations of ambiguities. We suggest that at least from the point of view of the scholar, if not from that of the practitioner of law, resort to the findings and methods of communication research may reveal a great deal about legal processes and functions in domestic and international societies that presently lies hidden under the traditional legal language and concepts. A communications approach seems particularly relevant to the study of international law in view of the paucity of authoritative third parties, the symbolic evidence of their presence, the linguistic and cultural impediments to effective communication, in addition to normal perceptual impediments to communication between parties pursuing divergent and possibly incompatible goals.

Laboratory experiments, including simulation and gaming, can be employed for research on communications, on the manner in which systems operate, on the effects of personality on decision processes, on negotiating behavior, etc. Project Leviathan, which Beatrice and Sydney Rome directed at System Development Corporation in Santa Monica, employed communications as the indicator of the effectiveness of a large organization. The project developed the important findings (1) that in the absence of norms their organization did not function effectively and (2) that the most important norm in producing a smooth-running group was the simple directive, "Take the system perspective."[51] Given the adaptability of the

[51] Beatrice and Sydney Rome, *Communications and Large Organizations,* Professional Paper SP-1690/000/000 Santa Monica: System Development Corporation, September 4, 1964), pp. 60-61. See also Muzafer Sherif, "Superordinate Goals in the Reduction of Intergroup Conflict," *American Journal of Sociology* 63 (1958): 349-56; Herbert A. Simon, "On the Concept of Organizational Goal," *Administrative Science Quarterly* 9 (1964): 1-22. For a suggestion based upon empirical and comparative studies, that the difficulties encountered by Dominicans in developing cooperation among themselves may be due to an extreme case by case approach that inhibits the building of superordinate or commonly accepted generalizations, see Bryant Wedge, "Communi-

Leviathan model to generalization, these findings are significant and certainly suggestive of additional research on the normative aspect as it relates to constitutional law and, given the locus of sovereignty in the state, for international law.

Reports on other simulations are included in our footnotes, and at this point in the text it suffices to call attention only to the Inter-Nation Simulation at Northwestern University which has provided Harold Guetzkow and his associates with a basic model[52] with which to investigate the Nth country problem, variables related to the outbreak of World War I (including personality variables), crisis decision-making, and differences in the decision-making behavior of high school students and diplomats stationed in Washington. The basic Guetzkow model was employed by Wayman J. Crow and John R. Raser of the Western Behavioral Science Institute to study the effects of capacity to delay response and to obtain a cross-national comparison of decision styles by conducting the simulation both in the United States and in Mexico.[53]

It does not seem unreasonable that the study of international law might extend its venture into simulation beyond the teaching device of the moot court. Indeed, Eduard Ziegenhagen has formulated and is revising a design for a simulation that would set the domestic appellate process under the pressures of domestic politics.[54] This is one direction in which simulation can be taken to provide training that supplements the moot

---

cation Analysis and Comprehensive Diplomacy," in Arthur S. Hoffman (ed.), *International Communication and the New Diplomacy* (Bloomington: Indiana University Press, 1968), pp. 40, 42.

[52] Harold Guetzkow, Richard A. Brody, Robert C. Noel, and Richard C. Snyder, *Simulation in International Relations: Developments for Research and Teaching* (Englewood Cliffs: Prentice-Hall, 1963).

[53] Crow and Raser, "A Cross-Cultural Simulation Study."

[54] Eduard A. Ziegenhagen, "A Student Handbook for A Simulation of Judicial Systems and Processes," mimeographed (Detroit: Wayne State University, July, 1968).

court experience. Other directions would stress negotiations and other norm-creating processes.

Aside from the fact that negotiations are often part of a lawyer's business, there are research possibilities to be exploited. Interest in negotiating styles might well be extended to include a possible distinctive "lawyer's style" by employing lawyers as subjects in a simulation that provides opportunities for comparisons with each other and with non-lawyers. We might learn more about the treaty-making process if an Inter-Nation simulation were structured to permit hard phrase-by-phrase negotiating instead of reducing the treaty-making time to five minutes or so in order to permit the simulated world to function for several simulated months or years. We know of no simulation structured to permit focus upon the role of legal norms in the conduct of relations between states—nor do we know of any simulation model that makes provision for either a norm-interpreting third party or for national legal advisers. The closest approaches to the study of the role of norms are, besides Project Leviathan, small group studies the most interesting of which is that of Thomas A. Cowan of the Rutgers Law School and Donald A. Strickland, a political scientist now at Northwestern University. The Cowan-Strickland study for NASA involved two groups isolated in simulated flight to the moon and gives attention to such things as leadership patterns, rule degradation, and emergence of new rules.[55] Observation of a later group in the NASA isolation experiment provided Walter O. Weyrauch with opportunity to note the emergence of standards in a small group and to

[55] Thomas A. Cowan, Donald A. Strickland, et al., "The Legal Structure of A Confined Microsociety (A Report on the Cases of Penthouse II and III)," Internal Working Paper No. 34 (Berkeley: Space Sciences Laboratory, Social Sciences Project, University of California, August, 1965).

find that some standards were violated only after the experimenter gave them express formulation.[56]

One objection that might be raised concerning simulation is that it amounts to small group research and suffers from the validation limitations imposed by the small group format. Certainly this would be true if the small group were isolated, not even linked by computer to other programmed small groups. It would also be true if the model set the small group in the wrong place and provided for face-to-face communications when simulating a situation in which the operative small groups would in reality be cabinets at national capitals communicating with each other through ambassadors.[57]

However, there is an answer to the above-mentioned objection, assuming proper structuring of the simulation. Too often we seem to have inherited a royalist concept of hierarchy that portrays hierarchies composed of individuals, culminating in a decision-maker whose word is final. This age of associations of all sorts displays organizations composed of departments, bureaus, sections, advisory groups, staffs, committees, commissions, and tribunals or their equivalents. An earlier age displayed guilds, estates, and other collegia. It might be more appropriate to think in terms of hierarchies of small groups tending to aggregate into associations and, like university faculties in particular fields, into interorganizational groups themselves subdivided into small groups. For a pluralistic world the small group, capable of aggregation with other small groups and of assuming a hierarchical rank, would seem to be an essential unit to account for in both partial and general theory. If so,

[56] Walter O. Weyrauch, "The Law of A Small Group," Internal Working Paper No. 54 (Berkeley: Space Sciences Laboratory, Social Sciences Project, University of California, 1967); condensed in "Law in Isolation: The Penthouse Astronauts," *Trans-action* 5 (June, 1968): 39-46.

[57] See Dina A. Zinnes, "A Comparison of Hostile Behavior of Decision-Makers in Simulate and Historical Data," *World Politics* 18 (1966): 496-99.

then the objection to small group research, whether or not in the form of simulation, is reduced only to a demand for proper structuring. And small group research has an enhanced contribution to make to theory.

Pre-Theory, Partial Theories, and Their Synthesis

WHEN DISCUSSING the current data now being collected and the accompanying interpretative literature, we remarked that the more general the theory needed to bring order, the more remote it appears to be. The flood of theoretically oriented literature adds to the chaos. Claims of generality are sometimes made, although often with a confining descriptive phrase, e.g., the "general theory of conflict." Or particularity is assured by the coverage; a theory of conflict that does little with conflicts at law and conflicts of law (in a broader sense than a synonym for private international law) is highly particular even in regard to the segment of life for which it seeks generality. The same is true of a general theory of law that does little or nothing with bargaining processes, legislative politics, interest group politics, and the like.[58]

No quarrel can be maintained against the avowed restriction of scope of a venture into theory-building. Nor is there objection, except perhaps to its quantity, to the literature directed "toward" a general theory of action or other theory. Even the most generalized venture is bound to be confined to something less than generality if the theorist lacks the interest or the technical skills for comprehensive and realistic study of all relevant subjects. Tomorrow's efficient computer retrieval will neither replace interest nor supply skill in handling retrieved data.

To produce another piece of "toward" literature or to produce avowedly partial theory or theory general only to a

[58] On these matters, see Joseph-Barthélemy, *La Conduite de la politique extérieure dans les democraties* (Paris: Publications de la Conciliation Internationale, 1930), and his "Politique intérieure et droit international," *Académie de Droit International: Recueil des cours* 59 (1937): 427-519.

particular portion of human behavior may well be to make a contribution toward general theory. So, too, might be the development of a "pre-theory" directed, as James N. Rosenau suggests, toward rendering raw materials "comparable and ready for theorizing" through similar processing. In respect to the specific matter of Rosenau's concern, foreign policy, this means translation into five sets of variables designated as idiosyncratic, role, governmental, societal, and systemic variables.[59]

It is unquestionably significant that among many social scientists a consensus has been developing that the present target for theoretical work should be so-called middle range theory. As Charles A. McClelland conceives the stages of research in terms of degree of abstraction there are five levels: (1) assembly of data, (2) low-level generalization, (3) highly generalized explanations based on conventional and socio-cultural data, (4) supracultural explanations, and (5) purely formal statements of universal scope.[60] The third stage in McClelland's classification is the target apparently gaining a consensus, although McClelland himself regards it as the most difficult objective and most likely to be reached by conjunction proceeding (a) from stages 1 and 2 and (b) from stages 4 and 5.

However, before lending support to that consensus, our predeliction for the fourth stage should be specified, for one of us has tried to base his exposition of international law upon foreign-language sources, English-language sources of foreign authorship, and American sources, while the other has expressed a concern that non-Western societies be taken into

[59] James N. Rosenau, "Pre-Theories and Theories of Foreign Policy," in R. Barry Farrell (ed.), *Approaches to Comparative and International Politics* (Evanston: Northwestern University Press, 1966), pp. 39-43.

[60] Charles A. McClelland, "Systems and History in International Relations: Some Perspectives for Empirical Research and Theory," *General Systems Yearbook* 3 (1958): 221-47. The order in which the five levels of abstraction are listed does not imply an unguided search for facts. Throughout his work McClelland refers to the use of organizing concepts when searching for data.

account. We have tried to meet the challenge of Hedley Bull's argument that current scientific approaches to international affairs represent certain American assumptions about foreign policy problems—assumptions about the moral simplicity of foreign policy problems, the existence of "solutions," the receptivity of policy makers to research findings, and the degree of manipulation that one state can exert over the whole diplomatic field.[61] Although Bull's comment may be only a revision of European objections to "international law, chiefly as interpreted by the United States," we cannot hold a brief for national or cultural boundaries to social science and would like to see more effort to overcome the burden of having been nationals before becoming social scientists.[62]

Endorsement of the middle range as the appropriate target is subject to additional strictures besides, in so far as possible, avoidance of the usually unseen bonds of culture. It could be that what is presented as a new theoretical advance might be no more than restatement of old concepts in newer terminology or with minor adaptations to cover modern developments such as the increased destructiveness of weapons and improved communications technology.[63] Moreover, what purports to be theory should not amount to a policy recommendation, whether pacifistic or belligerent, even if it might serve subsequently as a basis for the theoretician to attempt to influence responsible actors.

[61] Hedley Bull, "International Theory: The Case for A Classical Approach," *World Politics* 18 (1966): 375.

[62] If we can assume that an example of national conditioning exists in the use of the *New York Times* as the common news source for social scientists, then a warning is to be found in the report of differences between the *New York Times* and three European "prestige" newspapers' views of European integration. Karl W. Deutsch, "Integration and Arms Control in the European Political Environment: A Summary Report," *American Political Science Review* 60 (1966): 356.

[63] On the similarity between 18th-century balance-of-power thought and current debate on international affairs, see Per Maurseth, "Balance-of-Power Thinking from the Renaissance to the French Revolution," *Journal of Peace Research* 1 (1964): 120-36.

Theory should not be pushed beyond the limits of rationality and nonrationality models. Such models provide useful concepts but may fail to distinguish between the perspective rationality that expounds possibilities and strategies, the active rationality that makes action choices amid uncertainty and risk, and the retrospective rationality of the historian-philosopher that discovers an interaction of decisions made during conflict that was unknown to those who made the decisions.[64] If the findings of social psychologists are to be included in theory, as they should be, it is essential to probe the nature of men, if not of man, and their relation to nature. Doing so should include recognition of debts to political and social philosophers, including those whose interest in human nature led into psychology, without also becoming imprisoned in ideas acquired from those who have gone before and become socially acceptable among the scholarly professions.[65]

Perhaps the most important stricture that can be laid down as a guide to making middle range explanation and partial theory an eventual contribution to general theory is that the segments not be walled off from each other to prevent synthesis of many particulars into the general. Hopefully, present interdisciplinary endeavors have been penetrating terminological

[64] See Sidney Verba, "Assumptions of Rationality and Non-Rationality in Models of International Systems," *World Politics* 14 (1961): 93-117; P. Hassner, "Violence, rationalité, incertitude—tendences apocalyptiques et iréniques dans l'étude des conflits internationaux," *Revue française de science politique* 14 (1964): 1155-78. Cf. William H. Riker, "Bargaining in A Three-Person Game," *American Political Science Review* 61 (1967): 642-56, esp. pp. 655-56.

[65] On the need to reconstruct the particularities of political philosophers' efforts to understand the essential nature of political phenomena, see Richard Cox, "The Role of Political Philosophy in the Theory of International Relations," *Social Research* 29 (1962): 261-92. For experimental evidence of the high probability of sticking to a principle that worked once but no longer works, being a desire to be regarded as right in an approach to a problem, see A. S. and E. H. Luchins, "Einstellung Effect in Social Learning," *Journal of Social Psychology* 55 (1961): 59-66.

and conceptual barriers. Neither uniformity nor unification of theory has yet resulted, but if new barriers are not established by the emergent disciplines, it may be that a step has been taken toward the merging of theory whether multilaterally or, as Jerome Hall urged for political and legal theory, bilaterally.[66]

Care must be taken when employing models from alien fields. As Martin Landau has pointed out in the course of outlining a set of canons for the use of models, there exist several dangers to be guarded against when employing models from alien fields.[67] Among the dangers listed by Landau are: the introduction of vagueness when transfer to another field occurs and models are intermingled; failure to follow the rules and language of a model's original field; and, perhaps most important, the possibility of models from alien fields becoming mere metaphors. An illustration of the potential danger was actually presented in our reference to law as communication when the implication was made that not only the general public and the experts but also law books and computers have "memories." However, the risk of metaphor and vagueness may have to be taken when one is confronted with linguistic and other barriers to synthesis which mathematical representation alone proves an insufficient device for overcoming.

Despite the danger, partial theories have been constructed by synthesis without barring the door to further generalization. Almond's meshing of the functional approach with systems theory has already been mentioned. Hermann Weilenmann has produced a significant combination of historical study and participant observation to develop a theory of democracy based upon the opportunity of individuals to choose small group affiliations on the basis of what they prefer their own personal-

[66] Jerome Hall, "Unification of Political and Legal Theory," *Political Science Quarterly* 69 (1954): 15-28.

[67] Martin Landau, "Political Theory and Due Process of Inquiry," (Paper presented at the Annual Meeting of the American Political Science Association, Chicago, September, 1964).

ity structures and identities to become.[68] André Nicolai has developed a theory bridging the areas of economic behavior and social structure that seeks to explain and evaluate the dynamic union of structures and behaviors.[69] The bridge extends somewhat into the area of law or at least invites an excursion into it. In particular he explores the supports of structures maintained by individuals joined into groups. James M. Buchanan and Gordon Tullock conducted their examination of political organization and majority rule with the use of methods and concepts ordinarily used to study the economic organization of society, while Robert L. Curry and Lawrence Wade have resorted to exchange theory as a tool for political analysis.[70] Walter Isard and Julian Wolpert employ the methods of regional science to develop a hierarchical model of central places and service areas, charting vectors of influence and flow (communication, migration, etc.) to and from the world primary node, subregional primary nodes, and local community nuclei. A system of world law is postulated. It would entail adjudication grounded on multipliers or other bases for programmed decisions permitting compromise through the weighting of participation in decision-making, efficiency, and equality potentials.[71] Quite promising is Rum-

[68] Hermann Weilenmann, "The Interlocking of Nation and Personality Structure," in Karl W. Deutsch and William J. Foltz (eds.), *Nation-Building* (New York: Atherton, 1963), pp. 33-55, indicates directions to be taken by his theory of democracy. An earlier suggestion of the theory that would emerge may be found in his *Pax Helvetica: Die Democratie der Kleinen Gruppen* (Zurich: Rentsch, 1951).

[69] André Nicolai, *Comportement économique et structures sociales* (Paris: Presses Universitaires de France, 1960).

[70] James M. Buchanan and Gordon Tullock, *The Calculus of Consent: Logical Foundations of Constitutional Democracy* (Ann Arbor: University of Michigan Press, 1962; paperback edition, 1965); Robert L. Curry and Lawrence Wade, *A Theory of Political Exchange: Economic Reasoning in Political Analysis* (Englewood Cliffs: Prentice-Hall, 1969).

[71] Walter Isard and Julian Wolpert, "Notes on Social Science Prin-

mel's effort to develop a field theory of social action which is philosophically akin to the field theory of Kurt Lewin but differs mathematically by building in terms of vectors and angles rather than, as Lewin did, upon the mathematical ideas of topology. Rummel's theory is also similar to Quincy Wright's verbally structured field theory for international relations in its philosophy, emphasis upon coordinates, and its employment of a basic equation anticipated by Wright, among others.[72] The theory, developed for application with ordinal or nominal measurement, is also related to general systems theory in the hope of producing an advance in that theory.

All the preceding examples are ventures into theory that seek to bridge conventionally separated realms of discourse. They suggest what may become possible in the form of truly interdisciplinary theory, but it is not yet general theory and may never become such. These examples of synthesis may seem to be rather remote from the subject of international law. However, to the extent that theoreticians attack bridging problems, they can help to develop concepts that—in the hands of thinkers with the interest and skills to embrace international law in their theories—can advance international law beyond its reliance upon strictly legal theory. Venture into seemingly irrelevant theory, as well as among unfamiliar methods, at least promises innovation, a fruit that must be found before its quality is judged.

"Pure" Theory and Application

THE BATTLE between theory and application has been fought out in the physical and biological sciences and the old division between knowledge for its own sake and its translation into

---

ciples For World Law and Order," *Peace Research Society (International), Papers*, Ghent Conference, 1964, vol. 2 (1965), pp. 242-51.

[72] See Rudolph J. Rummel, "A Social Field Theory of Foreign Conflict Behavior," *Peace Research Society (International), Papers*, Cracow Conference, 1965, vol. 4 (1966), pp. 131-50.

socially useful forms has been largely erased—so much so, indeed, that federal spending, an indicator of socially useful payoffs, now underwrites much of what had come to be known as "basic research." In part, this new-found appreciation arises from the telescoping of the lag which once existed between the realms of theory and practice, or demonstration. The signal demonstration of this reduced time-lag is, of course, the case of Albert Einstein, whose life spanned the translation of the special theory of relativity's mass-energy equation into the realm of empirical reality. Although Keynes' life was comparable, this kind of vivid example is less commonly observed in the study of human behavior. For one thing, the paucity of theory reduces the opportunities. Nevertheless, there is no reason to believe that the same effect cannot be observed, helped along by the social sciences' well known characteristic, at times dangerous, of stimulating the very behavior predicted, i.e., the self-fulfilling prophecy.

But there is a second reason for the rapprochement between theory and application. Once it could be shown that the most abstruse theoretical work eventuated in developments that could be seen in everyday life, everyone suddenly became a kind of theorist. To the extent that the engineer's work depends upon prior work by the laboratory researcher or blackboard theorist, the engineer is himself a kind of theorist and his own applications feed back upon the work of subsequent theorists.

The overlap between the worlds of theory and practice becomes even greater when the interconnections are not consciously appreciated. The practitioner is always, in a very real sense, his own theoretician. Thus, every politician is his own political scientist, for if you probe for the rationales of his decisions, you will find them based upon a whole series of tacit propositions about political behavior. The practicing lawyer may never have taken a course in jurisprudence, yet his everyday choices must, of necessity, be informed by a set of assumptions about the nature of law and courts. Finally, the foreign-office policy-maker, despite protestations to the contrary, must hold his own theory of international relations. If he did not hold certain views on the *general* behavior of states, his own acts would be little more than random responses.

Science, as a way of thinking, can be set apart from everyday mental processes in at least two respects. First, like all genuinely creative activities, it centers upon the discernment of common properties in outwardly diverse phenomena. "In this sense, science is as much a play of imagination as poetry is."[73] Second, it depends upon making all of its assumptions and, indeed, its prejudices both conscious and explicit. Science ". . . unlike poetry . . . does not seek to exploit its ambiguities, but to minimize them."[74] This commitment to making the tacit explicit places science apart from the way in which we normally reason, since nonscientific mental activities are replete with all manner of hidden assumptions, telescoped reasonings, and undefined terms. These characteristics do not in themselves mean that any conclusions so drawn are false but only that there are sources of error that have not been eliminated.

International law takes in, at least by implication, an extremely wide gamut of human activity. This activity ranges from that of the individual policy-maker to that of a state which, though it acts as a single person, nonetheless encompasses the lives of tens of millions of persons. At various points, scientific, economic, psychological, sociological, and anthropological considerations impinge upon international law. International law, insofar as it includes a codification of behavioral norms, depends for its efficacy upon the truth of a great

[73] J. Bronowski, "The Machinery of Nature," *Encounter* 25 (November, 1965): 53.
[74] *Loc. cit.*

many assumptions about the ways in which individuals and states behave.[75] Now the social sciences, with some exceptions, have not been greatly interested in normative considerations. On the surface, indeed, most social scientists have been preoccupied with draining their research of all value judgments. But they have also been interested in investigating just those assumptions upon which the efficacy of international law depends. In their own endeavor to make the implicit explicit, social scientists, however inadvertently, have served to bring to the surface much that was submerged in international law.

Just as a scientist's theory must have links to the empirical world in order to possess any utility, so a legal system must bear some direct relationship to the behavior it wishes to regulate. This relationship may be conceived of as a correlation between "positive law" and "living law."[76] In other terms, law is a "subservient abstraction . . . to simplify the understanding of man's social and political history."[77] In any case, the linkage must be there. To the extent that the social sciences draw out, sharpen, and test the assumptions upon which international norms depend, they aid in the establishment of that linkage.

[75] William D. Coplin, "International Law and the Assumptions of the State System," *World Politics* 17 (1965): 615-34.

[76] F.S.C. Northrop, *Philosophical Anthropology and Practical Politics* (New York: Macmillan, 1963), p. 4.

[77] Anton-Hermann Chroust, "Law: Reason, Legalism, and Legal Process," *Ethics* 74 (1963): 1-38.

Chapter II: Patterns, Structure, and Units

Foundations of International Law

TEXTBOOKS ON international law frequently include a section on the foundations of international law that may elaborate a doctrine of natural law, of positivism, or of consensus. The doctrine then serves as a basis of discussion of the sources and evidence of positive international law or of occasional probes in the direction of sociological factors. The latter occur much less frequently than might have been expected after Max Huber's work of 1910. So rare is a probe toward biology such as that attempted by Georges Scelle or toward psychological foundations such as that attempted by Paul Therre and Ranyard West that they might almost be regarded as deviant scholars. Indeed, so deviant were they that neither Therre nor West were to be more than one-shot international lawyers while Scelle's search, however crude, for a link with biology is hardly the accomplishment for which he is best remembered.

Legalistic traditions, whether Continental or Anglo-Saxon, have prevailed and render the study of the foundations of international law little more than an exercise in logic. The exercise has been little challenged by the critics of international lawyers, since the critics have failed to familiarize themselves with the potential for probes in depth invited by such figures as Scelle, Huber, West, and Therre. Interestingly, the critics of international law have discovered that Julius Stone, Myres McDougal, Richard Falk, Kenneth Carlston, Wolfgang Friedmann, Roger Fisher, and Morton Kaplan with Nicholas Katzenbach have departed from tradition. But in no sense did the critics precede the international lawyers in discovering and appreciating the innovations. It would appear that there is a legal culture which, like other scholarly cultures, at one time shunts innovations to the sidelines, out of even the critics' view, and at a later time pushes innovation to the fore.

Traditional legal culture placed so-called foundations of international law either within the law itself or within doctrines about the law, e.g., moral philosophy. Thus Kelsen's *Grundnorm* stood at the apex of the legal hierarchy and to go beyond it, perhaps to morality or to sociological factors, was at most to go from the law to thought about the law. Such approaches, while not irrelevant, gave the impression of irrelevancy because they led only to conundrums, logically unsolvable, and to the island of the closed, self-contained system of legal theory. Such "islands," like all closed systems, are subject not to decreasing but only to increasing entropy.

The preceding criticism of closed systems of thought about the law does not imply rejection of such frequently suggested foundations of international law as the following: preexisting norms; the basic maxims of national, supranational, regional, and global systems; transnational legal cultures such as the Moslem or the modern Roman; or legal theory.[1] It only asserts that there are more foundations than are usually mentioned. Additional foundations are implied in conventional chapters, e.g., on territorial jurisdiction, boundaries, the high seas, and international air law. A political foundation is almost assumed, but hardly articulated in conventional international law texts.

Territorial jurisdiction has long been the core of international law for reasons which Richard Falk has endeavored to assess in terms of the global normative structure and the different properties of horizontal and vertical norms. More con-

[1] On the mystique, mythology, and masks that are among the supports of law, see C.A.W. Manning, *The Nature of International Society* (London: G. Bell, 1962), pp. 101-13. Anton-Hermann Chroust, "Law: Reason, Legalism, and the Legal Process," *Ethics* 74 (1963): 1-18; John F. A. Taylor, *The Masks of Society: An Inquiry Into The Covenants of Civilization* (New York: Appleton-Century-Crofts, 1966), chaps. I, IV.

crete is Alexander-Alexandrowicz's application of the horizontal and vertical categories to the global societal structure and its strata to demonstrate certain incompatibilities between national and transnational goals and the means for their realization.[2] Structural and political foundations are related to the geographical as the latter is modified by changes in the economics and technology of transportation and communication. There has been no legal system embracing units too remote in space and time to permit interaction. Between Marco Polo and the Chinese there could be reciprocal respect and courtesy, including the Italian's care not to offend the laws and customs of the Mongol Empire; but between Venice and China there was no common law because of an insufficiency of interactions, including deviant or offensive behavior, on which to base such a law. In more recent centuries Sino-European interactions, not requiring Arab traders and South China Sea sailors as middlemen, have required more guidance than a framework provided by etiquette.

Since this is not a treatise elaborating the foundations of international law, that particular task will not be pursued; implications, however, may be drawn from remarks at other points in this commentary. It suffices to say at this point that to the extent that "foundations" implies "resting" or a unidirectional dependence it is an inaccurate designation of the interactions that give rise to and change international law. Sociological, economic, and psychological foundations of international law, together with the time dimension, require integrated elaboration. Integration would give to time not its meaning for mathematical physics but its "social" meaning. Time, as is well known, both supports and undermines specific international norms. "The effects of time"—this is the subject matter to be examined for supports of international law and

[2] C. H. Alexander-Alexandrowicz, "Vertical and Horizontal Divisions of the International Society," *Indian Year Book of International Affairs* 1 (1952): 88-96.

for the termite-like action whereby certain living systems can damage or destroy those supports while others try to prevent or to counteract the damage.

Systems: Identification, Composition, Structure, and Processes

WITH EXTRAORDINARY rapidity postwar international relations scholars have sought to construct a theoretical framework to encompass world political interrelationships. These attempts have been quite adequately discussed elsewhere,[3] so that what follows represents simply a series of glosses on developments in international relations and history.

The search for patterned activity in the international scene might seem at first to occasion a dismal prognosis. The multiplication of international organizations of all kinds, particularly those whose claims are supranational, has lent some semblance of rational organization to international life, but the diffusion of power through an increasing number of state-subjects has maintained the appearance of radical decentralization and "diverse public orders." Nevertheless, some theorists have persisted in the search for underlying, indeed unconscious, continuities of behavior. This search for the reality of a pattern in the appearance of disorder has been most tenaciously pursued by the system theorists.

A debate which recurs from time to time is whether the word "community" or the word "society" can be properly applied to a nonhierarchical agglomeration of states, international and regional public organizations, nongovernmental international organizations, and, of course, individuals. Is there an international community or international society? In an older formulation fitting the days before the existence of inter-

[3] Richard C. Snyder, "Some Recent Trends in International Relations Theory and Research," in Austin Ranney (ed.) *Essays on the Behavioral Study of Politics* (Urbana: University of Illinois Press, 1962), pp. 103-71.

national organizations, is there a society of states, even when an extreme meaning of "sovereignty" is not attached to the idea of the state?

While we do not want to enter into a discussion of Tönnies' distinction between comparable German terms or to become embogged in other scholars' definitions and distinctions, certain problems do require attention. Was Cicero right in associating the idea of law with the idea of community—of having something in common which, in the case of the *ius naturale*, was identified as reason? Conversely, can there be law if there is no society or community? Can there be law if there is only an unstructured agglomeration? Bearing in mind that decentralization implies structure—a measure of organization above the zero level of an unstructured randomness—does the presence of law imply at least a minimum of structural association, laterally if not hierarchically? Or is the so-called presence of law at the international level only an illusion, a misperception produced by using personal or national moral standards to judge the international behavior of public officeholders?

What is needed is a concept that would do the following: establish a minimum requirement for the presence of law; account for the actual relationships of states and international organizations; permit the holding of something in common without imposing the standards of community or of society which we apply when individuals and groups less comprehensive than the state associate; carry no necessary global implications; and be valid for the period of the separation of Europe from the Americas, southern Africa, the Far East, and Southeast Asia, as well as for the relationships inaugurated by the Age of Discovery. This means that a concept is needed that would permit progressive developments from the simple to the complex, from the local to the global (and even the extraglobal now that space is being penetrated), and from the unifunctional to the multifunctional.

We suggest that one potentially useful concept is that of "system," more specifically, that of the "living system" which, in James G. Miller's view,[4] embraces seven levels from the cellular to the supranational and includes societies.[5] Because it can include the international level (supranational in Miller's language), the concept of system avoids the need either to prove that international associations are societies or communities or to admit a purely metaphorical employment of either or both terms.

Except for supranational systems which are said to lack an independent "decider," Miller's living systems share the characteristic of being "totipotential," that is, capable of carrying out all critical subsystem processes needed for life or survival. Those not capable of carrying out all subsystem processes required to sustain life, that is, "partipotential" systems, are either parasitic (e.g., viruses, for which another system carries out a critical process in exchange for nothing) or symbiotic (when another system carries out a critical process in exchange for something at a cost to the first system). The stress on capability should be noted, for a system can be totipotential but only partially rather than fully functioning. Moreover, in an age in which interdependence is more than ever before a characteristic of states, degrees of relative symbiosis must be taken

[4] What follows is based largely but not exclusively on James G. Miller, "Living Systems: Basic Concepts," *Behavioral Science* 10 (1965): 193-237, and his two additional articles, "Living Systems: Structure and Process" and "Living Systems: Cross-Level Hypotheses," in the same journal at pp. 337-79, 380-411.

[5] The levels are: cell, organ, organism, group, organization, society, supranational system. Supranational does not appear to embrace the distinction between international and supranational organizations that many students of international affairs make (Miller, "Living Systems: Basic Concepts," p. 213). Miller's systems form a hierarchy; each higher level is composed of lower level systems. For a similar conceptualization of a hierarchy of living systems, see J. C. Coleman, *Personality Dynamics and Effective Behavior* (Chicago: Scott, Foresman, 1960).

into account in analyses of pairs (dyads) and blocs of states and the true nature of their legal links. Indeed, system development through "community action" appears to include, among other consequences, symbiosis.[6]

"System" has been variously defined. It is not our purpose to examine exhaustively and to weigh the merits of the several definitions but only to call attention to a small number that may prove useful. David Easton distinguishes empirical systems from symbolic systems or sets of symbols employed to identify, describe, delimit, and explain the behavior of empirical systems. Empirical systems are seen as being of two sorts, natural and constructive. "Natural" systems are defined as sets of interactions that seem to share a common fate—that have elements that move together. In order to avoid a number of problems, among them the distinction between a system and a nonsystem and that of whether a nonsystem has later become a system, Easton chooses to deal with "constructive" systems, that is, with sets of variables selected by the observer on the basis of apparent interdependence, relevance, interest, and usefulness from the point of view of understanding.[7]

Miller prefers to follow Ludwig von Bertalanffy's lead to define a system as "a set of units with relationships among them." The word "set" implies that the units have common properties, the state of each of the coupled units being constrained by, or dependent on the state of other units. At least one measure of the sum of units must be larger than the sum of that measure of its units in the sense that a man with a head is something more than a man's body plus a head.

Miller distinguishes (1) conceptual systems composed of such units as words, numbers, or other symbols, (2) "con-

[6] Eugene P. Odum, "The Strategy of Ecosystem Development," *Science* 164 (1969): 265, 266.

[7] David Easton, *A Framework for Political Analysis* (Englewood Cliffs: Prentice-Hall, 1965), pp. 26-33.

crete" systems, and (3) "abstracted" systems. A conceptual system may be purely logical or mathematical, or it may be intended to have some formal identity or isomorphism with what is empirically determinable. Miller treats scientific advance as an increase in isomorphism between a conceptual system and objective findings about concrete and abstracted systems.

A "concrete" system is defined as a "nonrandom accumulation of matter-energy, in a region in physical space-time, which is nonrandomly organized into coacting, interrelated subsystems or components."[8] Nonrandomness stems from the circumstance that for a system to exist there must be a reduction of entropy, that is, disorder, disorganization, or lack of pattern. Since information entails varying amounts of formal patterning or complexity in a system and so is the negative of disorder or uncertainty,[9] a living system maintains a steady state of "negentropy," restoring its own energy and repairing breakdowns, even though entropic changes occur. Applying this conceptualization to legal systems may help to introduce clearer meaning to the idea that law acquires a life of its own, even though the expression is figurative and law has no life apart from human beings and their behavior.

An "abstracted" system, not to be confused with abstractions which represent a class of phenomena, is composed of relationships selected by an observer on the basis of his interests or theoretical or philosophical preferences. Some of these relationships may be empirically determinable but others may be only the observer's concepts. Clearly, Easton's "empirical" systems, in which interactions rather than nonrandom accumulations of matter-energy located in time-space are the units, are

[8] Miller, "Living Systems: Basic Concepts," p. 202.

[9] On the cybernetic concept and the possibility of a dual transition whereby negentropy becomes information, that is, the acquisition of knowledge, and information becomes negentropy, signifying the power of organization, see O. C. de Beauregard, "Sur l'equivalence entre information et entropie," *Sciences* 11 (1961): 54.

abstracted systems. So, too, is the systems concept of Talcott Parsons.

Later, particularly when considering intersystem relations, we will make reference to "functional" systems. This means (1) that we will be concerned with relationships such as the legal, political, and economic that can be isolated for analytical purposes, and (2) that these analytically carved-out systems consist of variables significantly related to one another. For example, an econometric model of the United States that seeks to evaluate the impact of different monetary measures involves the "arbitrary" construction of an economic system but also is governed by criteria of empirical relevance.[10] Analytical isolation does not, of course, mean existential isolation. Indeed, there is no necessary reason why an economic relationship cannot also be a political relationship. Nor does the stress on type of relationship mean that a functional system is an abstracted rather than a concrete system; for unless the relations are between units, they dangle meaninglessly between "nothings."

Miller gives five reasons for preferring concrete systems: (1) they are easier to use because they permit the theorist to profit from a lifetime of experience in space-time that has conditioned his thought processes; (2) variations in units appear to contribute as much or more to total system variance than variations in relationships and both must be taken into account to explain process; (3) for concrete systems one does not ascribe to relationships a life of their own apart from the units; (4) intrasystem relationships in concrete systems affect processes within and between concrete systems; (5) unification of the sciences would be accelerated if the social sciences made use of concrete systems as do the natural sciences.[11]

The concrete system might for most purposes be the more

[10] Gary Fromm and Paul Taubman, *Policy Simulations with an Econometric Model* (Washington: Brookings Institution, 1968), p. 9.

[11] Miller, "Living Systems: Basic Concepts," pp. 201-209.

useful for treating international law in a manner relevant to most people's concerns with international affairs. In the final analysis, we are hardly more concerned with the relationship between Red China's actions and the Vietnam war than we are with what attributes of China influence it to behave in certain ways when violence breaks out in Vietnam Units that "behave" and develop relationships arouse human expectations and worries. Hence there exists in the Red China–Vietnam problem not only a foreign policy problem but also a legal question. It is a legal question by virtue of the fact that the relationships involved are relationships between or among units that actually or potentially have the status of international legal persons, e.g., North and South Vietnam, the Viet Cong, Communist and Nationalist China, and the United States. Thus, only attention to the unit, South Vietnam, can permit a classification of the United States' action as intervention on behalf of a usurping regime or as response to an invitation by the legitimate government of an international person, that is, a state. And only attention to that same unit, South Vietnam, could have determined the status of the Viet Cong both as a domestic phenomenon and in relation to the states represented when the Vietnam situation was brought to the conference table.

The preceding does not constitute an argument that resort to abstracted systems cannot be useful for international law. Some matters may be clarified by resort to abstracted systems, among them, perhaps, the relationships of international law to municipal law. However, to be meaningful such an approach would require reference to the structure and processes of international systems, national systems, and subsystems of national systems.[12]

[12] For an attempt to deal with the municipal law–international law relationship that, despite an unrecorded effort to generalize at an appropriate level on the basis of relationships among relationships, could not avoid dealing with structures and processes and had to give

Our concern is with concrete systems that fall within Miller's categories. To identify living systems requires criteria derived from long observation by students of the whole range of living systems. These observations seem to distill themselves into the four criteria suggested by Donald T. Campbell: (1) physical proximity of units; (2) similarity of units; (3) common fate of units; and (4) distinct or recognizable patterning of units.[13]

Some question may be raised about the first two criteria. Physical proximity, which is not the same thing as contiguity, need not be permanent—e.g., an arbitration system may expand as may an originally European organization of sociologists. Nor need it be restricted to a territory smaller than the globe or, as may come to pass, the globe and its extensions in outer space. Perhaps it is sufficient to modify physical proximity by reference to speeds of communication and transportation, bearing in mind that modern speeds of both were not necessary for the existence of such noncontiguous imperial systems as those of Britain and Spain and such nonterritorial legal systems as existed in Europe in the Dark Ages.

More serious questions may be raised about similarity, a term which should not be confused with "sameness." Does not one need, as Aristotle suggested,[14] parts which are different that function in a reciprocal or a complementary manner in order to have a whole, a system? Clearly, one would not form a legislature of men and dogs, which suggests that there is need for the concept of similarity, but it should be qualified to per-

---

attention to system units and subsystem units, see L. Erades and W. L. Gould, *The Relation Between International Law and Municipal Law in the Netherlands and in the United States* (Leiden: Sijthoff; New York: Oceana, 1961).

[13] Donald T. Campbell, "Common Fate, Similarity, and Other Indices of the Status of Aggregates of Persons as Social Entities," *Behavioral Science* 3 (1958): 14-25.

[14] Aristotle, *Politics,* II, ii, 3-8.

mit international systems to include states and international organizations.

Concerning distinctive patterns, Miller sets forth as criteria at least the following: (1) multiple constituent units of the sort characteristic of the next lower level; (2) a boundary subsystem across which less matter-energy and less information is transmitted than within the system;[15] (3) a decider subsystem;[16] (4) several or all the other critical subsystems[17] carrying out their processes, or parasitic or symbiotic interactions with other systems; (5) a characteristic size and a characteristic duration of survival, neither of which is dependable because levels overlap in size and duration and, at some levels as in the case of states, both display extreme variation.

Miller identified nineteen critical subsystems necessary for

[15] On boundaries and linkage systems between national systems and the external environment, see Karl W. Deutsch, "External Influences on the Internal Behavior of States," in R. Barry Farrell (ed.), *Approaches to Comparative and International Politics* (Evanston: Northwestern University Press, 1966), pp. 8-10.

[16] On the requirement that to be an organization an entity must have a "will" of its own, see Paul Reuter, *International Institutions*, trans. J. M. Chapman (New York: Rinehart, 1958), pp. 214-16.

[17] Other critical subsystems may have a bearing on the degree of independence of the decider just as an injured leg can determine whether an athlete plays in a particular game. At the level of public entities a subsystem with the capacity to tax or otherwise independently raise funds is critical and its emergence is vital to transformation of a system from the status of partipotentiality (whether parasitic or symbiotic) to that of totipotentiality, that is, capable of carrying out all subsystem processes critical to life or survival. The history of the rise of national authority in England at the expense of the authority of local lords provides one piece of evidence. As evidence of the result of lack of a fund-raising subsystem free of dependence on the component units stands the United Nations financial crisis in the wake of the Congo peacekeeping venture. The tax-gathering, fund-raising subsystem would appear to be a part of the information processing subsystem that Miller calls the "internal transducer," since Miller classifies money as a form of information conveyed on a metallic or a paper marker. Miller, "Living Systems: Basic Concepts," p. 234; "Living Systems: Structure and Process," pp. 351-52.

existence, eight processing matter-energy, nine processing information, and two processing both.[18] Systems that survive carry out the several processes either through their own critical subsystems or through performance by another system of processes that neither parasitic nor symbiotic systems can carry out by themselves. This facet of systems theory can be particularly relevant if applied to such concepts as sovereignty, independence, statehood, the grounds for recognition, and the nature of international organization, particularly in the light of Miller's assertion that the "decider" or decision-making subsystem is so essential that a living system cannot exist if it is parasitic or symbiotic with another system for its decision-making. Given the interdependence or complementary symbiosis of states in today's world, it seems evident that the more traditional criteria for identifying and analyzing statehood require extension and adaptation to contemporary complexity. Systems theory provides an approach to studies of international personality and criteria for its determination, as well as for capability analyses of states. The latter take account of more elements of statehood than just the formal requirements for international personality and recognition.

When an international lawyer undertakes to write a textbook, he may be expected to begin by describing the units to be found in the international system and to distinguish among those units on the basis of whether they have "legal personality," that is, such capacities as those of entering into diplomatic relations and suing and being sued before international tribunals. In the course of making such a distinction, the international lawyer takes into account a unit's measure of independence or sovereignty. In Miller's general systems termi-

[18] "Living Systems: Structure and Process," p. 338. For similar but fewer subsystems for organizations, see James G. March and Herbert A. Simon, *Organizations* (New York: Wiley, 1958), p. 167; for social systems, see D. McLachlan, Jr., "Communication Networks and Monitoring," *Public Opinion Quarterly* 25 (1961): 194-95.

nology, this means that the international lawyer distinguishes totipotential systems capable of carrying out all processes, including independent decision-making, whether or not actually doing so, from partipotential systems, whether parasitic or symbiotic, at the international level. For example, the individual, possessed of his own decider, ordinarily has had to rely on his government's willingness to intervene diplomatically, treating the individual's rights as its own rights and injury to him as injury to the state, in order to press a claim against a foreign state. The individual has turned to a decider other than himself, namely, his government, not only for the purpose of pursuing a claim but even for the decision whether to pursue it. Internationally the individual has hardly been totipotential and so has *traditionally* not been treated as an international person or as a unit of the international system. As more avenues are opened to permit the individual to press his claims in his own behalf, he advances toward totipotentiality and the traditional denial of the individual's international personality becomes more a thing of the past.

The classification and distinction of units by the international lawyer is a venture into the realm of system structure. It may be that this venture does not present a framework as conceptually complete as the six possible systems of international relationships abstracted in Morton Kaplan's *System and Process in International Politics*. Incompleteness may be inevitable, for the international lawyer restricts his vision to a particular set of international relations. Nor does the lawyer attempt to present the framework of an international system other than that of the time in which he is writing, even though failure to do so may hinder any effort to distinguish currently viable rules from outmoded rules, fitting the structure and processes of an earlier system. For the earlier systems one needs the time-depth of a work such as Richard Rosecrance's *Action and Reaction in World Politics*.

Nevertheless, however unsatisfactory nonlawyers may find

it, the international lawyer's venture into system structure is of great importance. In doing so he implicitly, if he hasn't already done so explicitly, rejects the possibility that the condition of the international scene is one of entropy. Instead, the presumption of order, even though less than ideal in a subjective view, is present in international law textbooks. The lawyers' identification and classification of units, chiefly on the basis of the degree of independence of their deciders (governments), represent an attempt to order the international system into its components or subsystems and to carefully distinguish fully functioning from partially functioning units (e.g., neutralized states), subsystems (states) from subsubsystems (e.g., individuals, corporations), etc.

Once these fundamental distinctions of components are made—not necessarily with full accuracy, particularly in times of significant system change—the international lawyer can proceed to such questions as recognition, international adjudication, claims of private persons, the authority of international organizations, and the status of state agents and international officials. A verbal linkage is made between structure and process,[19] between the static spatiotemporal arrangement of a system's parts and the dynamic change in both matter-energy and information as time passes. A subsequent focus, for example, upon adjudication or upon a foreign policy appeal to legal argument involves (a) a particular process moving through (b) a structure that includes subsystems which (c) in terms of process or function may or may not be contained within the boundaries of a single component.[20]

Sooner or later the international lawyer, unless he is content

[19] And so, in Miller's view, a verbal linkage is also made between function and purpose which he equates with each other and with process.

[20] On the several complex relationships between subsystems and components which may in part account for Easton's preference for "constructive" over "natural" systems, see Miller, "Living Systems: Basic Concepts," pp. 220-21.

with a book or a course that merely catalogues norms, must deal with process. Hence, it is appropriate that he be at all times aware of the structure through which process moves. If process moving through structure is to be adequately understood and the components of structure, even at a particular moment, seen as what they were, what they are, and what they may become, sociological, political, economic, and other social science data must be combined with the legal. Lack of such combination in most textbooks, although not in the processes themselves, is the inadequacy that the social scientist finds in legal writings and often tends to attribute also to the processes.

The systems approach seems to be one way of integrating various categories of data to trace patterns of consequence for the content and effectiveness of international law. This is so even though systems theorists rarely adopt the terminology of international law. For systems theorists are preoccupied, like those ancients who wondered about the regularity of the seasons and the movement of heavenly bodies, with general problems of order. As we have seen, the very concept of system connotes pattern, regularity, and predictability. Adduced as a theoretical attempt to describe and explain the behavior of states and other international actors, system—concrete system since both units and relationships are of concern—provides an empirical counterpoint to the norms of international law. Kaplan and Katzenbach have presented, although without the depth, thoroughness, and sophistication of *System and Process in International Politics*, the first fruits of the system theorist's quest for pattern and the international lawyer's longstanding effort to translate the quest for pattern into legal order. Unreserved application of the systems approach, shedding light on structure, patterns, and processes, changes in behavior with legal implications, and the relative strength of global, regional, and national systems of order, still lies in the future.

Patterns, Structure, and Units

Current System Structure: System Mapping

To find patterns displaying system structure is not an easy task. A pluralistic world does not readily reveal the neat patterns of interrelated units as an aerial photograph does for the spatial relationships of cities, mountains, and prairies.[21] The magnitude of the difficulties emphasizes the need for and the utility of adequate "maps" of the pluralistic international system, which is only partially or incompletely arranged hierarchically.[22] Any map can only portray the relationships among units as they exist at a moment in time and in rapidly changing situations is soon outdated. Still the not too badly outdated maps can be revised with less effort than it took to make them in the first place. A scheme for mapping that successfully produces a map carries or suggests schemes for revision and even for improvement of its information-bearing qualities.

Crude "maps" of the international scene have been developed in the past and perhaps were adequate for their time. A rough map could be drawn by verbal specification of states considered to be members of the "Family of Nations"—of the European or Western State System. Beyond lay something else which might or might not come to be considered part of the European system, something analogous to the incomplete

[21] On the problem of pluralism, see Charles R. Dechert, "A Pluralistic World Order," *Proceedings of the American Catholic Philosophical Association* (Washington: Catholic University of America, 1963), pp. 167-86.

[22] For an attempt to apply the concept of stratification by combining the concept of development with the concept of blocs, see Irving L. Horowitz, *Three Worlds of Development: The Theory and Practice of International Stratification* (New York: Oxford, 1966). For more sophisticated steps toward system mapping by identification of hierarchical levels constituting an influence structure, see Steven J. Brams, "Measuring the Concentration of Power in Political Systems," *American Political Science Review* 62 (1968): 461-75; and "The Structure of Influence Relationships in the International Systems," in James N. Rosenau (ed.), *International Politics and Foreign Policy: A Reader in Research and Theory*, rev. edn. (New York: Free Press, 1969), pp. 583-99.

coastline of Antarctica or the African areas marked "unknown" on 19th-century maps. Within the European system, with sporadic extensions beyond geographical Europe, identification of states and classification of entities less than fully sovereign, alliance partnerships, trade relations, basic cleavages between commitment to liberalism and commitment to authoritarianism, and similar crude indicators could suggest rough patterns. A mysterious homeostatic hand called the balance of power provided the moving equilibrium of the system, at least as long as enough statesmen went along with it. However the nonhomeostatic situation of 1914—the rising level of positive feedback[23] even as the decision-makers saw themselves as attempting to maintain the balance of power—had outcomes demonstrating the inadequacies of crude maps that left only imagination and preconception to fill blanks and supply details.

There is no reason why the systems approach need produce any better maps than earlier portrayals of the international scene. The most that can be said is that it provides a possibility of doing so that warrants continued experimentation. Intuitive constructions can still be made to mislead as does the persistent historical reference to the actions of the Triple Alliance in 1914

[23] For suggestions for more study of positive feedback in addition to the concentration on negative feedback that has followed the rise to prominence of cybernetics, see Charles R. Dechert, "Positive Feedback in Political and International Systems," *American Behavioral Scientist* 9 (March, 1966): 8-14; Magoroh Maruyama, "The Second Cybernetics: Deviation-Amplifying Mutual Causal Processes," *American Scientist* 51 (1963): 164-79. In reference to a question by R. C. Buck as to whether a nonhomeostatic system might exist, Miller says that if a concrete nonhomeostatic living system were located, his conceptual approach, which by definition excludes such a possibility, would be in serious doubt. Miller, "Living Systems: Basic Concepts," p. 225, note 22; Buck, "On the Logic of General Behavior Systems Theory," in H. Feigl and M. Scriven (eds.), *The Foundations of Science and the Concepts of Psychology and Psychoanalysis,* Minnesota Studies in the Philosophy of Science, vol. 1 (Minneapolis: University of Minnesota Press, 1956), p. 235.

when the term Dual Alliance, preferred by Robert North and his associates in the Stanford study of the outbreak of World War I, would be more descriptive of significant patterns and relationships. Reliance can only be placed upon tools that provide a possibility of overcoming preconception. In the preceding chapter factor analysis was suggested as one tool holding out promise of better mapping. Statistical tools that permit identification of associations among variables aid in the charting of the international system and its components and in the location of divisions less prominent than the Iron and Bamboo Curtains.

An important part of a larger study on "The Correlates of War, 1815-1945" helps to delineate the international system structure at various times in the recent past. J. David Singer and Melvin Small have sought to identify the shifting and expanding membership of the international system over a century and a quarter (1815-1939), divided roughly into five-year periods, and to classify all members according to their attributed importance or status on the basis of scores established to reflect the numbers and ranks of diplomats accredited to each national capital.[24] Another attempted measure of membership was that of diplomatic recognition by at least half of the established system members, but it was found that the same results were obtained through World War I by the test of recognition by Great Britain and France. Those two states held the first two positions in the status ordering through 1879, and shared the first three positions with Germany in 1884-1904 and with the United States in 1909 and 1914. Clearly, for the period 1815-1914 Great Britain and France stood in the position of legitimizers whose stamp of approval in the form of diplomatic recognition had the effect of conferring membership in the expanding international system centering on Eu-

[24] J. David Singer and Melvin Small, "The Composition and Status Ordering of the International System: 1815-1940," *World Politics* 18 (1966): 236-82.

rope but embracing both European and non-European, Western and non-Western states. This circumstance of Franco-British legitimation is probably no more palatable to non-Western peoples than the idea that Europe as a Christian community was setting standards for non-Christians, even though this was undoubtedly related to the more recent role of Britain and France as the primary "liberators" of colonies.

Another attempt to determine patterns and configurations on the basis of numbers of career diplomats exchanged by pairs of nations, trade, and shared memberships in intergovernmental organizations was undertaken by Steven J. Brams.[25] Using obtainable diplomatic lists for 1963-64, trade data for 1962, and shared memberships for 1963, Brams employed the Savage-Deutsch model of transaction flows as modified by Goodman.[26] Having thus obtained criteria by which to define the "salience" of two nations for each other's trade, Brams applied some decomposition programs, each employing a different definition of a subsystem, to obtain "maps" of groupings of nations.

Rosecrance's undertaking to chart the international scene at various times since 1740, embracing more variables than the Singer-Small study but in nonquantified form, led to identification of nine "systems." The effort appears to be an intuitive ordering of historical data based upon a model that attempts to explain patterns of international outcomes in terms of actor disturbances traceable to two major states or groups of states, environmental constraints, and the regulator operative during each period. It appears possible to operationalize Rosecrance's scheme to make use of more data than can be gathered from secondary historical sources and to process the data in more

[25] Steven J. Brams, "Transaction Flows in the International System," *American Political Science Review* 60 (1966): 880-98.

[26] I. Richard Savage and Karl W. Deutsch, "A Statistical Model of the Gross Analysis of Transaction Flows," *Econometrica* 28 (1960): 551-72; Leo A. Goodman, "Statistical Methods for the Preliminary Analysis of Transaction Flows," *Econometrica* 31 (1963): 197-208.

ways than appear to have been employed in arriving at the representation of nine historical international systems.

A problem with the Rosecrance approach is that its restriction to two sets of actor disturbances does not really tell us very much about a system and its units. Nor does the characterization of environmental constraints by such terms as "abundance," "adequacy," and "scarcity" as related chiefly to availability of territories into which to expand. Missing is a satisfactory identification of units and subsystems and their interrelationships and interactions.

Setting aside the question of appropriateness of labels raised in the preceding chapter, the groupings that emerge from the factor analyses of Cattell, Russett, and Banks and Gregg seem at least to reveal cleavages that have potential consequences yet to be comprehensively set forth—cleavages such as an occasional historian may have discerned in isolated cases, like the one essentially along the 20th meridian between Slavs of Orthodox faith employing the Cyrillic alphabet and Slavs of Roman faith employing the Roman alphabet. Such cleavages raise pertinent questions about boundaries, communication channels, the extent of ingestion of matter-energy expressed in economic and similar terms, and the extent to which there may be penetration of systems and subsystems both national and functional by the dominant subsystem within a regional or cultural system.[27]

As demonstrated by one student in a term paper on treaty relationships, diagraming a particular type of relationship among states on transparent sheets can permit overlays demonstrating affinities and cleavages. Moreover, to overlay one set of cleavages with those of another type of relationship may reveal noncongruencies and even incompatibilities. Patterns of political relationships may not correspond to patterns

[27] On the concept of the "penetrated" system as applied to the broad fusion of national and international systems see James N. Rosenau, "Pre-Theories and Theories of Foreign Policy," in Farrell (ed.), *Approaches*, pp. 53, 65-71.

of legal relationships, to economic relationships, or to formal military alliances. For example, while on certain issues there is displayed a political affinity between Africans and Asians, their trade relations are not very strong, both regions being economically closer to Europe.[28] Issue-oriented political affinities are not reinforced by economic ties, nor economic cleavage by political affinities. The consequent cross-pressures could act to inhibit the manifestation of some future vengeance against Europeans and, more generally, against whites. In any case, absence of convergence of the economic and the political may indicate potential divisions among the African states or at least lack of a critical boundary for a regional system—critical in the sense that its violation would stimulate responses based on a variety of shared values.[29]

Economists' studies of payments balancing provide some of the clues needed for comprehension of system structure. Bilateralism has persisted in the Soviet bloc trade practice.[30] For

[28] *U.N. Yearbook of International Trade Statistics*, 1965; Arnold Rivkin, *The African Presence in World Affairs: National Development and Its Role in Foreign Policy* (New York: Free Press, 1963); and *Africa and the European Common Market: A Perspective*, Monograph Series in World Affairs, no. 4, 1965-66, 2nd rev. edn. (Denver: The Social Science Foundation and Department of International Relations, University of Denver, 1966); Rouhallah K. Ramazani, *The Middle East and the European Common Market* (Charlottesville: The University Press of Virginia, 1964); J. Russell Andruss and Azizali F. Mohammed, *Trade, Finance, and Development in Pakistan* (Stanford: Stanford University Press, 1965); Bruce M. Russett, *International Regions and the International System: A Study in Political Ecology* (Chicago: Rand McNally, 1967), pp. 135-38, 146, 147, 149.

[29] Brams, "Transaction Flows," pp. 889, 892, argues that "maps" based on the salient linkages of a number of transaction flows delineate critical subsystem boundaries.

[30] See David Cattel, "Multilateral Cooperation and Integration in Eastern Europe," *Western Political Quarterly* 13 (1960): 64-69; Istvan Ágoston, *Le Marché commun communiste: Principes et pratique du COMECON*, 2nd edn. (Geneva: Droz, 1965), pp. 146-48, 257-65. For economic indices that indicate the existence of two subsystems within the Soviet system and for indications that trade and cultural interaction proceed somewhat independently of political interaction and

65 countries of both non-Soviet and Soviet spheres in 1954-58 Michael Michaely's study showed a decline in multilateral balancing after 1948. No single country outside the Soviet bloc had as low a level of multilateral balancing as any country within the bloc. More bilateral balancing took place among the dollar countries, the United Kingdom, and continental Western Europe than among the Latin American non-dollar countries, the Overseas Sterling areas, and the rest of the world.[31]

C. P. Anderson suggested some years ago that multipartite treaties, such as the Versailles Treaty, are really collections of bilateral treaties.[32] Bearing this in mind, as well as the tendency toward bilateral balancing, one suspects that bilateral interaction may be so strong a feature of the international system that the whole system can be analyzed in terms of pair behavior.[33]

One should not expect a neat chart of component units interrelated in political, legal, cultural, and other subsystems. Aside from crosscutting private subsystems and semipublic subsystems in the scientific, business, communications, labor, political, and other fields, irregularities will be found in the forms of special treaty arrangements and historic privileges (e.g., the long established conduct of activities such as fishing off the coast of a foreign country or mutual investment in the development of a resource such as Canadian petroleum). Con-

---

conflict, see Edward L. Miles and John B. Gillooly, "Processes of Interaction Among the Fourteen Communist Party States: An Exploratory Essay," Research Paper No. 5, Stanford Studies of the Communist System (March, 1965), pp. 2-9, 25-26, 28-30.

[31] Michael Michaely, "Multilateral Balancing in International Trade," *American Economic Review* 52 (1962): 685-702.

[32] C. P. Anderson, "The Ratification of Treaties with Reservations," *American Journal of International Law* 13 (1919): 530.

[33] Analysis by dyads is employed by Brams, "Transaction Flows," and by Rudolph J. Rummel, "A Social Field Theory of Foreign Conflict Behavior," *Peace Research Society (International), Papers*, Cracow Conference, 1965, vol. 4 (1966), pp. 131-50.

struction of international petroleum and natural gas pipelines, whether formally international or international only in terms of territory traversed, creates special situations, interdependence, and consequent obligations not readily cast aside. Special functional relations of this type need not be forerunners of as broad a functional system as multi-nation economic integration. Even if only deviations from the norm, they represent patterns to be included in a chart of interrelationships.

Comparative Systems

ALTHOUGH the restriction of our observation to one populated planet prevents simultaneous comparison of global international systems in the manner open to students of comparative government, comparison of historical, real world international systems is not entirely ruled out. At least two obvious intertemporal methods are available.

One method of comparing international systems is to examine Western Europe and America at different times since the Middle Ages. Today, what is usually done is to compare the so-called classical balance-of-power system with the post-World War II system. Frequently, such comparisons have been grounded on the number of "poles" or major actors[34]—a symptom of postwar concern about superpowers and nuclear weapons. With the introduction of greater detail, comparisons can be made among several systems, if Rosecrance's designation is correct, or, if not, then among several manifestations of one or two systems. Without regard to definitional problems affecting the number of systems that have existed historically, it can be noted that both the rougher distinction between balance-of-power and bipolar system and the finer distinctions producing Rosecrance's nine systems present op-

[34] For an attempt to demonstrate the implications of the logic of numbers in a system of international relations, see A. Joxe, "Logique des relations de préference et nombre de protagonistes," *Stratégie* 4 (April-May-June, 1964): 41-58.

portunity for comparisons between or among successive stages of what passed for or was alleged to be "the" international system.[35] It may also be pertinent not to confine one's view to the military power factor. As Jay W. Wiley reminds us, there are differences between a world with a single financial center (e.g., England in the 19th century and the United States in 1945-58) and a world of many financial centers, even though they may be historically contiguous.[36] Historical contiguity may suggest caution lest one treat as recurrent in all systems those forms of behavior that may overlap temporally connected systems but for which there may be no evidence in systems not evolved from the European.

The second intertemporal method reaches farther into the European past and even beyond Europe to employ available information concerning systems that are extinct although not necessarily entirely without current influence (e.g., Vietnamese attitudes toward China). Extinct systems include those of Western Europe before modern times, systems usually not explored by international relations theorists who apparently see little profit in examining arrangements that preceded the classical balance of power. However, our concern is also with extinct systems not based on Western Europe. Despite the efforts of Baron de Taube to call attention to East European developments in the days of Byzantium,[37] very

[35] It is important to recognize that assertion of global scope for the European system became important only at a relatively recent period, roughly since 1856. The restraints represented by Castlereagh's phrase "the public law of Europe" and by Lord Stowell's judicial recognition that the European system did not extend to North Africa (*The Helena* [1801] 4 C. Rob. 3; *The Madonna del Burso* [1802] 4 C. Rob. 169) are too often overlooked when the "Family of Nations" concept is treated as only a manifestation of European ego.

[36] Jay W. Wiley, "Issues in International Economics: Gold, the Dollar, and CRU," *Indiana Academy of the Social Sciences, Proceedings, 1965*, n.s. 10 (1966): 28-36.

[37] Baron Michel de Taube, "Etudes sur la développement historique du droit international dans l'europe orientale," *Académie de Droit*

little has been done to examine international behavior and rules and customs produced by that system. To date the outstanding effort to look beyond Western Europe and, by its excellent use of the historic approach, to examine European systems preceding the classical balance of power is Adda Bozeman's study of intercultural relations before 1500.[38] Virtually unknown, certainly unused in English-speaking countries, is Isidoro Ruiz Moreno's employment of archeological evidence and analysis of religious, literary, and scientific works to demonstrate the existence of pre-Christian systems of international law and relations.[39] Indeed, Ruiz Moreno treated ancient, extinct systems as the materials for comparative analysis to find rules that are similar despite systemic differences. More than thirty years ago Frank M. Russell included in his then quite unparalleled survey of theories of international relations a review of Chinese and Indian systems and theories.[40] Some parallels to the European system appear even in Russell's condensation, for example, the blocking of the establishment of a Chinese dispute-settling organization by a ruler who held that there always had been and always would be war. Treatises on the Chinese and Indian systems of international law have tended to remain on bookshelves, although in recent years the objections of non-Western states have led to some interest in, for example, Kautilya's prescriptions.

Today, there are more opportunities for comparative work

International: Recueil des cours 11 (1926): 345-535; "L'Apport de Byzance au développement du droit international occidental," *ibid.* 67 (1939): 237-339.

38 Adda B. Bozeman, *Politics and Culture in International History* (Princeton: Princeton University Press, 1960).

39 Isidoro Ruiz Moreno, *El derecho internacional publico antes de la era Christiana* (Buenos Aires: Faculty of Law and Social Sciences, 1946). See also Roger B. McShane, *The Foreign Policy of the Attalids of Pergamum,* Illinois Studies in the Social Sciences, vol. 53 (Urbana: University of Illinois Press, 1964).

40 Frank M. Russell, *Theories of International Relations* (New York: Appleton-Century, 1936), pp. 16-50.

then ever before, particularly when one's concern is international behavior rather than a mere search for non-Western principles of international relations to incorporate into contemporary international law in hope of revising it into a scheme of globally congenial rules. For example, histories of the Mongol and Mughal Empires provide some idea of transcultural recurrences in the conduct of external relations, foreign trade, diplomacy, and treaty-making.[41] So, too, do histories of precolonial Africa.[42] Much is to be learned, as Ruiz Moreno suggested, from the study of extinct systems, appropriate comparisons with modern systems, and the bringing to bear of pertinent evidence related to intertribal relations and to the relations of archaic societies.[43]

If process can be viewed as something that, like osmosis, can occur in many systems, then it appears vital that every possible opportunity be used to ascertain how differences in structure alter the course, rate, and effects of process. In the absence of such a determination it is exceedingly difficult to distinguish that which is really attributable to system peculiarities from that which is the consequence of other variables.

Two other approaches to the comparative study of international systems warrant brief attention. The first, comparison between real world and laboratory systems can at most be regarded as having future potential, including a potential, if playacting can be avoided, for ascertaining whether real-world situations had to come out as they did. For the present, however, given the work still needed to develop further the simulation technique, the most relevant comparisons between lab-

[41] E. g., Michael Prawdin, *The Mongol Empire: Its Rise and Legacy*, trans. Eden and Cedar Paul, 2nd edn. (New York: Free Press, 1967); S. M. Edwardes and H.L.O. Garrett, *Mughal Rule in India*, 2nd Indian reprint (New Delhi: S. Chand & Co., 1962).

[42] E.g., Michael Crowder, *The Story of Nigeria* (London: Faber and Faber, 1962); J. D. Fage, *An Introduction to the History of West Africa*, 3rd edn. (Cambridge: The University Press, 1962).

[43] Christof von Fürer-Haimendorf, *The Apa Tanis and Their Neighbors* (New York: Free Press of Glencoe, 1963).

oratory simulations and real-world situations are those designed for validation of the former by reference to the latter.[44]

The other approach is to compare subsystems essentially regional in character, e.g., the European, the Atlantic, the inter-American, the Communist, the African, and the Southeast Asian. In some cases there may be some doubt about whether a particular region constitutes a subsystem. As has been indicated, lack of coincidence of economic, political, and treaty relations may render it questionable whether the region has the internal cohesion and boundary stability associated with living systems. Interactions of a region's states with distant states may be more numerous than with each other. Even so, such occurrences as the practice of bloc politics at the United Nations and the formation of regional organizations suggest treatment of Africa and Southeast Asia, for example, as at least embryonic subsystems. Regional organizations now facilitate the task of comparison. It is important to take account of the historical roots of regional subsystems. The African subsystem is relatively recent and not wholly unrelated to European colonial organization patterns, while Southeast Asia bears the imprint of Indian and Chinese empires and cultures.[45] These

[44] On problems and methods of validation, including a description of simulation of the outbreak of World War I with matched and with unmatched personalities, see Charles F. and Margaret G. Hermann, "Validation Studies of the Inter-Nation Simulation," Studies in Deterrence, no. 10, U.S. Naval Ordnance Test Station, China Lake, California. (December, 1963). For a comparison between a simulation and the Rummel-Tanter data on real world conflict behavior, see Paul Smoker, "Analyses of Conflict Behaviors in an International Processes Simulation and an International System 1955-60," mimeographed (Evanston: Northwestern University, August, 1968).

[45] Particularly useful treatments of pre-European empires in Southeast Asia and the absence of Western concepts of sovereignty are John F. Cady, *Southeast Asia: Its Historical Development* (New York: McGraw-Hill, 1964), and D. G. E. Hall, *A History of Southeast Asia*, 2nd edn. (London: Macmillan, 1964). For a geographical study that relates cultural clashes to political, economic, and other factors affecting the international politics of the region, see Charles A. Fisher, *Southeast*

subsystems may be compared with each other and with the international system. The latter comparison should lead to cross-level hypotheses and generalizations. In addition, comparisons should lead to some understanding of the extent to which uneven national and international development affects the comprehensiveness and substance of regional international norms. For example, at first glance the legal facets of the South and Southeast Asian subsystems appear to be limited to the five principles of *panch shila*, and those of the African to the three or four principles protective of statehood within existing boundaries that have been enunciated at inter-African conferences. However, analyses to date have concentrated on what has been indigenously generated and not upon what has penetrated these systems from the external international environment.

Units as Sources of International Law

The units that comprise the international system can be treated as sources of international law in two basic ways. One way is by interaction; the other is by unilateral action. The division may be somewhat artificial in that a unilateral action does not of itself produce law. To be more than an isolated incident, unilateral action must stimulate a response or be imitated by others. Even repetition by the party acting unilaterally cannot create more than an idiosyncrasy in the absence of response or imitation. However, our distinction is not affected by the need for response. The intent is to broaden the view of law creation at the international level beyond the limits of bilateral or multilateral expressions of the consensus of states.

Briefly, as we shall return to the subject later, the formal

Asia: A Social, Economic and Political Geography (London: Methuen, 1964). On the present state system of Southeast Asia, see Michael Brecher, *The New States of Asia: A Political Analysis* (London: Oxford University Press, 1963), chap. 3; Bernard K. Gordon, *The Dimensions of Conflict in Southeast Asia* (Englewood Cliffs: Prentice-Hall, 1966).

creation of law occurs through the familiar bilateral and multilateral negotiating processes that may include formal action by an international organization. In the case of lawmaking decisions by international tribunals, the lack of a formal, general, binding character is overcome by the additional law-creating steps of imitation by other tribunals and acquiescence through primarily national policy decisions at various operating levels or, to aggregate such decisions, state practice. More informally, custom arises through action, but the usual portrayal of such action is as state action, including action in response to deviation from expectations.

To an extent it suffices to say that such actions as virtually identical national statutes or court decisions can establish customary international rules. But formal national procedures are only a means of producing certain customs, not custom in its totality. Greater precision would be attained if distinctions were made between actions by state organs on state initiative and actions taken on their own initiative by private persons such as sailors, fishermen, traders in foreign lands, off-shore drillers for oil, and corporations with foreign affilliates or subsidiaries. Private persons' actions, particularly when generalized to produce expectations, may later receive governmental support in the form of diplomatic protest or comparable action or they may lead to prohibitive or regulative legal norms as governments engage in joint action against private behavior regarded as undesirable. An historical-sociological approach, reaching to the units of governmental and private subsystems, can reveal what traditional attribution of custom to state practice conceals.

Protection of Units

Among Morton Kaplan's rules for the balance-of-power system are two that relate to the preservation of the units. One rule requires that fighting be stopped before an essential national actor is eliminated; the other requires the readmission of defeated or constrained national actors into the system or their replacement by some previously inessential actor.[46] In Kaplan's view history shows that the same sort of protection was not accorded inessential actors and the partition of Poland is cited as an example.[47] Rosecrance takes a different view and holds that the *ancien régime* had refused to countenance the destruction of domestic state constitutions and that the partitions of Poland were an exception justified in part on the ground of Poland's exclusion from the general European system.[48] The 19th-century record appears to confirm Rosecrance's position on the elimination of actors, since the European states with populations of over 500,000 that were eliminated as actors were the eight German states absorbed into Bismarck's *Reich* and the five states joined to Sardinia and certain Hapsburg possessions to form Italy. Such is the record at least in regard to the elimination of national actors, major or minor.

In regard to intervention and interference in domestic affairs, the 19th-century record is somewhat different. Both reactionary and liberal states indulged in intervention when convenient, but their intervention raised protests. These protests expressed the principle of nonintervention, reflecting both the *ancien régime's* taboo and the conscience of nationalism on behalf of already independent states—the same nationalism that in 1919 supplied the principles for the dismemberment of the central Hapsburg actor and the peripheral Ottoman actor.

Across the Atlantic the Monroe Doctrine's declaration against intervention emanating from Europe and the later Pan-American proclamations of nonintervention by Western Hem-

[46] Morton A. Kaplan, *System and Process in International Politics* (New York: Wiley, 1957), p. 23.

[47] *Ibid.*, p. 33.

[48] Richard N. Rosecrance, *Action and Reaction in World Politics: International Systems in Perspective* (Boston and Toronto: Little Brown, 1963), p. 46.

isphere actors, even though carried to an extreme that threatened paralysis against attempted exports of Castroism,[49] represent efforts to protect even minor actors from outside interference symbolized by "the Holy Alliance," "the Colossus of the North," "capitalism," "Communism," and now "neo-imperialism." Additional thrusts in the same direction in the present century have taken the form of the doctrine of preservation of territorial integrity with particular reference to China, the Stimson Doctrine concerning nonrecognition of conquests, and the attempt to use nonrecognition in the case of the absorption of the Baltic States and in the cases of partitioned states.

Although Kaplan's speculation about the loose bipolar system does not indicate whether national actors are to be protected, it would appear that in the postwar world, even if due only to fortuitous circumstances, they and perhaps global and regional actors (i.e., intergovernmental organizations) are also to be protected. A number of principles can be regarded as contributing toward the objective of protecting both the existence and the indigenous functioning at least of national actors. These principles are (1) restraint in the treatment of national actors, (2) nonintervention, (3) territorial integrity, (4) nonrecognition of conquest, and (5) nonrecognition of absorption. What is not clear today is the line of demarcation between legitimate influence and intervention when a national boundary is subjected to such unspectacular penetrations as bilateral and multilateral aid, trade, private investment, and even "non-aid" when it is intended to influence policy.[50] It appears that a more general treatment of the matter could be undertaken through reexamination of the rules of

[49] C. Neal Ronning, *Law and Politics in Inter-American Diplomacy* (New York: Wiley, 1963), pp. 64-69, 72-73, 75-81.

[50] David A. Baldwin, "Foreign Aid, Intervention, and Influence," *World Politics* 21 (1969): 425-47; Andrew M. Scott, *The Functioning of the International Political System* (New York: Macmillan, 1967), pp. 210-11.

international law with reference to their contribution to system maintenance by protecting units. Doing so appears to be particularly relevant in light of such interesting African events as the collective decision to retain colonial boundaries, general failure to encourage Biafran secession by recognition of statehood, and global refusal to accept the white Rhodesians' declaration of independence.[51] Furthermore, if the perspective of protection of the units is a broad one encompassing more than national actors, such advisory opinions of the International Court of Justice as those dealing with United Nations finances and with injuries to individuals in United Nations service can be interpreted in terms of that perspective. This is not a greatly different view from that often employed in discussions of how boldly an international or supranational court can act and retain respect for its decisions. Thus, what is here suggested is a still more focussed and systematic examination of such opinions but as part of a military, political, and economic as well as legal complex of system-maintaining actions and presumably supportive rules.

Changes Within Units

System maintenance requires the protection of the units, and this requirement provides a key to the functions of potential or active revolutionary disturbance and reaction thereto in a particular system. We do not mean to imply either goodness or badness about the phenomenon of revolution. Nor do we mean to imply that either the "have nots" or the mission-oriented groups or an alliance of the two are necessarily the revolutionists and that the "haves," the conservatives, or an alliance of these groups are necessarily the system maintainers. John Locke's proposition that either set can act in rebellion covers the point.

[51] See, e.g., I. William Zartman, *International Relations in the New Africa* (Englewood Cliffs: Prentice-Hall, 1966), pp. 39, 50, 92; James Barber, *Rhodesia: The Road to Rebellion* (London: Oxford University Press for the Institute of Race Relations, 1967).

The effort of the Holy Alliance to prevent change categorized as rebellion employed intervention rather than protection of units. In the same category are more recent efforts to intervene in underdeveloped areas to project either Communist or anti-Communist images upon emergent nations through subversion and related activities. Both undertakings violate traditional notions about the protection of units. Whether to prevent or to impose change, intervention interferes with the internal dynamics of the units and by such interference can become an instrument affecting the maintenance of the international system.

System perspective may well be an ingredient essential to smooth functioning, and experimental evidence seems to indicate that taking a system perspective promotes a healthy state of units as parts of the whole, particularly if there is understanding of the responsibilities and potential contributions of the units.[52] It would appear that the healthier domestic societies are able to accord protection to their units without excessive concern that such protection invites destruction of the system. At the international level, at least since the days of predatory wars, protection of the units has denoted protection of the system and attack threatening the existence of the units[53] or their critical subsystems has signified rebellion against the system. The attacks of Napoleon and Hitler on other states represented such rebellion. It may be significant

[52] Beatrice and Sydney Rome, "Leviathan," *SDC Magazine* 8 (April, 1965): 23. See also Muzafer Sherif, "Superordinate Goals in the Reduction of Intergroup Conflict," *American Journal of Sociology* 63 (1958): 349-56. For indications of what a system perspective could mean for the development of a subfield of international law, see Myres S. McDougal and William T. Burke, "Crisis in the Law of the Sea: Community Perspectives versus National Egoism," in McDougal, et al., *Studies in World Public Order* (New Haven: Yale University Press, 1960), pp. 844-911.

[53] Such attacks are distinguished from limited wars to settle particular issues or, like Bismarck's war against France, to enhance status in the existing system.

that the activities of the 1930's in which Germany, Italy, and Japan were co-actors, albeit not in truly concerted undertakings characterized by common positive purpose, included defiance of a unit other than a state, namely, the League of Nations. Defiance of the League, coupled with attack on state-units, implies the interrelationship of protection of the units and system maintenance even though the League and the international system were not co-terminous.

Setting aside the exercise of judgment based on projection of one's own nationally parochial standards when passing upon the issue of recognition of governments, it would lend depth to the analysis of the recognition procedure if we were to treat nonrecognition as an attempt to preserve the international system by discouraging rebellion through internal attack on its units. Actually, internal attacks are against subsystems, and an uprising should be and sometimes has been differently characterized on the basis of whether what is attacked is only the government or also the social and economic subsystems. It should be pointed out that the objective of attack is a variable that can be independent of the method of attack such as a *coup d'état* or a war of rebellion. In recent years internal disturbances have become a major topic of social science research.[54] Study by international law specialists of the recognition of governments should benefit from the accumulating empirical research on various aspects of internal change.

Among the more important current scholarly developments has been a reconsideration of the nature of the *coup d'état*. Too frequently in the past there has been little effort to distinguish

[54] James Payne, "Peru: The Politics of Structured Violence," *Journal of Politics* 27 (1965): 362-74; Cyril E. Black and Thomas P. Thornton (eds.), *Communism and Revolution: The Strategic Use of Violence* (Princeton: Princeton University Press, 1964); Harry Eckstein (ed.), *Internal War: Problems and Approaches* (New York: Free Press; London: Collier-Macmillan, 1964); James N. Rosenau (ed.), *International Aspects of Civil Strife* (Princeton: Princeton University Press, 1964).

the *coup d'état* from revolution.[55] At the policy level, or at least in popular discussion of it in the United States, there has been an issue of whether governments coming to power by violence of any sort warrant recognition. However, the discussion seems to have had no practical effect other than a bit of delay when *coups* do not capture and hold headlines.

The work of Sebastian de Grazia on the technique and the significance of the *coup d'état* suggests that in some areas the *coup* is an established institution for changing governments, while Samuel Huntington accords the same quality to the type of *coup* that is directed toward achieving a change of policy by changing the party in control.[56] Whether resort to the *coup* is really resort to a substitute for an election requires specification of countries and occasions, including evidence either that the *coup* is employed because honest elections permitting a change of party are impossible or that the *coup* is a regular device to compel policy changes in difficult situations prior to the expiration of a constitutional term of office. The latter circumstance would be somewhat comparable to the parliamentary vote of "no confidence." Studies of the military in some countries indicate that a guardianship role is played and involves periodic withdrawal of support. That support actually amounts to "confidence" in the parliamentary sense may be a misleading metaphorical view of the issue.

A similar danger of metaphor exists in the "substitute for elections" concept. Metaphor is not needed to ascertain whether

[55] For an effort to distinguish the *coup d'état* and revolution that deals with those elements, particularly in Communist *coups*, that resemble revolution, see S. Tosti, "Movimenti revoluzzionari contemporanei," *Studi politici* 3 (1954): 128-32.

[56] Sebastian de Grazia, "The Coup d'État: Its Political and Military Significance" and "The Coup d'État: Modern Techniques and Countermeasures," Reports to Project Michelson, NOTS, China Lake, California (Princeton: Metron, Inc., November 27 and 30, 1961); Samuel P. Huntington, "Patterns of Violence in World Politics," in Huntington (ed.), *Changing Patterns of Military Politics* (New York: Free Press, 1962), pp. 32-40.

or not within a particular country the *coup* is a normal and acceptable way of changing governments. Outside the country the actions of foreign states may provide an indicator were a tabulation made, for example, of the frequency of employment of nonrecognition in cases of *coup* as compared with its use in cases of revolution. Or, it may be that the delay between seizure of power and recognition would provide an indicator of the international acceptability of the *coup*, perhaps giving rise to the inference that the law of recognition is really supportive of built-in national "safety valves."

The case of revolution through a general uprising, particularly if prolonged, introduces greater complexities than when only the recognition issue is involved. Studies of internal war seem to be delineating patterns and phases taken by revolutionary wars, particularly by successful revolutions. It would be difficult to say that such studies constitute guides aiding international lawyers to make recommendations concerning when and in what form recognition ought to be accorded to insurrectionists. What is provided is a guide to the nature of what might be called quasi-units, those either not yet in undisputed control of a country or not yet completely ousted from power. Conceivably, more systematic exposition of the pertinence of subjectively applied rules relating to insurgency may help to clear up some of the conceptual chaos, since recognition of "insurgency" was introduced to avoid full applicability of the laws of war entailed by recognition of "belligerency." Greater understanding of the patterns and phases of internal wars should also make more clear the forms and stages of involvement with external powers and the means of counteracting external aid. Without anticipation of early results, such clarification might ultimately contribute to a more satisfactory elaboration of principles protective of units than the present unsatisfactory mélange of legal doctrines of nonintervention and the practice of both unilateral and collective intervention.

Intersystem Relations, Conflicts, and Adjustments

In this section the level of reference of the word "system" will be changed to refer, according to context, to the national systems that are treated as the leading actors in most expositions of international relations and international law, economic and other systems not contained within national boundaries, regional systems, private transnational systems, etc. All would be treated as subsystems of the global international system dealt with in earlier sections. The reason for the change in reference points is to allow a view of a global system that develops from a condition of virtually no interactions and no minimal common purpose—the exchange of A for B not being the pursuit of common purpose as when both seek to establish and maintain condition X.[57] Much futile debate has been indulged in over the question of whether international law is superior to municipal law, or vice versa, or whether they are equal and coordinate. A debating posture on this question may be descriptive of a given moment or period of history. But if the general evolutionary direction is from the simpler to the more complex,[58] from tribe and city-state to empire, from duchy and fief to state to international and supranational organization—if it once was but is ceasing to be true that the state is the highest form of human organization—then there is gain in centering upon systems that during an important evolutionary stage could have been subsystems only of a hypothetical "mankind."

[57] The distinction is the same as that which Triepel employed to distinguish the *Vertrag* (contractual agreement) from the *Vereinbarung* (law-making treaty) and which students of negotiations have used to distinguish the objective of the exchange of different objects from that of a single arrangement or object. Heinrich Triepel, *Völkerrecht und Landesrecht* (Leipzig: C. L. Hirschfeld, 1899), pp. 35-63, 66-103; Fred Charles Iklé, *How Nations Negotiate* (New York: Harper & Row, 1964), pp. 2-4.

[58] See G. Sommerhoff, *Analytical Biology* (London: Oxford University Press, 1950), pp. 183-85.

Boundary subsystems are commonly stronger and tougher than most other subsystems. This does not mean that the military hard shell concept elaborated by John Herz[59] serves as an adequate model of a pre-missile national frontier zone. Even for the fortified state, the boundary was more than a military barrier.[60] In general, boundaries of all systems impede the ingestion of matter-energy (e.g., poison, foreign-made goods) and the input of information. They also impede extrusion, as the Berlin Wall dramatically demonstrates. A sudden decrease in the rate of flow of matter-energy or information indicates the presence of a boundary.[61]

Except in absolute isolation, which need not be wholly or even primarily spatial, there is still a flow of matter-energy and information, of goods and people and intelligence, across boundaries with varying degrees of transformation or distortion. For all practical purposes, too, when the relations of one system to another are limited to the occasional trip of a Marco Polo, we may regard those systems as in virtual isolation. However, it is not impossible that a system could exist that consists only of a succession of dyadic relationships, as between Europe and Arab traders and then between Arab traders and Cathay or Africa south of the Sahara. It might be best (particularly if each of a series of transactions is complete in itself) to treat these as series of dyadic systems, embryonic systems perhaps evolving into something more complex and permanent. At the least there exist intersystem relations, basically *ad hoc*. Such relations can exist even with so high a degree of inde-

[59] John H. Herz, *International Politics in the Atomic Age* (New York: Columbia University Press, 1959; paperback edition, 1962), pp. 41, 44, 47; and "Rise and Demise of the Territorial State," *World Politics* 9 (1957): 473-93.

[60] J. R. V. Prescott, *The Geography of Frontiers and Boundaries* (London: Hutchinson University Library, 1965), pp. 33-49.

[61] On description of the limits of an autonomous organization in terms of a communication differential, see Karl W. Deutsch, *The Nerves of Government: Models of Political Communication and Control* (New York: Free Press of Glencoe, 1963), pp. 205-206.

pendence of systems that the variables in one system alter in ways uncorrelated with those of a second system.

Intersystem relations can be relations between systems of the same functional order, that is, between political systems, between economic systems, etc. These systems may be on the same organizational level, e.g., state and state, or on different organizational levels, e.g., state and regional organization. The most commonly discussed relationship of the same order in treatises on international law is that between international law and municipal law and, more recently, that between the supranational law of the European Communities and the municipal law of the Six. In another vein, it is appropriate to consider relations of conflict between international or regional organizations and states in terms of their side-effects, e.g., the disagreement between the International Monetary Fund and Colombia that President Carlos Lleras Restrepo exploited to handle a foreign exchange crisis without subjection to the restraints and compromises usually imposed by politicians in the Colombian Congress.[62] Disputes between states and international organizations and their exploitation for domestic political purposes can be expected to have an impact, probably deleterious, on the development of the law relevant to state–international organization relations. At the level of state-to-state relations the need to investigate relationships between economic systems, as well as those between political systems, has been given eloquent expression by Wolfgang Friedmann.[63] In classical exposition it was the relations between state and state in Europe, regularized with the introduction of the resident ambassador, that gave rise to what became known as public international law.

[62] R. L. Maullin, "The Colombia-IMF Disagreement of November-December 1966: An Interpretation of Its Place in Colombian Politics," RAND Report RM-5314-RC (Santa Monica: RAND Corporation, June, 1967).

[63] Wolfgang Friedmann, *The Changing Structure of International Law* (New York: Columbia University Press, 1964).

The increased complexity of bilateral and multilateral international relations has been reflected in the formation of organizations increasingly durable and of both unifunctional and multifunctional scope. Both the output of treaty negotiations and the development of customs, almost faster than can be recorded by publicists, reflect this complexity. Whether and when, at the regional level and higher, interactions and penetrations of boundary subsystems—e.g., by regional community law—have increased to such a degree that units of the same level can be regarded as joined in a confederated manner or have erected a higher structure of which the formerly independent systems are now subsystems is likely to be a matter of more than academic debate.

An example of such an issue is the question of whether regional organizations such as the Organization of American States are free to act without prior authorization by the United Nations. It may be noted that, aside from security matters, OAS organs, particularly in the field of health, function on behalf of appropriate global agencies. The issue is whether the boundary around the Western Hemisphere represented by the Monroe Doctrine has been penetrated by the United Nations to an extent that converts the OAS into a United Nations subsystem. Whatever the correct answer at the moment, the point is that the question is one of consequence to international law and there may well be an identifiable time at which scholars, guided by the actions of statesmen, will have to conclude that the relations between the regional and the global organization are no longer those of two independent systems. Such a circumstance would then raise the issue of whether inter-American departures from general international law can or should be maintained.

Intersystem relations may also be between systems of different functional orders. Economic and political systems interact as do technological and economic systems, legal and technological systems, public and private systems,[64] and so forth. These different realms are systems in that organizationally, in internal interactions, and even in specialized language, there exist barriers crossed only with more effort than merely to approach them.[65] Relations among them are probably most easily dealt with by restricting oneself to one pair at a time. Thus, it is possible to use the methods of students of interest group politics and of public policy to examine just the relationships between economic and political systems or just those between the social conditions conducive to deviance and the law.

Most important of the relations among systems of different orders are the relationships of other systems with the political. It is, for example, commonplace to examine the penetration of finance by the influences of domestic and foreign policies on international capital movements. Somewhat less frequently

[64] Public and private interaction might be treated as interaction between organizational levels. However, where international activities are concerned it is difficult to make out a case for the subordination of international nongovernmental organizations to public international organizations. On one facet of public-private relations, see William M. Evan, "Public and Private Legal Systems," in Evan (ed.), *Law and Sociology* (New York: Free Press of Glencoe, 1962), pp. 165-84. On some aspects of the relations of private organizations with international organizations, see Peter H. Rohn, *Relations Between the Council of Europe and Non-Governmental Organizations* (Brussels: Union of International Organizations, 1957). For some preliminary suggestions for the study of the interaction of regional organizations that raises questions about the stimuli provided by and interactions with nongovernmental organizations and groups, see Karl Kaiser, "The Interaction of Regional Subsystems: Some Preliminary Notes on Recurrent Patterns and the Role of Superpowers," *World Politics* 21 (1968): 84-107.

[65] Miller, "Living Systems: Cross-Level Hypotheses," pp. 384-85. It is demonstrable that there are laws about the conduct of business that either have not penetrated the business world or have been altered in the intake process, and that there are relations in the business world that have not yet had impact on law. That extra effort is required to cross barriers or boundaries is revealed by the existence of lobbies, regulatory agencies, etc.

examined is the extent to which penetration of the realm of international finance by policy may be leading toward internationalization of domestic policies.[66]

Two thoughts concerning possible research topics come to mind in respect to internationalization that entails interpenetration of functional systems. An obvious topic for research would be the relationship of any trends toward internationalization or convergence of domestic policies to the effort toward harmonization of the laws of the EEC countries. As a minimum one could expect distinctions by countries, by economic, social, and political systems, and by function and subfunction of the circumstances in which private harmonizing and internationalizing activity—e.g., through cartels—comes first and the circumstances in which it does not.

Today, one of the most serious problems is politicization of the technical, including the technical aspects of such matters as law and justice, economic development, and social betterment programs. Perhaps it is the sickness of our time, to borrow the subtitle of Friedrich Grimm's book on political justice. Disarmament negotiations, the Arab-Israeli controversy over the uses of the Jordan River, and the East-West disagreement in the Economic and Social Council over whether underdeveloped states should first obtain basic industries or whether they should first obtain light industries, a market for the product of basic industries, are illustrations of the metamorphosis of issues from those of expertise to those of "national interest." Politicization of what could be and sometimes were essentially technical matters entailing problem solving rather than dis-

[66] Trends toward internationalization of domestic policies are dealt with in John Azad, *Der politische Faktor in den internationalen privaten Kapitalwanderungen* (Geneva: Descombes, 1961). On politicization of technical matters, see Ciro E. Zoppo, "Technical and Political Aspects of Arms Control Negotiations: The 1958 Experts' Conference," RAND Report RM-3286-ARPA (Santa Monica: RAND Corporation, September, 1962); David W. Tarr, "Military Technology and the Policy Process," *Western Political Quarterly* 18 (1965) 135-48.

tributive decisions and negotiations[67] is a matter to which international lawyers need to give more attention. Their work lies at a crucial point of the intersection of policy and law, the point of embedding policy in law, and so one basic point at which the boundary of the technical may be pierced by the political. An important weapon in the defense of the technical in any field is the law and its capacity to penetrate, to structure, and to bound the political—a factor most important in the development and preservation of democratic societies. That the law is subject to total politicization has been made evident by the internal processes of revolutionary and totalitarian regimes.[68] What is needed in this day of emphasis upon the supremacy of politics is the study of politicization as part of a reciprocal interaction between politics and law characterized by asymmetries varying over time and by subject matter. A similar approach could be employed to study interpenetrations of other functional systems.

What has been said above about interaction and even counteraction suggests conflict; and conflict is one of the primary forms of intersystem relations. Conflict between functional systems, as well as more passive structural incongruities, is to be anticipated and, perhaps, even welcomed provided that the struggle is not of such proportions as to negate the conflict-containing effect of cross-cutting pressures. Interorganizational conflicts, between organizations of different levels (e.g., regional and international organizations) or of the same level (e.g., two regional organizations) are a part of the international scene and part of the law-producing process. The most dramatic conflicts are, of course, those that involve states, although in recent years we have been treated to the spectacle

[67] For models of distributive and problem solving integrative bargaining processes, see Richard E. Walton and Robert B. McKersie, *A Behavioral Theory of Labor Negotiations: An Analysis of a Social Interaction System* (New York: McGraw-Hill, 1965), pp. 46-57, 137-43.

[68] E.g., Otto Kirchheimer, *Political Justice: The Use of Legal Procedure for Political Ends* (Princeton: Princeton University Press, 1961).

of conflict at arms between an international organization and a secessionist province. The European scene seems to have drawn most of the attention accorded interorganizational conflicts chiefly because the regional organizations in some cases were provided with overlapping functions (as in the transport and energy fuel areas) and sometimes displayed overlapping memberships (as in the case of Euratom and the European Nuclear Energy Agency). Interorganizational conflicts represent another source of law, an opportunity to observe law-in-the-making. To observe the evolution of organizations through makeshift arrangements such as the Inter-Executive Working Groups, the Inter-Executive Co-ordinating Committee, and various cooperative procedures among the European Communities is to watch the making of a living constitution. Along with the observation of nation-building, much data is being produced relevant to the generation of legal rules and legal systems. It is data that can hardly be tapped, let alone effectively processed, either by legalistically formal treatment alone or by social science approaches that do not incorporate the rich insights of legal scholarship.

Chapter III: International Societal Development

The Study of Societal Development

As FAR AS the outside observer is concerned, the process of integration is remarkably similar whatever units are involved.[1] Villages come together as towns, towns coalesce into cities, feudal demesnes fuse into states, states amalgamate to form new states, empires, and supranational entities. From the end of the Middle Ages until 1871, and once again with the South Slavs in 1919, the European map was periodically revised not only by conquests and cessions but also by the consolidation of national groups so that nationality and state boundaries approached congruence. At least some of the blame for the wars that followed is attributable to ineradicable incongruities between nationality and state. From one end of Europe to the other, the growth of nations followed the same consolidating process.[2]

There was also a concurrent disintegrative process, a process of fission whereby new political units were generated from old ones. The nation-building era of Europe, like feudalism before it, was a way of dealing with the debris of empire—territories joined in dynastic or personal union and not on the basis of nationality. Until freed from subjection to alien rule, some nationalities could not consolidate. World War I alone saw the fall of four empires, of which three not only were frag-

[1] Amitai Etzioni, "The Epigenesis of Political Communities at the International Level," *American Journal of Sociology* 68 (1963): 407-21; and *Political Unification: A Comparative Study of Leaders and Forces* (New York: Holt, Rinehart and Winston, 1965). See also Philip E. Jacob and James V. Toscano (eds.), *The Integration of Political Communities* (Philadelphia and New York: Lippincott, 1964).

[2] Karl W. Deutsch, "The Growth of Nations," *World Politics* 5 (1953): 168-95.

mented but also left such successors as Poland and Czechoslovakia, and such enlarged states as Rumania and Yugoslavia, with new nation-building tasks. Fragmentation of empire in the form of the post-war dismantling of English, French, Dutch, Belgian, and Italian overseas holdings has again left nation-building tasks—the conversion of state into nation instead of the other way around, as had been expected before 1919. Successor states present moderate but hardly insoluble problems to international law. Indeed, one of the latter's functions is to reduce legal disarray during the succession process which tends to resist regularization because of the uniqueness of each case.

The succession problems of new states are mild compared with the obstacles to societal development at the international level where no appeal to myths of common ancestry, national mission, ideals personified by national saints and heroes, etc., can be made.[3] Two difficulties in particular come to mind. One is that posed by new states to the extent that they are either unsocialized to international norms or are in active revolt against them. Such states represent unassimilated and potentially outlaw elements.[4] Even though they may in theory be proper subjects of international law, they may in practice bridle against subjection to it.

An even more serious but inescapable problem arises from the introduction of a new unit, politically significant and yet without a clearly defined legal status. The ambivalent legal status of supranational and international organizations represents an apparently common stage in political evolution that

[3] On the forms of nationalistic doctrines, see Florian Znaniecki, *Modern Nationalities: A Sociological Study* (Urbana: University of Illinois Press, 1952), pp. 35-45, 83-100.

[4] Richard A. Falk, "Revolutionary Regimes and the Quality of International Legal Order," in Morton A. Kaplan (ed.), *The Revolution in World Politics* (New York and London: Wiley, 1962), pp. 310-31; R. P. Anand, "Role of the New Asian-African Countries in the Present International Legal Order," *American Journal of International Law* 56 (1962): 383-406.

may foreshadow a time when a "supraunit" must make good its claims against its components. Analogically, the status may be that of an Anglo-Saxon King in relation to his Witanagemot, a Holy Roman Emperor to his Electors, or a Muscovite ruler to his boyars, and like theirs would tend to vary with the personality of the leader of the supraunit and the conduciveness of circumstances at different times to strong leadership.[5]

All of these problems are generated by political integration and disintegration. Political science, like international law, was long held in sway by its concentration on the state, for it seemed that it was a society of states in which we lived. Yet it is now clear that there are stateless societies that have politics, even as they have laws. It is also clear that the state is one type of political arrangement which happens now to be dominant, but was not always so in the past and need not always be so in the future. There is, consequently, something to be said for bringing attention to bear on the way in which political units change. Integration is one means of such change, an important means and one that is receiving its share of attention. The work of Karl Deutsch in particular has been associated with its study,[6] as has that of Ernst Haas.[7]

Rather less developed are the alternatives to the state and surmises as to future lines of development. The concept of "system" already discussed tends to free thought from the restraints of the concept of "state" which can, among other things, restrict the vision of a warless future to the lone possibility of a world state. Kaplan's hypothetical, nonhistorical

[5] In regard to the interplay of circumstances and personality it might be noted that Sir Eric Drummond commented that had each been in the other's post, both his methods and those of Albert Thomas would have failed. Stephen M. Schwebel, *The Secretary-General of the United Nations: His Political Powers and Practice* (Cambridge: Harvard University Press, 1952), pp. 3, 7, 232, note 42.

[6] See his essays in Jacob and Toscano, *The Integration of Political Communities*, chaps. II, III, VI, VIII.

[7] E.g., Ernst B. Haas, *The Uniting of Europe* (Stanford: Stanford University Press, 1964).

systems are illustrative of the system theorists' relative freedom from the concept "state."[8] The difficulty posed by the problem of international change is endemic in the social sciences, i.e., the near-impossibility of conducting controlled experiments to identify just what is most likely to evolve from the interplay of variables within particular structures. Two approaches offer the promise of new flexibility in this area. One is simulation; the other, the search for miniature analogues of the international system.

Simulation, the artificial construction of an existing or possible state of affairs, compensates for the absence of strict laboratory controls by creating, within the laboratory as it were, a replica of the social relationships being studied.[9] The application of simulation to international relations was preceded by its widespread use in war gaming and in the worlds of economics and business. Simulation is open to numerous criticisms, particularly the following: arbitrariness in the assignment of values to courses of action; the occurrence of role-playing or playacting in non-computer simulation; the charge

[8] Even Kaplan is not completely free from the inhibitions posed by the concept "state," for he holds that "the existence of a government is an unambiguous sign of a political system," that the rules of a modern political system "specify the areas of jurisdiction for all other decision-making units and provide methods for settling conflicts of jurisdiction," that it is both hierarchical and territorial, and that "no political system exists in the functional area which is subject to jurisdictional dispute." The international system is treated as lacking a political system or as being a "null political system." Morton A. Kaplan, *System and Process in International Politics* (New York: Wiley, 1957), p. 14.

[9] Excellent summaries of recent work can be found in Harold Guetzkow, et al., *Simulation in International Relations: Developments for Research and Teaching* (Englewood Cliffs: Prentice-Hall, 1963); William D. Coplin (ed.), *Simulation in the Study of Politics* (Chicago: Markham, 1968), pp. 7-111. A first comparison of simulation designs, reporting on use of the same basic scenario in three quite different games, has been made by Hayward R. Alker, Jr., and Ronald D. Brunner, "Simulating International Conflict: A Comparison of Three Approaches," *International Studies Quarterly* 13 (1969): 70-110.

that in computer simulation quantification has its limits; the oversimplification of complex phenomena; and the necessity for telescoping events that would in the real world occupy weeks, months, or years. While these are in no sense trivial criticisms, simplifying assumptions are one reason why science has achieved so much intellectual "leverage" over phenomena by enabling it to isolate some variables to the exclusion of others. In any case, policy-makers utilize numerous simplifying assumptions of their own, although they do not always make them explicit as simulation, particularly computer simulation, requires. Then, too, the refinement of simulation techniques has allowed controls to be placed on sources of error. Multiple "runs" through the same set of political conditions, use of policy-makers themselves as participants, and comparison of simulated past historical events with the actual historical records are among the means by which reliability and validity can be sought and tested. There have as yet been no simulations directly focused upon the role of norms in international behavior. But pilot studies involving simulated situations in domestic law indicate that simulation studies may ultimately become a major tool for the examination of the international arena.[10] This possibility is made more likely by the fact that numerous simulations of international relations per se already exist. In the study of the forms which international systems may take and how evolution from one system to another comes about, beginnings have been made both in Richard Brody's work on the Nth-country problem and in the work at the University of Chicago on the simulation of the balance of power and other models.[11]

[10] See, for example, Theodore L. Becker, *Political Behavioralism and Modern Jurisprudence*, (New York: Rand-McNally, 1965), pp. 88-115.

[11] Richard A. Brody, "Some Systemic Effects of the Spread of Nuclear Weapons Technology: A Study Through Simulation of a Multi-Nuclear Future," *Journal of Conflict Resolution* 7 (1963): 663-753; Morton A. Kaplan, "Some Problems of International Systems Research,"

The search for empirical microcosms[12] has been inspired by the same desire to find simplified versions of reality that has too often proved intractable when approached directly. Two promising analogues have emerged, namely, oligopolistic markets and tribal societies based on segmentary lineage. Of these, segmentary lineage systems have been the more intensively studied.[13]

In both cases, the initial reaction may be acute consciousness of the disparity between the world of international law and politics on the one hand and, on the other, the remote worlds of heavy industry and African tribes. Yet the crucial point justifying investigation of the analogues is structural similarity. One can at least proceed on the assumption that international law has the characteristics it has because of the uncentralized milieu in which it operates, a milieu widely at variance with that of domestic, state law but very much like the one in which segmentary tribes live.[14] In no sense is this to place any kind of value judgment on international law; the "equation" with certain kinds of tribal law indicates that structurally similar societies have similar ways of dealing with conflict, not that both are therefore "primitive." Since the comparison could equally well be made with oligopolistic markets of highly developed industrial societies, it is evident that

---

in *International Political Communities—An Anthology* (Garden City: Doubleday, Anchor Books, 1966), pp. 495-97.

[12] A brief discussion may be found in Richard C. Snyder and James A. Robinson, *National and International Decision-Making* (New York: Institute for International Order, 1961), pp. 31-32.

[13] Michael Barkun, *Law Without Sanctions: Order in Primitive Societies and the World Community* (New Haven: Yale University Press, 1968); Roger Masters, "World Politics as a Primitive Political System," *World Politics* 16 (1964): 595-619.

[14] On the desirability of cross-level search, abstraction, and generalization in systems analysis, see Herbert A. Simon, "The Architecture of Complexity," *Proceedings of the American Philosophical Society* 106 (1962): 467-68.

what is attempted is to isolate analytically the variable "decentralization."

As international society changes, it carries law with it, just as law is itself an agent in that change. If law is not to become a constant victim of extreme time-lag, some means must be found to determine the relationship between the content and effectiveness of legal norms and the rate and kind of change in the society. This can most easily be accomplished (1) by focusing on the functions that law in fact fulfills, regardless of the functions it consciously aims at, and (2) by determining, as far as possible, the consequence of changed conditions on international law itself or on legal systems that for purposes of analysis can be viewed as equivalent.

To accomplish these objectives it is desirable first to develop a typology of societies along a developmental scale that represents some reasonable correspondence to the varieties of societies that anthropology and history indicate have existed. Where historical data permits us to know the orders of several successions the scaling problem is relatively simple. Where it does not, as for nonliterate societies, the researcher may have to devise an ordering based upon the concept that evolution increases complexity or he may have to follow Tylor's early lead[15] and group societies on the basis of the presence or absence of certain characteristics that suggests a gradual succession of types in the absence of stagnation, decay, or rapid disintegration.

To develop a scalar typology implying a possible step-by-step advance through time entails dangers related to data quality, selection of adequate criteria for grouping societies and distinguishing stages, the selection of aspects of development

[15] Edward B. Tylor, "On a Method of Investigating the Development of Institutions; applied to Laws of Marriage and Descent," *Journal of the Royal Anthropological Institute of Great Britain and Ireland* 18 (1889): 245-72; reprinted in Frank W. Moore (ed.), *Readings in Cross-Cultural Methodology* (New Haven: HRAF Press, 1961), pp. 1-28.

to serve as signals announcing the classification of a society, and the meaning of "development" to be employed. For example, Organski's study of political development is clearly influenced by his awareness of the problems of economic development as well as those of nation-building.[16] His four stages of political development are: (1) primitive unification, (2) industrialization, (3) national welfare, and (4) abundance. To build upon Organski's typology, assuming that it could be translated to the international level, requires an economically oriented view of law coupled with the insights provided by the methods used in studying group politics. Were one to use Inis L. Claude's typology of the balance-of-power system, the collective security system, and the world state, his coupling of these systems to legal development would be of a definitely different nature than if one were to use the succession posited by Kaplan.

One typology, focusing upon units, has been employed in a study of societal development that takes law as a central concern. Elman R. Service's typology of societies from band to archaic state is used by Merrill Jackson, an anthropologist, to examine the organization, theory, and practice of medicine and jurisprudence in the handling of deviants at each of several stages of societal development.[17] A test is made of hypotheses derived from the basic theory that juridical and medical agencies become more complex internally and more special-

[16] A.F.K. Organski, *The Stages of Political Development* (New York: Knopf, 1965).

[17] Merrill Jackson, *A Study of the Evolution of Social Control: The Organization, Theory and Practice of Jurisprudence and Medicine*, Preprint 99 (Ann Arbor: Mental Health Research Institute, University of Michigan, July 1962); Elman R. Service, *Primitive Social Organization: An Evolutionary Perspective* (New York: Random House, 1962). See also Richard D. Schwartz and James C. Miller, "Legal Evolution and Societal Complexity," *American Journal of Sociology* 70 (1964): 159-69; Alvin W. Gouldner and Richard A. Peterson, *Notes on Technology and the Moral Order* (Indianapolis: Bobbs-Merrill, 1962).

ized with relation to each other as the structure of society becomes more complex. The findings appear to be of importance for the development of the concept of liability without fault and for the development of an intentionality mode in jurisprudence and an unintentionality mode in medicine. To carry Jackson's analysis to more modern societies, it would be useful to develop a typology that could be fitted into the Service typology. Furthermore, were the same thing done on the international level, it might well be found that certain forms of substantive law, certain procedures, and certain sanctions are correlated with particular forms of international societal development, that numerous attempts to draw principles and procedures from highly developed systems are premature, and that the principles and procedures needed are those akin to the ones that proved effective when domestic society evolved from the particular stage analogous to that of the current international system to the next more complex level of organization. Thus, for example, it may be that something akin to Judge John E. Read's suggestion for international itinerant justices might be desirable at the present or at a subsequent stage of international societal development.[18]

Jackson's method seems to open one of the more fruitful lines of approach to the correlation of legal, social, and political relations, fitted to organizational forms, including the governmental, that might be applied to both municipal and international law. Use of this approach, particularly in a systems context, should go a long way toward eliminating inhibiting comparisons with the state whereby Austinian misperceptions condition inference and interpretation. There is need to look beyond the simpler concepts of command, coercion, obedience, and deviance, to the contributions of law

[18] John E. Read, "Perspective in the International Plane," in David R. Deener (ed.), *Canada-United States Treaty Relations* (Durham: Duke University Press, 1963), pp. 78-79.

in its various manifestations to social coordination by providing inputs to, as well as receiving them from, society.[19]

Over time the international system requires study in terms of the transformation of an exclusively Western European system into a global system. To some extent this has been done, although earlier studies confined themselves to the formal "admission" of such states as the Ottoman and Chinese Empires. More recent publications have tended to lament the European imposition of its system and law upon non-Europeans.[20] The expansion of the European system from a regional to a global system, made possible by European technological advances and concomitant industrial requirements, did lead to intersystem and intercultural conflict and to impositions by Europeans, many of whom believed that they had a civilizing mission. What is now needed is not lament but acceptance of what has happened and more profound effort to explain and to understand the impact of the West on the non-Western world.

In the legal realm perhaps the most important question is whether European imperialism might not be looked upon as a lawgiving process comparable to the earlier lawgiving made

[19] Harry C. Bredemeier, "Law as an Integrative Mechanism," in William M. Evan (ed.), *Law and Sociology* (New York: Free Press, 1962), pp. 73-90.

[20] E.g., J.J.G. Syatauw, *Some Newly Established Asian States and the Development of International Law* (The Hague: Nijhoff, 1961), pp. 20-21, 46-52; S. N. Guha Roy, "Is the Law of Responsibility of States for Injuries to Aliens a Part of Universal International Law?" *American Journal of International Law* 55 (1961): 863-91. S. Prakash Sinha, *New Nations and the Law of Nations* (Leiden: Sijthoff, 1967), pp. 19-27, 137-45, holds that African and Asian criticism of rules of international law as alien does not explain their attitudes which he regards as based on perceived national interests. For a discussion of the Indian judiciary's tendency to apply statute law in preference to customary international law, see Kedar Nath. Agrawal, "The Indian Judiciary and Public International Law," *Indian Journal of Political Science* 25 (1964): 292-300.

possible by Roman conquests. The fact that Western negotiators may not have learned to communicate in terms understandable to non-Westerners[21] does not of itself mean that improper impositions have been made or that the process of the extension of rules originating in Europe is now halted.

Processes associated with the formation of the *ius gentium*, the common law, imperial law,[22] and the extension of international law beyond Europe might well be manifestations of a common process to be studied by utilizing the several tools of history, law, and social sciences. Attitude surveys are one tool that could prove useful, although to date we are not aware of any use of them relative to the evaluation of international law or of much use relative to international societal development. Nor do there seem to be content analyses of the editorial and news story reaction to law-relevant events.

In the absence of in-depth investigation of the processes of lawgiving and amalgamation of diverse indigenous standards, it is too easy to reach facile conclusions about contemporary circumstances. For example, one can easily assert that it is now insufficient to invoke a rule that summarizes a consensus antedating the independence of a complaining state. As argument for an effort to adapt international law to the interests and perceptions of today's new states, such statements are useful tools. As general descriptions, whether implying either that all rules are now challenged or that yesterday the mere

[21] See Robert L. Friedheim, "The 'Satisfied' and 'Dissatisfied' States Negotiate International Law: A Case Study," *World Politics* 18 (1965): 32-34.

[22] Particularly useful on the different ways in which conflicts of European laws and indigenous laws were handled by the various colonial powers is René Maunier, *The Sociology of Colonies: An Introduction to the Study of Race Contact*, ed. and trans. E. O. Lorimer, 2 vols. (London: Routledge & Kegan Paul, 1949), esp. vol. 2. On the continuation of the process in independence as official law displaces local law, see Marc Galanter, "Hindu Law and the Development of the Modern Indian Legal System" (Paper presented at the Annual Meeting of the American Political Science Association, September, 1964).

invocation of a rule silenced complaints, such lines are inaccurate. Danger lies less in an author's intentions than in his readers' failure to distinguish argument from description. Even social revolutions upset only parts and not the totality of legal relationships. A more scientific approach would suggest either withholding impressionistic statements or phrasing them in tentative form until investigation of the process of developing rules to bridge diverse local standards permits us to know how standards can be set rather than abandoned. The following circumstances will have to be taken into account: (a) the absence of consensus, (b) the evolution of consensus which must be expected as long as generations continue to succeed one another in positions of authority at about 15-year intervals, and (c) the need for rule standardization that arises when the turnover of system and subsystem components exceeds the rate at which components can develop less formal associations conducive to effective operations.[23]

Global Development

At the global level we are, of course, dealing with a system in which the integration process, if occurring at all, is minimal, far below the level reached in Western Europe. Centralization seems hardly to have occurred except, perhaps, to the extent that popular attention focuses on the United Nations and bloc leaders. Power is dispersed. This obvious fact is frequently stated without investigation into the reasons for it. Yet studies of regional integration and of federalism provide potential indicators of the conditions conducive to integration, given various combinations of pressures toward integration and disintegration.[24] Cross-level hypotheses and generaliza-

[23] Statement c is derived from a hypothesis that was set forth by E. G. Mishler in an unpublished paper on mental hospitals and that was suggested by James G. Miller as one which may be applicable at all system levels. "Living Systems: Cross-Level Hypotheses," *Behavioral Science* 10 (1965): 384.

[24] Too little has been done with the integrative and disintegrative

tions can be formulated that might facilitate understanding of the international system and its law, and the course of their evolution. Possible parallels and analogues may be explored, provided that neither is mistaken for evidence of identity.[25]

What is not clear is whether a global system can evolve to the degree of centralization at which there is no external environment on the planet or whether, in order to maintain a planetary environment, some minimum dispersion of functions and decisions must remain. It might be interesting to simulate a self-contained system-without-environment, if it is at all possible to shut subjects off from environments (e.g., even from the microsocieties of a simulated moon colony). In the past, one stimulus to the integration of societies, centralization of governmental organizations, and emergence of national leadership seems to have been an external threat,[26] although Karl

---

factors and the combination said by K. C. Wheare to produce federalism. *Federal Government*, 3rd edn. (New York and London: Oxford, 1953), pp. 37-54.

[25] On analogies, see Ernest Nagel, *The Structure of Science: Problems in the Logic of Scientific Explanation* (New York: Harcourt, Brace and World, 1961), pp. 107-17.

[26] Wheare, *Federal Government*, p. 37; Sidney Painter, *The Rise of the Feudal Monarchies* (Ithaca: Cornell University Press, 1951), pp. 86-88, 92-93; Quincy Wright, *A Study of War*, 2nd edn. (Chicago and London: University of Chicago Press, 1965), pp. 1016-17; Hans Speier, "Freedom and Social Planning," *American Journal of Sociology* 42 (1937): 470; Keith F. Otterbein, "Cross-Cultural Studies of Armed Combat," in Glenn H. Snyder (ed.), *Studies in International Conflict*, Research Monograph, no. 1, State University of New York at Buffalo, *Buffalo Studies* 4 (April 1968): 91-109, where it is found that in the 100 primitive societies studied, feuding does not occur if wars are frequent. For a theoretical framework that systematically embraces and generalizes about external factors, including threats, see Amitai Etzioni, *Political Unification: A Comparative Study of Leaders and Forces* (New York: Holt, Rinehart and Winston, 1965). For an experimental finding that contractual activity conducive to group cohesion may occur only when both an internal and an external threat to group survival appear simultaneously, see C. Faucheux and J. Thibaut, "L'Approche clinique et expérimentale de la genèse des normes contractuelles dans

Deutsch's analysis indicates that a common enemy is not essential for integration.[27] When present[28] the external threat also performs an integrative function for regional groups of states, e.g., the impact of Stalinist foreign policies, particularly the 1948 *coup d'état* in Czechoslovakia, on Western Europe was in large part responsible for the formation of NATO. In turn, East European integration has been a response to perceived counterthreats in the forms of NATO, Western European economic recovery and integration, remilitarization of West Germany, and later successes of EEC.[29] Indeed, Soviet memories

---

différentes conditions de conflit et de menace," *Bulletin de C.E.R.P.* 13 (1964) 225-43.

[27] Karl W. Deutsch, et al., *Political Community and the North Atlantic Area: International Organizations in the Light of Historical Experience* (Princeton: Princeton University Press, 1959).

[28] The external threat need not actually be present. It need only be perceived or alleged. Individuals and groups refurbish old enemies, operate as if an old threat still existed, or search for new enemies. The degree to which threat is felt may be a projection of unrelated factors independent of actual involvement with an enemy. David J. Finley, Ole R. Holsti, and Richard R. Fagen, *Enemies in Politics* (Chicago: Rand McNally, 1967), pp. 3, 154-55; Arthur Gladstone, "The Conception of the Enemy," *Journal of Conflict Resolution* 3 (1959): 132-27 For an earlier exposition of the political need for an "enemy" that first appeared in *Archiv für Sozialwissenschaft und Sozialpolitik* 58 (September, 1927), see Carl Schmitt, *Der Begriff des Politischen*, (Berlin: Dunker und Humblot, 1963). On the anticipation of a common enemy in the future, see Dean G. Pruitt, "Stability and Sudden Change in Interpersonal and International Affairs," in James N. Rosenau (ed.), *International Politics and Foreign Policy: A Reader in Research and Theory*, rev. edn. (New York: Free Press, 1969), pp. 401-402.

[29] Karl Kaiser, "The Interaction of Regional Subsystems: Some Preliminary Notes on Recurrent Patterns and the Role of Superpowers," *World Politics* 21 (1968): 88-89, 94-95, 100; articles by Karl Dietrich Bracher and by V. M. Khvostov and L. N. Kutakov in Joseph E. Black and Kenneth W. Thompson (eds.), *Foreign Policies in a World of Change* (New York: Harper & Row, 1963), pp. 127-28, 246-48; Marshall D. Shulman, "The Communist States and Western Integration," in Francis O. Wilcox and H. Field Haviland, Jr. (eds.), *The Atlantic Community: Progress and Prospects* (New York and London: Praeger,

of German invasion and obsession with Hitlerian aggression and terror have produced a paradigm of association between Western integration, German remilitarization, and aggression.

An external entity provides stimulus not only by being a threat. When it can be perceived as a success, it has impact through imitation or a comparable response. Marshall D. Shulman, employing the analogy of electrodynamic induction, has asserted that "integration in western Europe is producing integration by induction in eastern Europe."[30] Other scholars have noted that EEC and even the Central American Common Market have had a "demonstration effect" on Latin America by providing models for problem-solving and examples of ways of gaining international political status and of more effectively defending interests.[31] Of course, imitation or utilization of an external pattern of interaction and its corresponding structure as a model are not the only policy responses. Dean G. Pruitt points out that changes in a level of output by one party have an effect on another party's output, possibly but not necessarily on the same dimension. Moreover, reciprocal changes can be sequenced in various ways including both vicious and benevolent circles.[32] On the global level not

---

1963), pp. 131-44; Harold K. Jacobson, "Economic and Political Integration: From Schuman Plan to European Common Market and Euratom," in Andrew Gyorgy and Hubert S. Gibbs, *Problems in International Relations*, 2nd edn. (Englewood Cliffs: Prentice-Hall, 1962), pp. 156-59, 161-63.

[30] Shulman, "The Communist States," p. 142.

[31] E.g., Kaiser, "The Interaction of Regional Subsystems," p. 96; Sidney Dell, *A Latin American Common Market* (New York: Oxford, 1966); Christopher Mitchell, "The Role of Technocrats in Latin American Integration," *Inter-American Economic Affairs* 21 (Summer, 1967) 3-29; Philippe C. Schmitter, "The Process of Central American Integration: Spill-Over or Spill-Around?" Monograph Series, mimeographed (Berkeley: Institute of International Studies, 1967).

[32] Dean G. Pruitt, "Reaction Systems and Instability in Interpersonal and International Affairs," in Snyder, *Studies in International Conflict*, pp. 3-25.

just external threats but also external models are necessarily absent.

Under these circumstances it is not surprising to find an inward search for models and examples of the integration processes displayed in such images as "world government" and "world federalism," or in generalizations derived from regional or functional international organizations. One can employ such models in an attempt to visualize a global utopia, conceived less as an ideal than as an improvement on the present, or as an attempt to understand how men have dealt with such persistent questions as inter-community violence, trade barriers, and divergent values.

In terms of what the use of historical models as guides might mean for the evolution of international law, one must assume that methods of managing conflict are related to the forms and conditions of social structures as modified by such factors as rates of communication and capacities to produce and distribute goods. Whenever we make use of the past, we must remember that most historical models reflect low energy, not high energy, societies. Models of the recent past reflect a world of disparities and change: most countries are still low energy societies, while some, like Russia and Japan, have been converted only recently into high energy societies. Even a deterministic scheme would have to account for the vast differences between, for example, the England that produced the Common Law and the infant global society of the 20th century whose first inclusive attempt to organize formally was undertaken but a half-century ago.

However, it must be remembered that in history the unique has often emerged and that the unique is what the scientist has been unable to predict.[33] Social circumstances have compelled man to evolve organizations without models to guide

[33] Kenneth E. Boulding, *The Image: Knowledge in Life and Society* (Ann Arbor: University of Michigan Press, 1956; paperback edn., 1961), pp. 70-71.

him.[34] Perhaps the most notable period in the history of the West occurred during the Dark Ages when such structures emerged as the municipal organization of the burgesses and trading groups of merchants in need of caravans and convoys for protection from robbers and pirates.[35] It is noticeable that most accounts of Western political theory leave a gap between St. Augustine and either the investiture controversy or St. Thomas Aquinas, thereby omitting much basic material on the forging of the institutions that emerged from the disintegration of both Roman and tribal structures.

Primitive law provides analogues that can help scholars to gain understanding of legal processes in other decentralized systems. But potential legal developments in the future must be inferred from the several possibilities of societal change. It is probably going a bit far to suggest that a reasonable estimate of probabilities can be made in the near future, for much still needs to be done to blend anthropological and historical research and to organize the data in a manner that will indicate progressions from primitive to modern law.

Unquestionably, since a progression involves, among other things, structural change, a matter of prime interest is organizational growth. But organizational growth is only part of the problem, even when one does not restrict his vision to the Austinian requirement that law exists only in conjunction with the state. For, as studies of international systems of the past have demonstrated, not all changes in system structure are organizational changes in a narrow sense. If there is any

[34] On the irrelevance of the state as a model for world society and the consequent need for new modes of thought, see B. Landheer, "The Sociological Approach to International Problems," *Higher Education and Research in the Netherlands* 6 (Summer, 1962): 3-14; Ernst Jünger, *Der Weltstaat, Organismus und Organisation* (Stuttgart: Ernst Klett, 1960), pp. 30-31.

[35] Henri Pirenne, *Economic and Social History of Medieval Europe*, trans. I. E. Glegg (New York: Harcourt Brace, 1937; paperback edn., n.d.), pp. 52, 93.

lesson to be learned from history, it is that many structures are possible and one ought not be astonished by whatever emerges in the human quest for social order. As has been pointed out with regard to national development, there is today a tendency to present an overly restricted concept of development by employing as the standard for its measurement the condition of the United States in the third quarter of the 20th century.[36] By such a standard, neither Rome nor Han China was developed or modern. Moreover, use of the United States as a standard tends to set political participation or popular politics as a *sine qua non* of development, thereby ignoring (1) possible prerequisites of participation without excessive instability—e.g., what Almond and Verba refer to as "subject competence" or "administrative competence" but understress in comparison with participation—and (2) forms of participation other than those of modern democratic politics.[37]

For international development, participation or popular politics is not and probably will not soon be an ingredient in the development process. The involvement of governments in international organizational politics is no more a case of popular participation than was the conciliar movement. Indeed, it is hard to find structural comparability between current international bodies that contribute to lawmaking and the Model Parliament of 1295. Structures such as the Model Parliament

[36] For criticisms, see Herbert Blumer, "The Idea of Social Development," *Studies in Comparative International Development*, vol. 2, no. 1 (St. Louis: Washington University, Social Science Institute, 1966): esp. 7-8; Abdul A. Said, "The Impact of the Emergence of the Non-West Upon Theories of International Relations," in Said (ed.), *Theory of International Relations* (Englewood Cliffs: Prentice-Hall, 1968), pp. 93-106; C. D. Hah and J. Schneider, "A Critique of Current Studies on Political Development and Modernization," *Social Research* 35 (1968): 130-58.

[37] Gabriel A. Almond and Sidney Verba, *The Civic Culture* (Princeton: Princeton University Press, 1963), pp. 19, 23-26, 214-29; Lucian W. Pye, *Aspects of Political Development: An Analytic Study* (Boston and Toronto: Little, Brown, 1966), pp. 124-25.

preceded and became vehicles for popular participation. What may be suggested is that the important clues to developmental progressions, however varied their outcomes, lie in what *preceded* Plantagenet Parliaments, the Estates General of Philip the Fair, and comparable bodies.

Strengthening of royal authority, disarming the competitive power centers, improving methods of dispensing justice, acquiring revenue, employing oaths of allegiance to the king, and relying upon military forces subject only to central authority—none of these was achieved overnight but all were vital aspects of development.[38] Such facets of development are pertinent in that they are responses at least as much to internal as to external stimuli. In our time, French acceptance of the Coal and Steel Community and of Western defense arrangements was a response more to a perceived German, that is, internal Western European threat than to the external Soviet threat.[39] Absence of an external threat on a global scale implies that stimuli toward integration are to be found in internal threats and that historical analogies suggestive of appropriate integrative responses must lie among community-building responses to internal threats. In an age when the so-called balance of terror renders conquest a technique for suicide rather than global integration, it is important to remember that past routes to integration were not all military or political. Nor, lest the "common market" phenomenon be misinterpreted, did economics provide a lone integrating force. EEC rests on the earlier evolution of Europe. Furthermore, as the ancient uniting of China and its preservation suggests, vision should not be restricted to the Western world as though it had a monopoly on integrative processes and values.

[38] Painter, *The Rise of Feudal Monarchies*, pp. 14-17, 33-38, 40-42, 49, 53, 58-62, 80-83; Ferdinand Lot, *The End of the Ancient World and the Beginnings of the Middle Ages*, trans. Philip and Mariette Leon (New York: Harper Torchbooks, 1961), pp. 351-53.

[39] Jacobson, "Economic and Political Integration," pp. 159, 161, 162.

International Societal Development

Another approach to international development might examine whether there is a progression from the tangible to the spiritual or vice versa. One facet of regional societal development in Europe would suggest a movement from the occasional missionary's ideas of Christianity to the highly bureaucratized organization of Innocent III. On the other hand, in more mundane matters the progression of functional organizations from the Central Rhine Commission (1804) through those like the Universal Postal Union and the International Telegraphic Union to the League of Nations suggests that, in relation to objects and transactions that cross borders, organizational structure progresses from such tangible things as rivers, telegraph wires, railroads, letters, and goods to matters lying more in the realm of attitude and opinion, e.g., politics, economic coordination, labor standards, etc. It is possible that a sequential pattern of integration might indeed appear, even on more than one level of social organization—e.g., tolls for passing the borders of counties and marches were abolished through assertion of central controls over commerce. If so, it becomes possible to gain a more solid grasp of where global society stands vis-à-vis national sovereignty and developing regional authority than has to date been provided by studies concentrating on current national and regional integration. In the absence of any systematic integration of data from past and present, only the vagaries of intuition provide estimates of the current state of international development in terms of the comparative authority of global organization, regional authority, and national government.

Sovereignty, Nationalism, and Security

On the subject of sovereignty we can be brief. This is the problem of the independent decider, the critical subsystem which Miller identified as necessary to the existence of a living system in a totipotential rather than a parasitic or a symbiotic condition. For a state, the independent decider is its political subsystem, of which the crucial segment is the government. Fear of loss of the decider's independence from foreign influence has helped to keep the international system dispersed even after it had become technologically feasible to produce and maintain a more centralized international system.

How much independence should be retained by governments has been sufficiently debated. The task for scholars is not that of judging this debate but of ascertaining what pressures make for various degrees of subordination and, on the legal side, what responsibilities can be effectively imposed on the constituent units of the international system at its various stages of development. Among the circumstances to be studied is the level of technological development. Besides such frequently discussed matters as economic interdependence and mutual self-interest in avoiding nuclear destruction, such problems as air and water pollution are much more serious than at the time of the *Trail Smelter Arbitration* (1941). To these may be added the problem of establishing appropriate procedures to prevent the spread of diseases. And a virtually unexamined issue is that of responsibility for mob acts against foreign states, particularly when compounded by government complicity in mob-making or, as in 1966 in Poland, by police or soldier participation in the violence.[40]

[40] The only study of which we are aware that focuses upon the problem as it relates to international law is Harold D. Lasswell, "The Impact of Crowd Psychology upon International Law," *Philippine International Law Journal* 1 (1962): 293-309. On the incident in Poland in which Polish soldiers and police joined in throwing missiles at the American Embassy to produce an American protest and the Polish Foreign Minister's apology, see the *New York Times*, July 20, 1966, p. 2; July 21, 1966, p. 2. For a useful comparative analysis of the dynamics of the Hungarian uprising of 1956, the Panamanian mass demonstration of 1964, and three Dutch demonstrations during World War II, see Henry L. Mason, *Mass Demonstrations Against Foreign Regimes: A Study of Five Crises*, Tulane Studies in Political Science, vol. 10 (New Orleans: Tulane University, 1966).

What system changes might provide effective restraints so that each state meets its responsibility to other states is a topic to be examined with concern for more than desirable rule content. This area of responsibility of state to state is one in which systems analysis can be put to the service of policy. In doing so, one could interrelate responsibilities, the need of the international system to maintain its components in a state of relatively high efficiency and low cost, and the consequent need to assure independent national decisions whenever knowedge of the local system and circumstances is essential to an effective decision. In this regard, it must be recalled that national symbols, among which is the national legal system, are today more likely to elicit effective response than are the still remote symbols of international authority and community.

Clearly, one direction for research, a direction getting at the nature of the sense of obligation activated by law, is to investigate more thoroughly the multiple loyalties problem (which to date largely focused on the problem of the personnel of international military and peacekeeping bodies).[41] Some attention to the loyalty problem appears in Efimenco's categorization of four forms of integration—accommodation, legal universalism, institutionalization, and transformation—that might bridge the reality of the state and the concept of world community.[42] But, aside from occasional efforts, this area of great importance to the effectiveness of international law has yet to be exploited. Perhaps something might be learned from the processes by which men developed loyalties to entities larger than Ticino, Hanover, and Scotland. Studies of the learning and socialization processes might provide in-

[41] Harold Guetzkow, *Multiple Loyalties* (Princeton: Center for Research on World Political Institutions, 1955). On the problem of the loyalties of the personnel of an international force, see H. V. Dicks, "National Loyalty, Identity, and the International Soldier," *International Organization* 17 (1963): 425-43.

[42] N. M. Efimenco, "Categories of International Integration," *India Quarterly* 16 (1960): 259-69.

sights relevant to the international problem and to the role of law.[43]

Recently, some interesting examinations of the role of the national have produced hypotheses relevant to issues concerning the law of nationality, treaty-making, the law of diplomacy, nationalization of foreign enterprises, and the nature of claims and demands. A penetrating article by Albert Breton employs an economic view of nationality to develop a hypothesis that nationality is a form of capital. The ideology of nationalism entails encouraging the investment of present scarce resources for the alteration of either interethnic or internation distribution of ownership. Some of the implications of the hypothesis are presented in terms of English-Canadian claims and demands on the United States, and French-Canadian demands on English Canada.[44]

Still more penetrating is Stewart E. Perry's social-psychological examination of the national. Viewing the nation-state as a consensus of effective or motivational behavior in a collection of individuals who regard themselves as being together, Perry sees the national role as a mobilization of the members of one society against those of another, demanding loyalty, and in crises even taking precedence over the family. He treats official representation of one's country as the most rigid definition of the national role, the most difficult to modify, and the most misunderstood by extra-nationals. Perry regards the concept of the national role as useful for the examination of propaganda activities and of international negotiations.[45]

[43] The role of law enters into Richard M. Merelman's application of psychological learning theory to the theory of political legitimacy. "Learning and Legitimacy," *American Political Science Review* 60 (1966): 548-61.

[44] Albert Breton, "The Economics of Nationalism," *Journal of Political Economy* 72 (1964): 376-86.

[45] Stewart E. Perry, "Notes on the Role of the National: A Social-Psychological Concept for the Study of International Relations," *Jour-*

In dealing with the same topic, Daniel Katz, Herbert Kelman, and Richard Flacks develop some hypotheses concerning symbolic, normative, and functional commitment. Viewing symbolic commitment as essential in the early stages of national existence and during crises but as weak and unstable in the long run because prolonged subordination of other roles to a national role is both psychologically untenable and sociologically dysfunctional, the authors see a need for a system of norms and sanctions in order to maintain conformity. Developed normative mechanisms relegate symbolic mechanisms to a secondary position. In the absence of any threat switching commitment to the symbolic, normative commitment is thought to be accompanied by a lack of interest in international affairs and acceptance of any foreign policy appearing to have a general approval.

Normative commitment would persuade the American lower, middle and working classes, but a national system depends on functional integration. Katz, Kelman, and Flacks perceive a functional commitment that helps to maintain the institutions to which the upper-middle and upper classes are tied or in which they hold positions essential to effective functioning of the national system. These people are highly interested in international politics but tend to conform to the established foreign policy.[46] If the authors are correct in their hypotheses, then the pressures on the elite to conform to exist-

---

nal of Conflict Resolution 1 (1957): 346-63; reprinted in James N. Rosenau (ed.), *International Politics and Foreign Policy* (New York: Free Press of Glencoe, 1961), pp. 87-97.

[46] Daniel Katz, Herbert Kelman, and Richard Flacks, "The National Role: Some Hypotheses About the Relation of Individuals to Nation in America Today," *Peace Research Society (International), Papers*, Chicago Conference, 1963, vol. 1 (1964), pp. 113-27. For the report of an experiment on conformity to group goals rather than individual goals, see E. E. Smith, "Individual versus Group Goal Conflict," *Journal of Abnormal and Social Psychology* 58 (1959): 134-37.

ing policies would seem to impede development of a commitment to international law and institutions and accompanying pressures on the government to function as an agent of the international system. Alternatively, it could mean that the government is freer to act in support of international law and institutions than its sensitivity to "public opinion" appears to permit.[47] To get at the question of which is the correct inference and through it to the role of nationalism in international policy formation, resort almost certainly must be had to studies of national decision-making, particularly with respect to foreign affairs.

Internal Decision-Making

THE EXPERT as an expert has been curiously neglected by the social sciences.[48] Perhaps this simply indicates the extent

[47] Cf. Karl W. Deutsch, "Mass Communication and the Loss of Freedom in National Decision-making: A Possible Research Approach to Interstate Conflicts," *Journal of Conflict Resolution* 1 (1957): 200-11. A recent study of the Kennedy years suggests that governments can be rather free of public opinion, although not of their own perceptions of public opinion, provided that they mobilize their bureaucracies before making public announcements of policies and proposals and provided that they avoid creating a credibility gap. National-security-minded segments of the elite are a particular concern and may stimulate a government into a semantic response, e.g., an equation of a nuclear test ban with nuclear superiority or a distinction between "offensive" and "defensive" weapons. To the extent that freedom to act depends upon level of trust in other governments, what appears essential is not mass or elite trust in another government but trust in one's own government to the extent of accepting an administration's statements that others can be trusted. Wesley L. Gould, with the assistance of William Klecka and Charles Weyant, "The *New York Times* and the Development of Assurance Between Adversary Nations: Six Case Studies, 1961-1963," Studies of the Social and Psychological Aspects of Verification, Inspection and International Assurance, Technical Report No. 2, United States Arms Control and Disarmament Agency (W. Lafayette, Indiana: Purdue Research Foundation, December, 1968), pp. 51-56, 58, 62, 66, 198-99, 262-64, 266-67.

[48] One of the few studies is George A. Kelly, "The Expert as Historical Actor," *Daedalus* 92 (1963): 529-48. More recent attention has

to which expertise of some sort has been accepted as the norm rather than the exception. In any case, the interaction of international law and the formation of foreign policy involves the intersection of various kinds of expertise. It is a matter not only of content—the norms themselves—but of the cast of thought, the way of approaching a problem, that is important.

On the substantive side, law serves two functions. First, a policy's congruence to it makes that policy appear legitimate in the eyes of the members of the community. We know little enough about the role of legitimacy in human action but the desire for approbation by both one's peers and one's successors seems to be a powerful motivation. Second, legal rules have a fact-component as well; they are, as Holmes suggested, predictive generalizations.[49] They tell the "badman" what he may reasonably expect of society, but they go further. They embody their own social science component, their own set of generalizations about how people behave.

A working legal system involves a correlation between the law of codes and law books and the "living law" of human behavior.[50] While this is generally true, it is all the more cen-

been focused on scientists and their role in policy-making, e.g., Don K. Price, *The Scientific Estate* (Cambridge: The Belknap Press of Harvard University Press, 1965); Robert Gilpin, *American Scientists and Nuclear Weapons Policy* (Princeton: Princeton University Press, 1962); Donald A. Strickland, *Scientists in Politics: The Atomic Scientists Movement, 1945-1946* (Lafayette, Indiana: Purdue University Studies, 1968), esp. chaps. 4-6; Eugene B. Skolnikoff, *Science, Technology, and American Foreign Policy* (Cambridge: M.I.T. Press, 1967), esp. chaps. 11, 12. On scientists as negotiators, besides Gilpin, see Strickland, "Scientists as Negotiators: The 1958 Geneva Conference of Experts," *Midwest Journal of Political Science* 18 (1964): 372-84. On the role of experts and their relations with politicians in Latin America, see P.J.H. Frías, "El Papel de los expertos en la vída política de América Latina," *Revista de estudios políticos* 128 (1963): 193-99.

[49] Oliver Wendell Holmes, "The Path of the Law," *Harvard Law Review* 10 (1897): 457-548. See also H.L.A. Hart, *The Concept of Law* (London: Oxford University Press, 1961), pp. 38-41.

[50] Eugen Ehrlich, *Fundamental Principles of the Sociology of Law* (New York: Russell and Russell, 1962), p. 493.

tral to a system like international law which, for all the proliferation of treaties, remains largely customary. The anthropologist, Ward Goodenough, states that customary norms can fruitfully be regarded as the "modal tracks of behavioral events,"[51] i.e., behavior that by sheer repetition has come to be regarded as *the* way of doing something. The analysis of legal norms tells us not only what *should* be done but what *has* been done, what *is* done, and what, hopefully, *will* be done. The effects of law are felt not only in the past but in the present and future. Apart from cause-effect relationships, law expresses generalizations about how people do in fact interact with one another.

Legal propositions have an "if-then" form, and analysis of the if-clauses ought to yield some information of verifiable character. There is a model of society, a theory about the way it operates, implicit in every legal system, including international law. As a test of the centrality of legal considerations in policy-making, it is worth asking the extent to which the law-derived model compares to the model utilized by policy-makers. For law enters the policy process not simply as a set of norms useful in dealing with choice situations but as a way of conceiving problems and determining the range of alternatives available. Snyder, Bruck, and Sapin see the policy-maker as "carving out" of the total range of phenomena before him something he conceives to be the problem at hand.[52] But how is this done? Could "the problem" be conceived in

[51] Ward Hunt Goodenough, *Cooperation in Change* (New York: Russell Sage Foundation, 1963), pp. 252-54.

[52] Richard C. Snyder, H. W. Bruck, and Burton Sapin, "Decision-Making as an Approach to the Study of International Politics," in Snyder, Bruck, and Sapin (eds.), *Foreign Policy Decision-Making: An Approach to the Study of International Politics* (New York: Free Press of Glencoe, 1962), pp. 65-66, 81-82. See also Dean G. Pruitt, "Definition of the Situation as a Determinant of International Action," in Herbert C. Kelman (ed.), *International Behavior: A Social-Psychological Analysis* (New York: Holt, Rinehart and Winston, 1965), pp. 393-432.

different ways? What determines the version of the problem that is finally brought forward for solution?

International law provides a way of viewing events in the international arena. Its norms constitute a structure for processing information[53] that offers the decision-maker an alternative perspective. It may, in fact, be determinative in the sense that it provides the decision-maker with his preferred conception of the problem or, in other terms, definition of the situation. But whether determinative or not for a particular decision, international law competes with other views of international events.

Different professions look at the world in vastly different ways and many of these differences have already been recognized and studied. Indeed, the notion of the differing world-views of scientists and artists has become so much a part of intellectual discourse that only in recent years have writers come forward to explicitly challenge it.[54] One difference that has not as yet been challenged is that presumed to separate the scientist and the lawyer. So far the kind of study directed at, say, the Wall Street practitioner[55] has not focused on the international lawyer. Nevertheless, a body of material of a related kind does exist and, indeed, embraces studies of the legal profession in non-Western countries.[56]

This material concerns itself with the thought patterns of lawyers per se and with their activities within the larger arena of government. Legal training and professional experience is

[53] Harold M. Schroder, Michael J. Driver, and Siegfried Streufert, *Human Information Processing: Individuals and Groups Functioning in Complex Social Situations* (New York: Holt, Rinehart and Winston, 1967), pp. 11-12.

[54] E.g., J. Bronowski, *Science and Human Values* (New York: Harper, 1956).

[55] Erwin O. Smigel, *The Wall Street Lawyer* (New York: Free Press of Glencoe, 1964).

[56] E.g., J. Murphy, et al., *The Korean Legal Profession: The Judicial Scrivener and Others* (Dobbs Ferry: Oceana, 1967); "Lawyers in Developing Societies," *Law and Society Review* 3 (1968-69), entire issue.

thought to leave its mark so that the lawyer sees events in a different way, forms his judgments in a characteristic manner, and tests those judgments in a style of his own.[57] Notwithstanding the institutional separation that has from time to time set international law apart, the international law specialist also bears the imprint of his professional legal training and socialization. Indeed, the authority of the lawyer derives in large measure from general recognition that his training has imbued him with an expertise. The phenomenon of lawyers in government is as old as the republic, but the growth of federal administration has produced a recognizable "Washington lawyer." Studies of the "Washington lawyer" take the effect of training and socialization one step farther: from the abstract formulation of thought patterns to an inquiry into the way those thought patterns enter the policy process.[58]

In the course of wedding law to policy, the official who is trained in international law couches policy proposals in the language of his profession. The interaction of law and government thus provides a mass of raw material for legal analysis, material unsanctified by citation in treaty or court opinion but still freighted with implications for the understanding of international law. White papers, memoranda, communiqués, statements to the press, and position papers do not fall within the accepted range of legally significant materials. Yet day-to-day formulations of problems and alternatives do offer glimpses of the influence of the law-trained mind on the outcome of events.

The role of the expert is intertwined with the roles of many other persons in the policy process. Furthermore, like the politician, the expert is constrained by existing domestic

[57] Theodore L. Becker, *Political Behavioralism and Modern Jurisprudence* (Chicago: Rand McNally, 1964), pp. 117-24, 126-30; Vilhelm Aubert, "Researches in the Sociology of Law," *American Behavioral Scientist* 7 (December, 1963): 16-20.

[58] Charles Horsky, *The Washington Lawyer* (Boston: Little, Brown, 1952).

policies that impinge upon the range of choice and by influences exerted by the legislature, political parties and party strife, the mass communication media, other experts, and administrative departments acting as pressure groups.[59] We may also assume that the expert in government service is subject to constraints related to rank, a felt need to protect relations with superiors and informants, and to differences between bureaucratic and professional goals and standards.[60] Of course, even if such constraints do not impede upward communications, there is no guarantee that the expert's advice will be heeded.[61]

To what extent legal advice is sought and heeded is difficult to say. David R. Deener's important study of the Attorneys General and their treatment of international law is the lone work in that area and is more concerned with what the Attorneys General said than with their role in the decision process.[62] The only real attempt to probe the area of the role of law, lawyers, and legal advice in the foreign policy decision process is represented by the conference of legal advisers to foreign offices held in 1963 under the auspices of the Ameri-

59 On military policy as a bargain struck between contending forces, see David W. Tarr, "Military Technology and the Policy Process," *Western Political Quarterly* 18 (1965): 135-48. On interdepartmental conflicts that have affected foreign policy, see, e.g., W. L. Dorn, "The Debate Over American Occupation Policy in Germany in 1944-1945," *Political Science Quarterly* 72 (1957): 481-501; Jere Clemens King, *Foch Versus Clemenceau: France and German Dismemberment, 1918-1919* (Cambridge: Harvard University Press, 1960); Raymond G. O'Connor, *Perilous Equilibrium: The United States and the London Naval Conference of 1930* (Lawrence: University of Kansas Press, 1962).

60 For a report on a relevant experiment, see Arthur R. Cohen, "Upward Communication in Experimentally Created Hierarchies," *Human Relations* 11 (1958): 41-53. See also Peter M. Blau and W. Richard Scott, *Formal Organizations: A Comparative Approach* (San Francisco: Chandler, 1962), pp. 60-63, 173, 244-47.

61 See Général Gauché, *Le Deuxième Bureau au travail (1935-1940)* (Paris: Amiot-Dumont, 1954).

62 David R. Deener, *The Attorneys General and International Law* (The Hague: Nijhoff, 1957).

can Society of International Law.[63] This beginning has made it clear that there are many interesting questions to be explored concerning legal advice. For example, it appears that whether a question is legal or political in nature depends on the size of the legal adviser's staff and the current backlog of work. When a Ministry of Justice monopolizes legal advice, the tendency of a Foreign Office to seek such advice even before signing a treaty may be related to the spatial relationship of the two offices and the means of communication available. The form and consistency of legal advice may be related to the frequency of rotation between the diplomatic service and the legal adviser's office. Or, as the last two sentences suggest, they may be related to the organizational pattern determining who shall supply legal advice on foreign affairs to whom.

Even if the legal adviser is assigned a purely technical task such as advising whether a particular action can or cannot be taken, how to carry out a particular action without offending another government, or to justify what has already been decided, it would be useful to ascertain whether and under what circumstances a legal adviser's action precludes a policy decision-maker from later changing his mind. For example in the case of the Cuban blockade, did the work of Department of Defense lawyers between Friday evening, October 19, 1962, and the next morning in drawing up a blockade proclamation in harmony with planned naval operations restrict freedom of decision on Saturday afternoon, October 20?[64] Or had the President been in fact, if not formally, committed on Thursday, October 18, to the blockade as the first step to get the Soviet missiles out of Cuba?[65] On the basis of presently

[63] For the summary report and background papers, see H.C.L. Merillat (ed.), *Legal Advisers and Foreign Affairs* (New York: Oceana, 1964).

[64] On activity at the office of the Judge Advocate General of the Navy, see the declassified log of Rear Admiral Robert D. Powers, Jr., *Memorandum for JAG Files*, JAG:001, fvs, 5 November 1962.

[65] Theodore C. Sorensen, *Kennedy* (New York: Harper & Row,

available information the latter seems more probable, but the former is not ruled out even for the missile threat to national security.

The subject of legal advice has many intriguing facets to be examined. In this endeavor to determine the parts played by law and lawyers in the foreign policy decision process, the techniques used by the student of decision-making and the student of organizational behavior, as well us those used by the international law specialist, are forces that could profitably be combined to lift what has amounted to a veil of mystery. Have the decision-makers been, as sometimes charged, too legalistic in their approach to foreign policy? Or, as is sometimes lamented, have they subordinated the law to policy? To date we can guess but do not know.

1965), pp. 776-80; Robert F. Kennedy, *Thirteen Days: A Memoir of the Cuban Missile Crisis* (New York: Norton, 1969), pp. 36-37, 43-44.

Chapter IV: Functions, Purposes, Obligations, and Reciprocity

Law in International Relations

IT MAY BE assumed that, with the exception of writers whose sense of "realism" impels them to argue that law is non-existent in international relations, those individuals who turn their attention to international law hold the conviction that law has something to do with international relations. Not only must this be the case for the publicist, it must also be the case for the practitioner, whether a legal adviser to a Foreign Ministry or a member of a law firm, for otherwise there would be nothing of international scope on which to practice the lawyer's art.

That there is something on which to practice the lawyer's art does not mean that there is agreement on what that something is, what functions it performs, and to what uses it is put in international affairs. Much of what has been written about the matter has been highly speculative. The paucity of truly empirical studies of the nature, functions, and uses of law in international relations leaves speculation virtually unrestrained. Anecdotal support for various optimistic and pessimistic portrayals of law's place in the international scene hardly carries knowledge beyond the limits imposed by acceptance of either the myth of the rule of law or the myth of the dominance of power. Nor do conceptualizations based upon what are really no more than scraps of evidence introduce order into the study of law's international functions and uses. Need remains for a multipronged categorizing of data in forms conducive to statements about the functions and uses of law in international affairs.

International law has been subjected to the onslaughts of a fierce polemical literature, but, strangely, its detractors never deal with life in a hypothetical world without either international lawyers or the semblance of international law. Untestable as such a life is in the real world, it is worth examining in the simulated worlds of the imagination. A world constructed in this fashion would be unlikely to remain long in its "out-law" state. Law, like Voltaire's deity, would have to be invented.

The concepts taken for granted in international law—sovereignty, ambassador, refugee, citizenship, territorial waters, etc.—are in fact symbolic representations of certain events and facts in the world of international relations. Law is a system of symbolic representation,[1] a shorthand for taking in the panoply of events and making some sense of it. By functioning as a picture of the world—albeit a simplified one—a legal system of any kind performs more than coercive functions. First and foremost, to the extent we accept it, it gives us a grip on reality. The human propensity for image-making impels us to construct models of our environment. The same environment is, of course, subject to an indefinite number of representations. The international lawyer sees the world in one light, the economist in another, the geographer in a third. But whether one sees the world as made up of legal subjects, producers and consumers, or topographical forms, the important fact is that in some sense one sees the world through message-bearing symbols. One's vision of the world is restricted to what can be conveyed, often ambiguously, by those sets of symbols that he has learned to use.

International law is enunciated in a logically interrelated set of metaphors. Thus, it is possible to avail oneself of the informational aspect of international law quite independently of international legal institutions. Even if there were no inter-

[1] Anton-Hermann Chroust, "Law: Reason, Legalism, and the Legal Process," *Ethics* 74 (1963): 1-18. See also Walter Probert, "Law and Persuasion: The Language-Behavior of Lawyers," *University of Pennsylvania Law Review* 108 (1959): 35-58.

national legal institutions, a shared international legal system would perform a function. It would orient decision-makers to their world. And the more widely decision-makers share this system, the more it will also function as a means of communication between them. There is, in fact, a substantial congruence between the language of international governmental communication and the language of international law. The avenues for this communication have traditionally been the legally approved diplomatic channels. Contemporary departure from these channels may be less a deviation from the law than one of the periodic exercises in law revision that brings the law into line with the capabilities of modern weapons and modern means of communication.

The acceptance of a standard language of discourse and standard means of exchanging messages implies socialization. The concept of "socialization" is a new one as far as international law is concerned. It means, simply, the learning of and submission to rules appropriate to the social system in which one finds oneself.[2] The processes of habituation and education which this usage implies have affected different states over different periods of time. The traditional long-lived states of the West would never even think of their acceptance of international law in these terms, so removed are they from the roots of socialization. To the newly emerging nations, on the other hand, the socialization process is an ongoing and painful experience.

Within a society special institutions, of which educational institutions are an important component, are set up to systematically socialize members. International society, less well-developed institutionally, nonetheless performs the socialization function.[3] The requirements of diplomatic procedure

[2] E.g., Paul Bohannan, *Social Anthropology* (New York: Holt, Rinehart and Winston, 1963), pp. 17-19.

[3] Chadwick F. Alger, "United Nations Participation as a Learning Experience," *Public Opinion Quarterly* 27 (1963): 411-26; "Personal

tend to be adopted even by those states ideologically opposed to them. The young United States overcame its original abhorrence of ambassadorships, even as the Soviet Union is now replacing revolutionary iconoclasm with a fine sense of diplomatic style. Diplomatic procedures, while they have no explicit sanctions behind them, are in a way self-enforcing. To the extent that a state wishes to have relations with other states, it must conform. To do otherwise is to court international isolation.

Attention has been focused upon communications and socialization by three developments. First, the United Nations, by channeling diplomatic activity, has opened the question of why states maintain contacts in some ways rather than in others. Second, the concept of socialization has been seen to apply to states as to individuals.[4] Third, political scientists have begun to interest themselves in the theory of communication.[5] The importance of information for the survival of a political system, once taken for granted, has been approached afresh. Indeed, it has been the hallmark of modern political science to cease studying what had been the prime objects of research and transfer attention to the least conspicuous and least studied; this occurs in the belief, verified in many cases, that external magnitude has no necessary relationship to political significance.

Information theory and legal theory meet in the pivotal con-

Contact in Intergovernmental Organizations," in Herbert C. Kelman (ed.), *International Behavior: A Social Psychological Analysis* (New York: Holt, Rinehart and Winston, 1965), pp. 523-47.

[4] For the most complete discussion of the place of socialization and communication in international law, see William D. Coplin, *The Functions of International Law: An Introduction to the Role of International Law in the Contemporary World* (Chicago: Rand McNally, 1966), esp. chap. V.

[5] E.g., Karl W. Deutsch, *The Nerves of Government: Models of Political Communication and Control* (New York: Free Press of Glencoe, 1963), esp. chap. 9.

cept of "order." Degree of "order" may be translated into "degree of information." Perfect order is a situation about which one has complete information, a situation from which what we commonly call the "element of chance" has been totally removed. A situation about which we know everything is totally ordered; nothing will happen which has not been foreseen. This concept of order is similar to the concept of a legal rule as a predictive generalization. The more legal rules are obeyed, the more order exists, and the more the legal rules tell us about the society. Conceivably, an information theorist might study the degree of information provided by legal rules, as measured against observable behavior, and derive from this juxtaposition an index of international order. In any case, the order-information relationship offers a concept of legal order grounded in observable phenomena.

The foregoing discussion has at no point referred to sanctions or to a legal system as a set of sanctioned rules. The important point is that laws are *sometimes* sanctioned rules, but they are *always* something more. As instruments for socialization, communication, and the ordering of events, they perform functions irrespective of the existence of a sanctioning apparatus. These functions may be latent in terms of the ideal of coercive institutions, but they are performed nonetheless.

Presumably, empirically-grounded probes of the functions and uses of international law should also reveal a good deal about how and why particular international norms come into being and how they have changed over time. No doubt a most useful approach would be to emphasize process; but it also appears unquestionable that human purposes in particular situational contexts would come to the fore in descriptions and explanations of the genesis and evolution of particular international norms. To take an obvious example, it would be difficult to narrate the coming into being of norms concerning jurisdiction over the continental shelf without reference to uses for petroleum and natural gas and the development of means for exploration and exploitation. Whether from such specific instances of purpose it would be possible to generalize to an overall purpose underlying international law is debatable.[6] For the present, at least, it would seem more fruitful to treat international law as a multipurpose phenomenon having systemic functions as well as more parochial instrumental uses for actors on the international scene.

Purposes Derivable from the Intent of Actors

INSTRUMENTAL purpose, inferable from a study of the actors in international relations, their objectives, and their methods, can be approached through the literature and underlying source materials on diplomatic history, foreign policy, and the related decision processes. Although the literature on diplomatic history and foreign policy has to date supplied essentially anecdotal evidence susceptible to use as support for prejudgments of the uses of international law and the relative importance of each identified use, that literature at least provides a number of case studies. No conclusions but the beginings of an examination of the uses of international law and the constraints upon choice among uses is possible. A framework such as Richard C. Snyder's for decision-making should assist in the aggregation of the scattered data provided by case studies on foreign policy and diplomatic history, permitting the data to be put into a common form as requested by James N. Rosenau in his plea for a pre-theory of foreign policy.[7] Of course, this assumes that attention is paid to the uses made of law in the relevant decision and negotiating processes, masked as they are by the incompletness of the rec-

[6] On this point, see Wesley L. Gould, *An Introduction to International Law* (New York: Harper, 1957), pp. 162-71.

[7] James N. Rosenau, "Pre-Theories and Theories of Foreign Policy," in R. Barry Farrell (ed.), *Approaches to Comparative and International Politics* (Evanston: Northwestern University Press, 1966), pp. 39-43.

ord and by our virtual ignorance of the frequency and conditions of resort to, let alone the persuasiveness of, legal advice.

Literature on diplomatic history and foreign policy constitutes one set of sources for identifying the uses of international law and subsequently inferring its instrumental purposes. There are other sources. Assuming that the level-of-analysis problem is resolved in favor of actors, it is still necessary to determine on which actors to focus. Traditionally, the state has been the primary focus. Focus upon it can be justified on the grounds that the state is the meeting place of pressures generated in both domestic and international politics, the holder of a quasi-monopoly of armed force in a defined territory, and the possessor of the capacity to enter into the most important treaties or, more broadly, to make the most important decisions.

The conceptual dangers inherent in focus upon the state, among them anthropomorphism, are well known.[8] Hence, besides an investigator's particular interests or his perception of information and similar needs, avoidance of dangers inherent in the state concept may lead to focus on other units, perhaps upon international organizations, perhaps upon interest groups that may affect foreign policies. Explanatory power accrues only when decisions are discussed in a framework that concentrates upon the actual decision-makers rather than upon the collective entity to which certain decisions are imputed. Hence, the literature on international organizations and on the units embraced in national systems yields data on the actors' uses of international law. However, the particular focuses of students of internal units, especially their overriding concern about domestic issues, mean that in general relatively little has been done by social scientists—Ernst B. Haas being a notable exception—to explore the attempts of domestic in-

[8] See, e.g., Vernon Van Dyke, *Political Science: A Philosophical Analysis* (Stanford: Stanford University Press, 1960), pp. 63-64.

terests to utilize international instruments, including international law, to advance or to protect those interests.[9]

In other words, there remains a need for a catalogue of the instrumental uses to which international law is put. Such a catalogue is incomplete unless the cast of actors includes other units in addition to and often, for precision, instead of the state.

Purposes Derivable from the Nature of the System

On the assumption that healthy parts are essential to the existence of a healthy whole, some instrumental purposes could be treated as system purposes. To do so invites the dysfunctional projection of part upon whole and the resultant subordination of system purposes to the aspirations of a particular member or members (as when Kaiser Wilhelm II equated himself with the balance-of-power system).[10] Accuracy would be promoted by treating system purposes as a category distinct from instrumental purposes. System purposes could be treated as instrumental only when, as with regional and functional international organizations, a system is in turn a subsystem of a larger whole. In this case, we mean a subsystem that as a unit is striving for something by manipulation of the larger system. For the term "purpose" to be relevant, the subsystems must be individuals and articulate groups, that is, those creatures and their aggregates that are capable of both purpose and manipulation. Otherwise, one can speak of "function" and "process" but not of "purpose."

In the simpler dichotomization into system and unit, dis-

[9] Lester W. Milbrath, "Interest Groups and Foreign Policy," in James N. Rosenau (ed.), *Domestic Sources of Foreign Policy* (New York: Free Press; London: Collier-Macmillan, 1967), pp. 231-51, concludes that interest group influence on foreign policy is slight.

[10] See the references in Martin Wight, "The Balance of Power," Herbert Butterfield and Wight (eds.), *Diplomatic Investigations: Essays in the Theory of International Politics* (London: Allen & Unwin, 1966), p. 165.

tinction of instrumental and system purposes does not preclude overlaps. Indeed, the assumption that a healthy whole requires healthy parts suggests a presumably conflict-free overlap, however difficult such an overlap may be to identify and demarcate. But overlap is not the same as identity. To institutions and to channels—whether the latter be arteries of commerce, acoustic nerves, or intelligence services—can be ascribed purposes independent of the purposes of the units creating or using the channels. In the case of an anatomical network such as the nervous system one cannot attribute purpose to a creator except by metaphor or by reference to an anthropomorphized god. In a social system, independent systemic purposes may sometimes be ascertainable from the intentions of those creating channels and institutions. But the analyst may have to look beyond the creative act and original intentions, for the creators may not monopolize a channel or institution, their successors may not employ them for the uses originally intended, and the impact of other elements of the system may produce unplanned system purposes.

To the extent that what may be labeled as "system purposes" exist independently of the volition of human creators or managers, system purposes are the same thing as functions. The purposive element can be retained to the extent that such terms as "communication" and "survival" imply purpose in the sense of permitting something to be done regardless of why a particular doer may undertake an action. In the case of a communication system what is implied is a process, communication, permitting a particular action, namely, the sending of a signal to a receiver—a purpose inchoate as compared with the more specific purposes of senders and receivers. Nevertheless, there is a closer relation to purpose than is suggested by a nonpurposive designation such as the simple transmission of electrical impulses. The purposive element derives from the occurrence of process in a definable structure and from human concern with both. For example, the processes of stress and strain have no purposive aspect in regard to a remote, abandoned farmhouse. Let people return, then purpose can again be attributed to the forces that prevent the building's collapse. The probability returns that the concepts of process, function, and instrumental purpose will be intermingled.

Analytically, clarity is gained if it proves possible to conceive of process, function (or system purpose), and instrumental purpose in a manner that does not confound one with another. What can be discerned as serving *system purposes* and thus possessed of a function is not immune from simultaneous subordination to the *instrumental purposes* of actors. At the same time, discernment of system purposes may of itself carry normative weight with actors to engage their actions in ways that contribute to the proper use, maintenance, and functional effectiveness of systems.

As with instrumental purposes, system purposes are referred to in the plural. International law has not merely had a peace-maintaining function; it has also had a war-regulating function. How many functions can be identified as system functions and how closely these have corresponded to the categories represented by Morton Kaplan's systemic rules has yet to be carefully and systematically investigated. Only a few system functions or purposes are set forth here. Survival of the system is not included, since it is not clear whether the rules of any international system are actually conducive to its survival or, instead, to its ultimate destruction and replacement. Nor do we propose to deal here with the conundrum of whether sudden change, let alone more gradual change, constitutes maintenance of the one ever-changing system or its succession by a new system.[11] The existence of an international system, whatever its type and its degree of continuity with what

[11] More specifically, is the post-1945 system a new system or the old system with different weightings of power? Was the rigid bipolarity that developed after 1871 a different system from that preceding the Franco-Prussian War or was it the same system improperly operated?

preceded, is assumed. Within it, as within what preceded, is an institution called international law that has systemic functions. Some of these functions are discussed in the next three sections.

Communication and Information Functions

INTERNATIONAL law may be regarded as a form of communication chiefly among governments but including among the intended recipients all persons and groups performing activities to which a particular international custom or agreement is relevant.[12] Such communications can be treated as stored in memories that include treaty collections, statute books (particularly in the case of non-self-executing agreements), court reports, treatises on international law, and, at least in part, human memories. Traditional concern for promulgation and publication is evidence that law serves as a medium for the transmission of admonishments to potential offenders, indications of reward upon compliance with certain requirements,

[12] For a general discussion of communications models see Karl W. Deutsch, "On Communications Models in the Social Sciences," *Public Opinion Quarterly* 16 (1952): 356-80; and *The Nerves of Government*, esp. chaps. 5, 9. For a treatment of law as a substitute for continuing communications flows among the components of a system, see Charles R. Dechert, "A Pluralistic World Order," *Proceedings of the American Catholic Philosophical Association* (Washington: Catholic University of America, 1963), pp. 167-86. For an attempt to use communication theory to buttress an argument for the interpretation of treaties by reference to all of a community's basic goals including the shared expectations of the contracting parties, see Myres S. McDougal, Harold D. Lasswell, and James C. Miller, *The Interpretation of Agreements and World Public Order: Principles of Content and Procedure* (New Haven: Yale University Press, 1967), pp. 371-72. For the opinion of one of the above authors that communication theory, conceived as largely made up of the three elements of decision theory, symbolic logic, and semantics, is irrelevant as a guide for decision and sometimes even as a guide for analysis of the context, see Miller, "Research Tools Available to Lawyers," in Layman E. Allen and Mary E. Caldwell (eds.), *Communication Sciences and Law* (Indianapolis: Bobbs-Merrill, 1965), p. 27.

and instructions to those having tasks to perform in the distribution of rewards, punishments, and reparations.[13] It could even be said that John Austin's characterization of law as the command of the sovereign was a crude communication theory of law.

The concepts of communication theory and information theory, as well as the research findings in the three dimensions of syntactics, semantics, and pragmatics, are potentially applicable in efforts to ascertain the functions of international law and the effectiveness of related performance. In this sense, performance would reflect the information-order relationship referred to above and be included in the construction of an index of international order. Performance, even though seldom represented in quantitative terms, is generally treated as a measure of the effectiveness of a law in producing conformity. But performance by itself is not necessarily an indicator of effective communication which can be said to rest on co-orientation, that is, on the simultaneous orientation of communicators toward each other and toward objects of communication.[14] The concept of co-orientation is analogous to

[13] For a report of six experiments that give rise to some useful hypotheses on the effectiveness of norms as sources of information, see Edward L. Walker and Roger W. Heyns, *An Anatomy for Conformity* (Englewood Cliffs: Prentice-Hall, 1962), pp. 41-53.

[14] On the concept of co-orientation with reference to human groups, see Theodore M. Newcomb, "An Approach to the Study of Communicative Acts," *Psychological Review* 60 (1953): 393-404. A criticism of the McDougal use of communication theory (see note 12 above) on the grounds that deference to textual provisions will normally best realize the contracting parties' "genuine shared expectations" by restricting the latitude of interpreters could be carried further by employing the concept of co-orientation, as could McDougal's version. The criticism really differs from McDougal in terms of "how to do it" when assessing the parties' intentions. Gidon Gottlieb, "The Conceptual World of the Yale School of International Law," *World Politics* 21 (1968): 108-32. Experiments on the uses of norms as sources of information together with conclusions concerning the variables on which the effectiveness of information sources depend, are reported in Walker and Heyns, *Anatomy for Conformity*.

that of coding in the mathematical theory of communication and to that of coupling or matching systems in electronic engineering. Co-orientation is dynamic as a result of both exchanges of communications and feedback.

The degree of co-orientation at a given moment may or may not be indicated by the outward manifestation of agreement. Or it could be indicated by either relatively continuous or sporadic messages and actions over a period of time. Bearing in mind that communicative action need not receive verbal expression, what is needed but may be unattainable is a measure of co-orientation that would take account of both verbal interpretation and performance as transmitted over a communication network. The network, given delays in response to communications stored in printed texts, may be quite different from the networks over which a norm of international law was originally transmitted.[15]

Such a measure, if it could be devised, might conceivably isolate the residue of co-orientation potential after distortions arising in the communication network were identified and separated.[16] At the present time it is not clear whether the apparent ineffectiveness of certain segments of international law is due to an insufficiency of "redundancy"—the measure of the interdependence of signals—to counteract the noise, including semantic noise or ambiguity, of feedback and to permit sender and receiver to learn a mutual language, or whether it is due to an insufficiency of co-orientation potential caused perhaps by mutually incompatible culture patterns and cogni-

[15] On the United Nations as an instrument of change in the international communications network, see Chadwick F. Alger, "Participation in the United Nations as a Learning Process," *Public Opinion Quarterly* 27 (1963): 411-26.

[16] On forms of distortion, see John R. Kirk and George D. Talbot, "The Distortion of Information," *ETC.: A Review of General Semantics* 17 (1959): 5-27.

tive structures, as well as inadequacies in the communication network.[17]

Employed with care, the three approaches to human communications of mathematical theory, social psychology, and linguistic anthropology can each in its own way illuminate the communication function of international law hitherto only incidentally considered. In applying the concepts developed through these approaches it must be borne in mind that although communication theory deals in part with the information content of signals, information content is a concept related to the idea of selection or discrimination. The mathematical theory of communication concerns the signals themselves and the measurement of information content regarded as a property or potential of the signals. It is abstracted from questions of meaning, basic to the study of communications among men but insufficient in itself as explanation of the communication process.[18] As the lawyer well knows, the end product of meaning is vital and when the legal process leads to the courts there arises a clash over meanings, e.g., interpretations of events, statutes, precedents, and customs which lead

[17] On the functions of redundancy, see Anatol Rapoport, "What is Information?," *ETC.: A Review of General Semantics* 10 (1953): 247-60; Josiah Macy, Jr., Lee S. Christie, and R. Duncan Luce, "Coding Noise in a Task-Oriented Group," *Journal of Abnormal and Social Psychology* 48 (1953): 401-409, which also deals with the effects of different communication networks and differences in their built-in redundancy. On the effects of feedback, see Harold J. Leavitt and Ronald A. H. Mueller, "Some Effects of Feedback on Communication," *Human Relations* 4 (1951): 401-10. For a rigorous application of the concept of feedback to human behavior in general that helps in the understanding of the complexity of feedback and its contribution to co-orientation, see W. T. Powers, R. K. Clark, and R. I. McFarland, "A General Feedback Theory of Human Behavior," *Perceptual and Motor Skills* 11 (1960): 71-88.

[18] Colin Cherry, *On Human Communication: A Review, A Survey, and A Criticism* (New York: Wiley Science Editions, 1961), p. 9.

to results not necessarily those intended by, for want of a better term, a lawmaking communicator.[19]

Also of consequence, particularly to the lawmaking process, is the study of the relationship between the lawmaker and the particular audience or audiences, including courts, with whom he is attempting to communicate.[20] Such studies can be directed not only to the technical problem of draftsmanship but also to the problem of the dissemination of information about the law (whether by government or by nongovernmental media of mass communication) and the problem of the accuracy of such secondary information as affected by such nonprejudicial factors as the process of translation into laymen's language.[21]

In respect to mass communications, there is a relatively unexplored area that could be investigated with some profit to the discipline of international law. To what extent and with

[19] On the range of meanings that can be attached to political events and the consequences of interpretative diversity for the political system, see Murray Edelman, *The Symbolic Uses of Politics* (Urbana: University of Illinois Press, 1964). Edelman's approach can be adapted to provide focus on the legal system and on legal communications and symbols. On the close connection between political and juridical expressions, see Richard Koebner, "Semantics and Historiography," *Cambridge Journal* 7 (1953): 131-44. For a suggestion that communication can be analyzed into three components—namely, transmission of information, instruction, and motivation—and the definitions of these components in terms of purpose, see R. L. Ackoff, "Towards a Behavioral Theory of Communications," *Management Science* 4 (1958): 218-34.

[20] For some interesting propositions drawn from a nonlegal context, see Raymond Bauer, "The Communicator and the Audience," *Journal of Conflict Resolution* 2 (1958): 67-77.

[21] Gabriel A. Almond and G. Bingham Powell, Jr., *Comparative Politics: A Developmental Approach* (Boston and Toronto: Little, Brown, 1966), pp. 169, 180. A related problem, particularly in regard to the mass media, is that of source credibility. I. Hovland and W. Weiss, "The Influence of Source Credibility on Communication Effectiveness," *Public Opinion Quarterly* 15 (1952): 635-50; Leslie W. Sargent, "Communicator Image and News Reception," *Journalism Quarterly* 42 (1965): 35-42.

what degree of accuracy international law issues are accorded dissemination by the press has not been investigated.[22] As a start, in order to employ easily identifiable events, one might examine the attention given to a sample of International Court of Justice decisions. While the Court's decisions may seem of minor consequence to American scholars, there is evidence that such cases as those concerning South West Africa have created, both before and after the decision, a fair degree of anxiety and excitement in the public press of interested countries.[23] Indeed, one of the authors of this book found that when in Europe during an early stage of the *Interhandel Case* he was frequently asked by waiters and others who had identified him as American, "Why is a big country like the United States afraid of a little country like Switzerland?"—a reference to the Connally Amendment. This experience suggests that, besides an examination of newspapers that would include use of the tool of content analysis, it might be desirable, resources permitting, to use opportunities to follow the chain of communication in what has been called its two-step flow from mass media through face-to-face channels.[24] Attention could thus be paid to communications structures as well as to meanings.

Setting aside structure for the moment, it is evident that the

[22] A bit of attention has been given to the problem of getting adequate press coverage of the United Nations, A. Arnold Vas Diaz, "The World Press and the United Nations," *Gazette: International Journal for Mass Communications Studies* 9 (1963): 217-26. For a comparison of the coverage of the 1960 General Assembly by the *New York Times* and the Hungarian party central daily, *Nepszabadsag*, see George Gerbner, "Press Perspectives in World Communication: A Pilot Study," *Journalism Quarterly* 38 (1961): 313-22.

[23] *New York Times*, July 19, 20, 23, 24, 1966, with accounts of reactions overseas to the rejection of the case brought by Ethiopia and Liberia.

[24] Elihu Katz, "The Two-Step Flow of Communication: An Up-To-Date Report on an Hypothesis," *Public Opinion Quarterly* 31 (1957): 61-78; A. V. van den Ban, "A Revision of the Two-Step Flow of Communications Hypothesis," *Gazette: International Journal for Mass Communications Studies* 10 (1964): 237-49.

problem of meaning renders it desirable to give attention to the work of semanticists. For example, if communications are to be effective globally, a real problem is created by different language structures and word meanings.[25] Even in the relatively simple situation of interpretation of a treaty between two states, the text in the language of each being authoritative, significant differences of meaning can require decision concerning which meaning is to govern.[26] Alexander Ostrower's study of national, international, and diplomatic languages of yesterday and today provides a comprehensive view of the problem of communicating intended meaning and the utility of technical and international languages.[27] Such investigation can probe deeply into those aspects of diplomatic and legal language that are derived from social factors of which a diplomat or a lawyer may be unaware or over which he has no control.[28] The probe should be both in the direction of the communicator and in that of the recipients. The latter objective seeks a partial explanation of what happens to the message with the passage of time.

Such variables as cognitive structures of particular individ-

[25] E.g., Yu-kuang Chu, "Interplay Between Language and Thought in Chinese," *ETC.: A Review of General Semantics* 22 (1965): 307-29. According to Fred Blumenthal in *Parade*, July 14, 1968, a Sunday magazine section of the *Washington Post* and a number of other papers, at Vienna in 1961 Khrushchev became angry whenever "miscalculate" was translated. Afterwards, President Kennedy asked Major General C. V. Clifton to investigate. Clifton found that "miscalculate" has no Russian equivalent and that the term employed, the most literal rendering for the Russian mathematical term, meant "inability to count," implying that Khrushchev was "stupid."

[26] E.g., *Mavrommatis Palestine Concessions* (P.C.I.J., 1924), series A, no. 2, pp. 19, 20.

[27] Alexander Ostrower, *Language, Law and Diplomacy: A Study of Linguistic Diversity in Official International Relations and International Law*, 2 vols. (Philadelphia: University of Pennsylvania Press, 1965), esp. Part III which relates to several international law problems.

[28] See Suzanne Keller, "Diplomacy and Communications," *Public Opinion Quarterly* 20 (1956): 176-82.

uals may be beyond investigation, but a number of sociological and situational variables may be susceptible to research.[29] Thus, the investigation of language, i.e., of what is sent and received, and meaning can proceed into the examination of relationships, structures, and processes.

Communication is a process necessarily occurring within and between structures subject to the effects of information taken in from the environment, e.g., the visual locating of a mountain pass, which is not communicated in the sense of being transmitted by another human's deliberate act. Once those communications processes that are fundamental to the functioning of the global international system or of a regional subsystem are isolated, it becomes possible to identify that portion of the communications system that can be called the "legal system." By then searching for sources, messages, meanings, channels, immediate recipients, and audiences, sets of relationships can be established and structure delineated.[30]

To the extent that messages do not stay within the same system, the investigator can identify intersystem relationships and perhaps even obtain a crude measure of the degree of affinity between the systems that display communication links. One step in the mapping of intersystem communications channels entails identification of intended and actual audi-

[29] See the suggestions of P. H. Ennis, "The Social Structure of Communication Systems: A Theoretical Proposal," *Studies in Public Communication* 3 (1961): 120-44.

[30] It has been argued that the procedure outlined has the merit of converting problems of definition into empirical problems. Richard R. Fagen, *Politics and Communication* (Boston and Toronto: Little, Brown, 1966), p. 21. This argument assumes that definition has been attended to when bounding the political system and examining its operations prior to isolating communication processes. There would, however, still exist the problem of whether, for example, a message providing health statistics is a political message or, for present purposes, a legal message. A problem of definition would exist unless characterization of the message could be derived from the channel through which it is transmitted or the audience or both.

ences for particular types of legal messages. A subsequent step might be to employ the type or basic content of messages to relate audiences to each other. It can be argued that the latter has already been done in studies of treaty relationships. The reply to such an argument is that the treaty message is often directed to a more specific audience than the state, its whole populace, or even its government in the sense of an undifferentiated unit.

What legal messages are intended for legal technicians? For politicians untrained in law? For other functional elites? For the general public? What types of legal messages have what kinds of impact upon these groups? How do differing situations, e.g., crisis and noncrisis, affect receipt of the various types of legal message by each audience? To what extent is there distortion by elites, especially by legally-trained technical elites, as a result of socialization to the national system prior to exposure to legal training? In what ways does training with emphasis on national laws and legal procedures reinforce prior socialization and intensify resistance to penetration by messages originating externally? Does socialization introduce "noise" into the processing of messages? What countervailing attitudes and socialization processes can increase boundary penetrability by international legal messages and reduce noise?

What may pass from the legal communications system into other systems will in volume be less than what is transmitted within the system. Moreover, it may be distorted in a manner similar to the press distortion of a judicial decision or a government statement, as much through incompetence as design.[31]

[31] On incompetent reporting and other barriers to accurate message transmission, see W. Phillips Davison, *International Political Communication* (New York: Praeger for the Council on Foreign Relations, 1965), pp. 14-22. For some examples of distortion by a newspaper supporting an Administration's foreign policy see Wesley L. Gould, with the assistance of William Klecka and Charles Weyant, "The *New York Times* and the Development of Assurance Between Adversary Nations:

Diminution in frequency, together with distortion in the zone of diminution, provides evidence both of the existence of system boundaries and of the character of intersystem relations. Diminution and distortion result even though the formulator of a message (e.g., the International Court of Justice) may intend that the message be transmitted not just within the international legal system but also into the political, economic, or social system for impact there.

All types of messages can be affected by two problems, namely, channel capacity and information load. Formulae such as Claude E. Shannon's mathematical expression for the maximum capacity of a channel to communicate information[32] may be too closely tied to telecommunications to be of practical value for legal systems so subject to human variables. Even so, the concept of maximum capacity suggests a standard for the assessment of efficiency. Presumably, an effective communication system will display a systematic relationship between the information entering and leaving it.[33]

Clearly, simple information overload should increase selectivity and reduce the number of categories employed to classify

---

Six Case Studies, 1961-63," Studies of the Social and Psychological Aspects of Verification, Inspection and International Assurance, Technical Report No. 2, United States Arms Control and Disarmament Agency (W. Lafayette, Indiana: Purdue Research Foundation, December, 1968), passim. For a more generalized view of directions of bias, see Donald A. Strickland, "Content Analysis," Studies of the Social and Psychological Aspects of Verification, Inspection and International Assurance, Technical Report No. 3, United States Arms Control and Disarmament Agency (W. Lafayette, Indiana: Purdue University, Herman C. Krannert Graduate School of Industrial Administration, September, 1968), pp. 23-29.

[32] For a concise report on Shannon's work see Warren Weaver, "The Mathematics of Communication," *Scientific American* 181 (July, 1949): 11-15.

[33] George A. Miller, "The Magical Number Seven, Plus or Minus Two: Some Limits on Our Capacity for Processing Information," *Psychological Review* 63 (1956): 81-82.

information.[34] This is all the more true of perceptions of threat, with short decision time, that appear to reduce the dimensionality of thinking and receptivity to information.[35] It may well be asked what effect the hundreds of thousands of Nuremberg Trial documents had on the decision process. Do international judges and arbitrators perceive a threat from the political world that affects their technique in such a way as to inhibit innovative judgments, awards, and advisory opinions? Does increased selectivity under threat tend to filter out legal information from among the constraints on foreign policy decision-makers and reduce its significance to the status of a rationalizing instrument? Or is the constraining effect already minimal because the quantity of information contained in treaty collections and expositions of customary international law is too great to handle?[36] The human being is clearly not the most rapid information processing system, and there is evidence that the maximum channel capacity of living sys-

[34] James G. Miller, "Information Input, Overload, and Psycho-pathology," *American Journal of Psychiatry* 116 (1960): 695-704. Simplified classification, processing by hierarchic structures, and filtering out information under stress apparently occurs sooner in structures mediating the intake of information than in decision-making structures. Harold M. Schroder, Michael J. Driver, and Siegfried Streufert, *Human Information Processing: Individuals and Groups Functioning in Complex Social Situations* (New York: Holt, Rinehart and Winston, 1967), pp. 97-101. For the case of an overload of legal messages about the treatment of enemy subjects in Brazil during World War II with consequences that included the taking of anti-enemy measures against Jewish refugees and some Brazilian citizens but not against Austrians, see Antonio Chavez, *Os suditos inimigos* (São Paulo: Gráfico Editoro "Lex," 1945).

[35] Dean G. Pruitt, *Threat Perception, Trust and Responsiveness to International Behavior*, Technical Report No. 11, Office of Naval Research, Washington, D.C. (Newark, Delaware, January 9, 1964); Schroder, Driver, and Streufert, *Human Information Processing*, pp. 75-88, 154-57.

[36] See Richard W. Edwards, Jr., "Electronic Data-Processing and International Law Documentation," (A Summary Report of a Meeting held at The American Society of International Law, Washington, February 25-26, 1966), pp. 4-5.

tems drops with increased complexity.[37] Adding the problem of the quantity of legal data now stored in books, a real problem exists to bring to the fore and to translate into sufficiently nontechnical terms to assure understanding the many legal considerations that may potentially bear upon a foreign policy decision.

Concerning the reception of information, Karl W. Deutsch suggests that the effectiveness of reception depends on two classes of conditions. First, some parts of the receiving system must be in a state of highly unstable equilibrium in order that a small amount of energy carrying a signal will set off a larger process of change. Second, the selectivity of receivers is related to both the richness and the specificity of the information that has already been stored in them.[38] Deutsch suggests that the first of these technical relationships may have parallels in politics. It would appear that seeking instabilities conducive to change would generally require examination of legal communication systems, among others. Measurement of the intake from the legal into other communication systems should provide some clues of the relative effectiveness of a society's legal system in the performance of its legitimating function and as an instrument for changing domestic or international societies. However, one should be cautious about attributing stability or instability to a society in which competing messages are preferred to legal messages; for messages can flow into as well as from the legal system and, judged on the degree of its receptivity, it may prove to be the sole overly stable or unstable element.

As for selectivity of receivers if reception is more restricted

[37] For an examination of five information processing systems ranging from neurons in the frog sciatic nerve to a small social institution, see James G. Miller, "The Individual as an Information Processing System," in William S. Fields and Walter Abbott (eds.), *Information Storage and Neural Control* (Springfield, Illinois: Charles C. Thomas, 1963), pp. 301-28.

[38] Karl W. Deutsch, *The Nerves of Government*, pp. 147-48.

when rich and specific information is already stored in memories, it may be that herein lies an explanation for the relatively slow change of private law noted by Maxwell Cohen.[39] Although it would entail a rather boring task of counting, it should not be overly difficult to obtain a quantitative confirmation or rejection of the hypothesis that the rate of change in the major categories of law is related, among other things, to the number of rules already established. Confirmation would have to be explained in terms of broader societal processes including learning processes.

Selectivity of the receiver is a factor which, apparently, has to be taken into account by the communicator. It may be that the apparent slowness with which the progressive development and codification of international law takes place is a consequence of trying to communicate simultaneously with a variety of receivers whose receptivity differs according to cultural biases, linguistic structures, and thought patterns. For example, Friedheim noted that at the Geneva Conferences on the Law of the Sea the Western use of legalisms impeded communication with non-Western delegations.[40] Wedge found that Brazilian students could not be persuaded by evidence but could be persuaded if one either argued on the basis of a general theory or employed emotional association.[41] Chu raises questions about the modification of both Western and Marxist ideas when rendered in Chinese in light of the relationship between language structure and thought processes.[42]

[39] Maxwell Cohen, "'Basic Principles' of International Law—A Revaluation," *Canadian Bar Review* 42 (1964): 449-62.

[40] Robert L. Friedheim, "The 'Satisfied' and 'Dissatisfied' States Negotiate International Law: A Case Study," *World Politics* 18 (1965): 30, 31, 33-34.

[41] Bryant Wedge, "Communication Analysis and Comprehensive Diplomacy," in Arthur S. Hoffman, *International Communication and the New Diplomacy* (Bloomington: Indiana University Press, 1968), pp. 31-34.

[42] Yu-kiang Chu, "Interplay Between Language and Thought in Chinese," *ETC.: A Review of General Semantics* 22 (1965): 307-29.

The above references to the variety of variables and the quantity of information that is available as inputs into the legal communications system suggest a high probability that legal systems function inefficiently. Inefficiency can be quite serious if we assume that communications have such systemic purposes as avoidance or reduction of surprise and its consequences and reduction of the number of variables to be manipulated in decisional situations. If this high probability of inefficient functioning is the reality, we must distinguish between systemic purposes such as those mentioned and instrumental purposes whereby units or actors in the system may, as in a contest at law, deliberately insert the element of surprise or produce an information overload. Careful distinction would permit the measurement of "noise" produced in the system to be seen as a symptom of inadequacies in the communication system itself and not as disturbance traceable to the actors pursuing, as they might be expected to do in any system, their own particular ends.

Integrative Function

ANOTHER systemic function that may be attributed to international law is integration. This function is closely related to the communication function, for, aside from the order-information relationship, it is not possible to conceive of the coordination of physically separated parts without the transmission of messages. Indeed, even physically connected organisms cannot function in an integrated manner without message transmission. Thus, from a process standpoint the integration function may be regarded as subordinate to or dependent on the communication function, while from a teleological standpoint integration may be regarded as a purpose served by the communication process.

Study of integration, of the coming or bringing together of previously separated parts, is a study of progression over time with due attention to inferred causal relationships. Some of these relationships may be traceable to law and, indeed, much attention is currently given to the law's impact on Western European integration. With the attention given to societal development and the integration process in other sections, it may suffice at this point to suggest that law can promote integration insofar as it serves to express and to disseminate common values and to provide a basis for the conduct of conflict, since conflict has an integrative potential. Lawyers, motivated by the reference to "general principles of law" in Article 38 of the Statute of the International Court of Justice, have tended to accord attention to the development of common values, while political scientists and sociologists, as well as apologists for war, have attempted to identify the integrative effects of conflict.[43]

One further comment is suggested by a recent study by William M. Evan and Mildred A. Schwartz on law and the emergence of formal organization. The authors conceive law to be an intervening variable in the process of social change rather than a mere consequence of other institutional structures. In their view, the values embedded in law, the efficiency of enforcement provisions, and the social units affected stimulate responses in the form of private formal organizations, some functional and some dysfunctional in terms of promoting societal objectives.[44]

[43] E.g., Robert C. North, Howard E. Koch, and Dina A. Zinnes, "The Integrative Functions of Conflict," *Journal of Conflict Resolution* 4 (1960): 355-74; Herbert Spencer, *Principles of Sociology*, 3 vols. (New York: Appleton, 1891-97) 2: 241-64; Georg Simmel, *"Conflict,"* trans. Kurt H. Wolff in *Conflict and The Web of Group-Affiliations* (New York: Free Press, 1955; paperback edn., 1964), esp. pp. 17-20; Lewis A. Coser, *The Functions of Social Conflict* (New York: Free Press, 1956; paperback edn., 1964), esp. chaps. I, V, VII, VIII; Robert F. Murphy, "Intergroup Hostility and Social Cohesion," *American Anthropologist* 59 (1957): 1018-35.

[44] William M. Evan and Mildred A. Schwartz, "Law and the Emergence of Formal Organization," *Sociology and Social Research* 48 (1964): 270-80.

Without confounding organizational goals with system purposes, further investigation might well show that under various conditions and over time responses to certain types of laws produce tendencies toward integration and even more centralized organization. Perhaps the conditions conducive to the acceleration of integration may be distinguishable from those producing dormant periods. To borrow from an anthropologist's suggestion, made after studying African rituals expressive of social conflict, that it may be more desirable to judge a society's level of organization than its degree of stability,[45] it may be that more attention should be given to the *types* of organizations that have resulted from the growth of international law. Such a study of the law-organization relationship should provide more fruitful insights into the function of law in the international community than the more common tendency, at least in the Anglo-Saxon tradition, to work within the constraints of Austinian positivism. Moreover, it should help to render unnecessary the treatment of international law by means of analogy, express or implied, with modern national law.

The Adaptation of Man to his Environment

A SELDOM mentioned function of law, perhaps taken for granted, is the adaptation of man to his natural and social environments. Socialization, mentioned early in this chapter, is conceived as that part of adaptation which relates to the social environment. It occurs only through its component processes of teaching and learning. Messages embodied in legal norms and those conveyed when legal procedures are conducted and observed or studied are one means whereby teachers can communicate with learners. This is true not only for socialization but also for adaptation to the natural environment. Not only does the natural environment impose the engineering prob-

[45] E. Norbeck, "African Rituals of Conflict," *American Anthropologist* 65 (1963): 1254-79.

lems of utilization and noncontamination; human inventiveness and venture open new segments of the natural environment to exploitation and thereby produce new sets of human interactions and new coordination requirements.

Lynton K. Caldwell has called attention to the need for a systematic formulation of a comprehensive environmental policy. A comprehensive policy might guide legislative, administrative, and judicial decision-makers and avoid the waste and confusion of fragmented action. Industrial man has assumed that he can exploit nature with impunity, while nations have acted on gross assumptions about the extent of harm and deprivation that may lawfully be inflicted on other nations.[46] Nations have harmed and deprived others not just by wars and raids but by self-centered exploitation of the resources of the land and the sea and now by pollution of the atmosphere.

It might well be argued that until the present century international law had aided rather well the adaptation of men to the age of wind and soil, to the coming of steam, to the era of dynastic quarrels and alliances, to the earlier manifestations of the nation-state's power, and to the essentially aristocratic politics that preceded the breakdown of 1914. Doubts may be entertained concerning more recent times with mounting population pressures and great disparities between high energy and low energy societies. It might be asserted that the adaptation function of international law is impaired perhaps because of a more rapid rate of invention, perhaps because the norms of aristocrats are not suited to politics featuring mass appeal techniques, or perhaps because the makers of international law suffer from perceptual and information-processing inadequacies.

[46] Lynton K. Caldwell, "Environment: A New Focus for Public Policy?," *Public Administration Review* 23 (1963): 132-39; and "Biopolitics: Science, Ethics, and Public Policy," *Yale Review* 54 (1964): 1-16.

However that may be and however complicated by ongoing technological change,[47] the function of assisting man's adaptation to his social and natural environments remains. Wolfgang Friedmann's well-known exposition of the expanded scope of 20th-century international law provides evidence of the function of assisting, well or ill, more men and organizations to fit into more spheres of international activity than at any preceding time.[48] In fact, even though the adaptation function may be taken for granted, emphasis on rules and procedures in the traditional international law course is emphasis on how to get along in the perceived social and natural environments.

For the individual or group actor an instrumental purpose is present. What is derivable from the system and can be classified as a system purpose is adaptation to the "objective" environment in which the perceptions of actors are among the realities.[49] Here arises a basic problem that no system, regardless of its own dynamics, can avoid. The adaptation function cannot be performed if only the components of a system adapt to environmental changes. Performance of the function also requires adaptation at a higher level, that is, adaptation of the system itself, in this case, of the international system and its law.

[47] For a series of papers on the problems confronting diplomacy as a result of scientific advances, particularly in chemistry, medicine, agriculture, energy, geophysics, and outer space, see Karl Braunias and Peter Meraviglia (eds.), *Die modernen Wissenschaften und die Aufgaben der Diplomatie* (Graz: Styria Verlag, 1963). See also Samuel D. Estep, "International Lawmakers in a Technological World: Space Communications and Nuclear Energy," *George Washington Law Review* 33 (1964): 162-80.

[48] Wolfgang Friedmann, *The Changing Structure of International Law* (New York: Columbia University Press, 1964), esp. pp. 11, 13-15, 17.

[49] Cf. Harold and Margaret Sprout, *The Ecological Perspective on Human Affairs with Special Reference to International Politics* (Princeton: Princeton University Press, 1965), pp. 28-29, 132-41.

Adaptation, i.e., change, of the system is accomplished through the actions of the perceivers; among these, state leaders are the most important. Some perceivers have sought to change the environment itself—to fit it to themselves and their visions—rather than to adapt themselves. They tend to reject the legal system rather than to fit it more closely to the existing environment. The violent proportions of some attempts to change the perceived environment and the existing system of rules facilitating adaptation hardly needs comment. But adaptation, although not necessarily free of violence, is a more modest undertaking that accepts both the environment as it is at any moment and its inevitable changes. Regardless of the degree of violence employed by perceiving actors, the adaptation function itself is stimulated by perceived environmental changes, requires change in the legal system, and entails the evolution of old norms and the genesis of new norms.

Crimes and International Criminal Law

THE DEFINITIONAL problems that have plagued the development of an international criminal law are not without their domestic counterparts. However, the aura of certainty that has long clothed municipal law has tended to cast these problems into the background. Only as municipal law has achieved a rapprochement with the social sciences, have the definitional problems assumed their true proportions. A definition of "crime" and "criminal" is neither simple nor, once made, immutable. A pioneering criminal law casebook[50] directs its attention precisely to these questions and rescues them from the oblivion of foregone conclusions. In fact, as its editors make clear, the category of "crime" is intimately tied to notions of legal function. It is not an automatic process, but rather emerges out of a coherent view of the purposes of law. What ends is law supposed to achieve and how can a crimi-

[50] Richard C. Donnelly, Joseph Goldstein, and Richard D. Schwartz, *Criminal Law* (New York: Free Press of Glencoe, 1962).

nal law serve as a means to those ends? Further, as municipal law has escaped the positivist penchant for law-as-legislation, attention has been directed to the enforcement process. The ambiguity of many legislative enactments has turned effective lawmaking power over to the courts and police, whose exercise of discretion may ultimately determine which acts are criminal and which are not.[51]

In a self-help system such as international law, enforcement has always been a peculiarly fluid and discretionary process.[52] In municipal law, the police and courts have either arrogated control of the process to themselves or have stepped in when legislatures have defaulted. International law, on the other hand, has put the same kind of power in the hands of the enforcers but it has been placed there as a matter of right and necessity. Students of American law are only now discovering what international lawyers have long known, namely, that there is a crucial nexus between legislation and enforcement. American jurisprudents have discovered to their dismay that legislative policy may be amended or *de facto* repealed by differential enforcement or no enforcement at all, and that in fact the "living law" may contain norms never reduced to writing. Within the framework of the American constitutional system, this new reality is a deviation from the norm. International law has long accepted the fact that what states do to enforce rules alters the nature of the rules themselves.

This perhaps brings some focus to the question of international crimes, for the crucial definition of criminal behavior is more apt to manifest itself in action than in writing. The growth of an international criminal law is a response to specific

[51] Frank J. Remington and Victor G. Rosenblum, "The Criminal Law and the Legislative Process," *University of Illinois Law Forum* 7 (1960): 481-99. See also Austin T. Turk, "Conflict and Criminality," *American Sociological Review* 31 (1966): 338-52.

[52] Cf. Thomas D. Eliot, "A Criminological Approach to the Social Control of International Relations," *American Journal of Sociology* 58 (1953): 513-18.

events, not a set of deductions from self-evident principles. Despite the fact that genocide has received explicit legal definition only in our own time, the seeds for its legal recognition lay in such far-off events as the Czarist pogroms and the nearly-successful attempt by the Turks to destroy the Armenian people.

As the Eichmann case was to do later, the London Agreement and the subsequent Nuremberg Trials stirred up considerable thoughtful opposition. The opposition is itself an indication of the indissoluble relationship between legislation and enforcement. These trials were themselves part of the norm-generating process. Francis Biddle, one of the American judges at the war crimes trials, caught this with remarkable perception when he remarked that he then knew what English judges must have felt during the formative years of the Common Law.[53] International and Common Law share this characteristic, that both grow incrementally from the very invocation of the legal process. While it is commonly accepted that the American legal system will not tolerate *ex post facto* legislation, this is an oversimplification. In the absence of a prolix legal code, and given the legislative leeway American judges have exercised as a matter of right, the law is indeed changed in the very act of applying it, just as it is either changed or reinforced in the act of making an arrest.

International law is in a sense the extreme version of Common Law methodology. Nowhere is this more evident than in the international law of crimes. It, too, is advanced in case-by-case fashion, yet the "cases" here are less likely to be the output of courts and more likely to be historical events perceived as being the raw material of international legislation. It is no coincidence that the same acts normally placed under the rubric of "international crimes" are in recent years also being categorized as elements of the *ius cogens*. The latter may

[53] Francis Biddle, *In Brief Authority* (Garden City: Doubleday, 1962), pp. 369-487.

be seen as an anachronistic offshoot of natural law. Like the British concept of "natural justice," *ius cogens* does partake of this ancient tradition. Yet the overlap between *ius cogens* and the evolving law of international crimes[54] tells us something about how criminal acts are defined as well. Since the *ius cogens* comprehends those norms which no treaty can revoke and still remain valid—unless the treaty itself were an acceptance and recognition "by the international community of states as a whole"[55] as a modification of the *ius cogens*—its norms differ qualitatively from the run of international customary and treaty law.

In the first place, breaches of the *jus cogens* violate or fall outside what we may call the rules-of-the-game. International law allows a state great but not complete latitude to do many things that we might regard as morally wrong. Within the limits set by international law, states may pretty much do as they please and have a more than even chance of justifying their actions. International criminal acts are so considered not because they are morally wrong (we might think many permissible acts were as well) but because they transcend even those broad powers that a state may legitimately exercise. A state may thus do much to its citizens that outsiders would regard as unfair and do it with impunity, but to reduce large numbers of them to the status of disposable chattels is to risk forfeiting one's position as a state.

Second, a state may legitimately involve itself in a good deal of conflict with other states, even violent conflict. But there is a tacit assumption that all such conflicts are what Thomas C. Schelling calls "mixed motive games."[56] They are competi-

[54] Alfred Verdross, "*Jus Dispositivum* and *Jus Cogens* in International Law," *American Journal of International Law* 60 (1966): 55-63; Egon Schwelb, "Some Aspects of International *Jus Cogens* as Formulated by the International Law Commission," *ibid.* 61 (1967): 946-75.

[55] Article 50, Draft Conventions on the Law of Treaties, *International Legal Materials* 7 (1968): 770, 793-94.

[56] Thomas C. Schelling, *The Strategy of Conflict* (New York: Galaxy, 1963), p. 89.

tions in which the competitors still share some common interests, however tenuous. Even an interest so vague as a desire not to utterly destroy each other's populations would be sufficient. The laws of war are an explicit recognition of common interests between belligerents. To reject the possibility of common interests is to risk placing oneself literally "out-law." The tentative gropings[57] toward a legal prohibition of aggression are the result.

Third, international criminal law was earliest associated with the acts of individual international entrepreneurs, namely, pirates and slavetraders. In retrospect it is easy to see how they could provide a starting point for the new legal category of "international crimes," since states could almost never be adversely affected either materially or symbolically by their prosecution. Furthermore, not only did no state stand to lose, but most stood to gain. It demonstrates once again that economic relationships stand at the advancing edge of international law. It shows, too, the pivotal role of the individual in international law, even in periods when he may formally stand outside it. Notwithstanding the extralegal character of the individual, it was the acts of individuals that stimulated an international criminal law.

A most interesting development is the tendency for international law, having begun with individual anti-social acts, to come full circle back to the individual. For what we see now in tentative and still unestablished activities of the United Nations[58] is a transition from emphasis on the deviant activities of the minority to emphasis on the "human rights" of the majority. In part the international concept of human rights is the reverse side of the law of crimes. Once it was accepted that

[57] Julius Stone, *Aggression and World Order* (Berkeley: University of California Press, 1958).

[58] Myres S. McDougal and Gerhard Bebr, "Human Rights in the United Nations," *American Journal of International Law* 58 (1964): 603-41.

individual acts could adversely affect the interests of states it was simply a matter of time before it was recognized that individuals per se were significant international actors who themselves were also the major victims of international crimes. Hence, current efforts to solidify negative reactions toward specific historical events into general rights serve to structure the future rather than just to react to what has already been done.

Obligation, Obedience, and Effectiveness

To TACKLE the problem of legal obligation and its correlative problems of obedience and effectiveness is to enter into a realm of intellectual activity that has produced much futile speculation. In the past there have been efforts to relate obligation to God, Nature, human nature, consent, and other less well-known foundations including the functioning of several internal organs that were seen as contributing to the "organic secretion of thought" by the brain.[59] In legal literature speculation concerning the nature of obligation tended to subside after the late 19th-century German attempts to explain the status of German states under Bismarck's Constitution produced little more than futile argument and disagreement. More generally, positivists became entangled in the intricacies of consent theories. J. L. Brierly later attempted to escape those intricacies by arguing that states are bound because they think they are bound. But this argument only begs, perhaps unwittingly, for psychological and sociological explanations by removing the search for the basis of consent from the body of law.

At present it is possible to attack the problem of obligation from several directions and, in the process, to treat obligation as the link between the law and obedience. One could get a simple measure of obedience by a tabulation of the number of known violations, something which has been done only

[59] Pierre Jean Georges Cabanis, *Rapports du physique et du moral de l'homme*, 2 vols. (Paris, 1802), 1: 147-49, 161.

in special cases such as the Roosevelt-Litvinov Agreements and ILO treaties.[60] The tabulation needs extension to account for various types of states, agreements, and forms and circumstances of violation. Given a reasonably accurate record of obedience, clues to the nature of obligation, which need not be the same for all types of treaties and states, might emerge. Custom may be too elusive for such treatment, although some progress might be made by taking court records and diplomatic protests as indicators of the incidence of violation.

Given data of the type suggested, it might be possible to construct a scale starting with total disobedience and ranging through various degrees of partial obedience. In doing so it is necessary to bear in mind that most laws allow an appreciable degree of disobedience, a phenomenon relatively little studied except with regard to penal law.[61] It is tempting to treat an obedience-disobedience scale as a measure of effectiveness. However, before doing so one must ask the question of whose level of obedience is being measured. The potential thief, debtor, aggressor, or treaty violator is not the only actor whose obedience is required for effective law. So, too, is the obedience of the other actors, including those who would normally be concerned with the law only as subjects (e.g., witnesses, jurors, the suppliers of peacekeeping forces).[62] Since the latter would

[60] Donald G. Bishop, *The Roosevelt-Litvinov Agreements: The American View* (Syracuse: Syracuse University Press, 1965); E. A. Landry, *The Effectiveness of International Supervision* (London: Stevens, 1966).

[61] J. Carbonnier, "Effectivité et ineffectivité de la règle de droit," *L'Année sociologique*, 3rd series (1957-58), pp. 3-17.

[62] Hans Kelsen, *General Theory of Law and State*, trans. Anders Wedberg (Cambridge: Harvard University Press, 1945), pp. 53, 60-62; and *Law and Peace in International Relations* (Cambridge: Harvard University Press, 1942), pp. 23-26. On the liability of English jurors to reprimand, fine, or imprisonment, at various times prior to *Bushell's Case* (1670), see W. O. Ault, *Private Jurisdiction in England* (New Haven: Yale University Press, 1923), pp. 127, 174; F. W. Maitland,

include, particularly in decentralized systems, the retaliators,[63] they must be taken into account when constructing a scale of effectiveness. For international law one could compile not just a record of states' obedience but also an additional record of responses to violations and outcomes produced by the responses. This would provide opportunity to differentiate ineffectiveness resulting from rejection of international legal norms by the subjects of international law from ineffectiveness traceable to the nonresponse of injured parties and third states. It would also provide indications of commitment which may be treated as expressive of an underlying feeling of obligation.

An approach to the nature of commitment has been suggested by Howard S. Becker. Essentially conceptual and definitional and relying in good measure on Schelling's notion of commitment in bargaining and on Goffman's discussion of commitment to a front or "face" in interaction, Becker's concept is that commitment comes into being when a "side bet," possibly resulting from participation in social organizations, links extraneous interests with a consistent line of activity. Understanding a commitment requires an analysis of the value of the system in which side bets are made.[64] Becker's concept may have the effect of avoiding the tautology present in most definitions of commitment, but its utility can be ascertained only if it can be shown to establish the desired linkage between activities and extraneous interests.

Experiment with internationalist and highly isolationist

Select Pleas in Manorial and Other Seignorial Courts (London: B. Quaritch, 1889), pp. 90, 97; Maitland and F. G. Montague, *A Sketch of English Legal History*, edited by J. F. Colby (New York: G. P. Putnam's Sons, 1915), pp. 133-34.

[63] In a broad meaning, "retaliators" would include the initiators of civil suits, as is asserted in a well-known passage in Rudolf von Ihering, *The Struggle for Law*, trans. from the 5th German edn. (1877) by John J. Lalor, 2nd edn. (Chicago: Callaghan, 1915), pp. 1-4.

[64] Howard S. Becker, "Notes on the Concept of Commitment," *American Journal of Sociology* 66 (1960): 32-40.

subjects has shown the former to be more cooperative while the latter exercised more real choices. It may be that a syndrome, similar to that for authoritarianism, is associated with internationalism.[65] Such experiments may provide one clue to a psychological foundation of international law. It is not a clue to a characteristic of particular leaders subject to manipulation from abroad; but, if combined with a technique similar to that by which simulators have sought to identify personality characteristics of the chief statesmen of 1914,[66] it might assist anticipation of what statesmen are likely to do under various circumstances.

Still another approach is suggested by Morton Kaplan's behavioral rules for the balance-of-power and loose bipolar systems.[67] Earlier, we suggested the possibility of investigating whether international legal norms change, as Kaplan suggests the behavioral rules change, when one system is replaced by another. Kaplan's suggested rules are requirements imposed by a system upon acting units under the assumed objective of maintaining the system. We now suggest, as we did not earlier, that Kaplan's rules can be regarded as rubrics potentially permitting classification of more detailed international norms.

In our present uncertainty as to whether Kaplan's categories are the only ones representing operative system rules and our uncertainty concerning the accuracy of their fit to empirical evidence, we suggest still another approach. The rules of international law for the balance-of-power and loose bipolar periods could be grouped in categories of increasing generality to see whether a few axiomatic rules, generally not represented by traditional international law rubrics, emerge. The same thing

[65] Daniel R. Lutzker, "Internationalism as a Predictor of Cooperative Behavior," *Journal of Conflict Resolution* 4 (1960): 426-30.

[66] Charles F. and Margaret G. Hermann, "Validation Studies of the Inter-Nation Simulation," Studies of Deterrence, no. 10, U.S. Naval Ordnance Test Station, China Lake, California (December, 1963).

[67] Kaplan, *System and Process in International Politics*, pp. 23, 38-39.

might be done for identifiable behavior patterns without regard for their embodiment in the corpus of international customary law but taking care to distinguish behavior reflecting an actor's "strategic rules" for manipulating the international system for his own benefit from behavior reflecting systemic rules that identify legitimate goals and actions and their limits. Besides serving as a test of Kaplan's categories and permitting their revision to achieve greater correspondence with identifiable reality, the two sets of categories for each of the systems could be compared. What might emerge would be a clue to the nature of the international legal obligation that relates it to the degree of correspondence of the two patterns. Incautiously handled, this procedure might do no more than confuse systemic rules and "strategic rules" and thereby buttress the pragmatic position that law is what is done. Rather than waste the effort, what would be sought, without immediate regard for violations and deviance, would be the conformity of the legal categories of each system with the behavioral patterns identified. A presently unknown degree of discrepancy is probably tolerable. But if none or very few of the legal categories matched the behavioral categories, or if the legal categories of the loose bipolar period matched the behavioral categories of the balance-of-power period, it would be possible to make meaningful statements about effectiveness, expected obedience, and therefore about the obligation of international law at the times chosen for study. These statements would leave room for some conduct not in harmony with particular rules while at the same time relating obligation, important for the effectiveness of specific rules, to the legal system's degree of correspondence to the basic aspects of the totality of international behavior.

To make brief reference to an approach to be dealt with more fully later, the concepts of reciprocity and responsiveness may also be brought into play in the effort to probe the nature of international obligation. It is possible to make an Austinian approach to reciprocity by treating it as a link between command and obedience and as such bearing a relationship to power.[68] Such an approach may have a bearing upon obedience in certain situations but, as Rousseau has pointed out, it places the emphasis on prudence rather than upon any moral "ought." For a law that combines the consensual and the customary and resorts to command only on rare occasions, a command-obedience reciprocity is an inadequate explanation of international obligation. It explains very few happenings, most of them transient *de facto* superiority-inferiority relationships existing at times of breakdown in the more common unit-to-unit reciprocity. Unit-to-unit reciprocity presents the more fertile approach to the problem of obligation because it relates obligation to system processes.

Reciprocity, Sanctions, and Rewards

THE CAUSES of legal efficacy are no more certain today than when Aristotle wrote. It is the great unsolved problem of jurisprudence. That this should be so is odd, for it is an area where theoretical and practical concerns overlap. The legislator and judge run the risk of deploying their resources in vain if they have no clear idea whether their efforts are bringing about the desired results. Although even under the best of circumstances international law is incomparably more difficult to reform, there is still every reason to determine the limits of possibility. Yet, as Arthur Larson has remarked:

> Much of the discussion of the potentialities of world rule of law is carried on under the unproved assumption that the only motivation for obedience of law is fear of the exercise of force. . . . Certainly this is an issue which need not be left to speculation and rhetoric and which is amenable to the techniques of research. . . . It is quite likely that at least a

[68] E.g., J. Gaudemet, "Esquisse d'une sociologie historique du pouvoir," *Politique* 19-20 (1962): 195-234.

> half-dozen factors would be identified as motivating compliance with law, in addition to mere threat of punishment.[69]

On reflection it is extraordinary that great systems of ideas and weighty social institutions should be reared upon so uncertain a foundation. The only substantial body of data concerns the deterrent value of capital punishment and it tends to contradict the commonly accepted belief that the more severe the punishment, the less likely the crime.

The very concept of "sanction" is itself confused. Despite the fact that it is usually equated with "punishment" or "deprivation" there is no necessary reason for so limiting the concept. The ambivalence of "sanction" may be traced by briefly examining its etymology and usages. Its Latin root, *sancire*, means "to render sacred or inviolable, ordain, decree, ratify." In a less theologically burdened vocabulary, it meant simply to "legitimate" and thus was only indirectly tied to enforcement processes. By extension it came to mean in the 16th century a law or decree, particularly one of an ecclesiastical nature. In the course of the 17th century, the connotation of a penalty was engrafted to it, and at the end of the century it came also to include the "provision of rewards for obedience."[70]

What are we to make of this tangled history? In the first place, it suggests that we may trace the problem of obedience in terms of the gradually loosening ties of supernatural authority and the supersession to social control functions by temporal forces. Second, it suggests that obedience may be prompted by considerations other than fear of punishment; indeed, although there is more than a suggestion of divine punishment, there is also the connotation of harmonization with divine norms. Third, we learn from an examination of

[69] Arthur Larson, *The International Rule of Law* (New York: The Institute for International Order, 1961), pp. 66-67. See also Richard D. Schwartz and Sonya Orleans, "On Legal Sanctions," *University of Chicago Law Review* 34 (1967): 274-300.

[70] *The Oxford English Dictionary* (Oxford: Clarendon Press, 1933), pp. ix, 82.

early usage that our own equation of sanction with punishment, ignoring the concept of differential rewards as sanctions, is in fact something of a throwback.

The point of this excursion into English usage is that a multifaceted concept of sanctions conforms much more closely to what we know of human behavior than does the simple juxtaposition of sanction and punishment. Learning theory has accepted both rewards and punishments as efficacious in influencing behavior.[71] "Positive reinforcement" and "negative reinforcement" both control an individual's responses, the former tending to increase the probability that the response will recur, the latter decreasing the probability of recurrence.[72] Even though our thinking tends to be solely in terms of punishment, much modern municipal legislation is predicated upon the use of rewards. The tangle of "reward," "punishment," and law receives perhaps its penultimate expression in Mr. Justice Cardozo's opinion in *Steward Machine Co. v. Davis* (1937):

> The difficulty with the petitioner's contention is that it confuses motive with coercion. "Every tax is in some measure regulatory. . . ." In like manner every rebate from a tax when conditioned upon conduct is in some measure a temptation. But to hold that motive or temptation is equivalent to coercion is to plunge the law in endless difficulties.[73]

Regardless of the policy objectives the Court was attempting to achieve, its essay into reward and punishment flies in the

[71] For an application of learning theory, together with the theory of cognitive dissonance, to the theory of political legitimacy, with reference to positive and negative sanctions as reinforcements, see Richard M. Merelman, "Learning and Legitimacy," *American Political Science Review* 60 (1966): 548-61.

[72] Bernard Berelson and Gary A. Steiner, *Human Behavior: An Inventory of Scientific Findings* (New York: Harcourt, Brace & World, 1964), p. 141.

[73] 301 U.S. 548 at 589-90.

face of what we know about what makes people behave in particular ways.

What is clear is that fear of punishment vies with desire for reward in determining conduct, that at this point we have no way of knowing which is the more important, and that there is no reason to believe that these two conditions are the only ones of any importance. For example, the thoroughly random introduction of rewards may create highly tenacious behavior patterns. This is the kind of "learning" involved in behavior that we would commonly call "superstitious":

> The more frequent the rain dance, the greater the chance that it *will* be reinforced some of the time . . . the less frequently reinforcement occurs, the greater the tolerance for failure. According to this analysis, such superstitions persist largely *because* they work infrequently and sporadically, not in spite of the fact.[74]

Sheer habit is capable of producing consistent behavior long after either rewards or punishments have been dispensed with.[75] Thus there is an inertial component in human behavior capable of imparting consistency to it irrespective of the probability of gain or loss.

What are we to make of this evidence from the standpoint of law in general and international law in particular? If we think of obedience to legal rules as correct responses, then several considerations may enter in: reward, punishment, the frequency with which either is administered, and sheer habit. Indeed, even reward and punishment can be seen as less than wholly separate categories, for to reward the majority is relatively to deprive the minority. The operation of these factors may be spelled out in the rule itself, as is the case with formal

[74] Berelson and Steiner, *Human Behavior*, pp. 156-57.

[75] *Ibid.*, p. 136. In front of the house where one of us lived, the stop signs for the north-south street at a four-way stop intersection were removed. Eight years later several drivers every day travelling north or south were stopping their cars.

legislation. It may also be largely dependent upon the discretion of administrators and police. Finally, the extent to which the subject has internalized the norm and made it his own may take the matter wholly outside the framework of coercive institutions. We might do well to examine the socialization process.

The multiplication of considerations that must be dealt with in determining when and how a rule is to be obeyed has a special significance for international law. As long as punishment in the narrow sense of physical coercion was the only way of looking at obedience, international law required means of wielding force in the absence of central institutions. That, in turn, has entailed all sorts of problems concerning the legal status of war and has introduced a profound degree of ambivalence into legal theory; for at one and the same time war has been proclaimed to be both the international crime par excellence and the closest analogue to municipal police action.

As our concept of sanctions grows in breadth and sophistication, we are in a position to see new forces buttressing legal rules. Richard A. Falk has aptly pointed to the distinction between coercion and reciprocity that divides vertical legal relationships from horizontal legal relationships.[76] Reciprocity in itself means that there is a network of penalties and rewards. If states are tied together economically, socially, militarily, and culturally, the severance of those bonds produces mutual losses. Schelling implies that interstate relationships themselves, rather than independent institutions, may hold the key to the rule of law, since these relationships contain built-in reward and deprivation structures.[77] If sanctions in fact inhere in interactions no less than in formal legal institutions, efforts to

[76] Richard A. Falk, "International Jurisdiction: Horizontal and Vertical Conceptions of Legal Order," *Temple Law Quarterly* 32 (1959): 295-320; and "The Reality of International Law," *World Politics* 14 (1962): 353-63.

[77] Schelling, *The Strategy of Conflict*, chap. 4.

build explicit international police forces at all costs may be misplaced and premature.

Of course, this broad conception of sanctions has its defects, principally its uncertain efficacy. It was commonplace on the eve of World War I to argue that the economic interdependence of Europe made war impossible.[78] A nation may be willing to gamble future losses against present gains. Or it may fail to calculate its advantages in a rational manner, deliberately forsaking what game theorists call a "minimax" strategy, one that cuts maximum possible losses to the bone. These failings notwithstanding, the interactions are a reality. Thus, for the time being it may be more prudent to tailor legal expectations to the existing capacities of the system rather than to pitch them at a level which cannot be met. International law in our century has been afflicted with periodic bouts of disillusionment,[79] generated by excessive expectations. Just as "legal institutions" has constituted a bogey diverting efforts from the norm-creating realities of behavior, so "sanctions," narrowly defined, has thrust into international legal thinking biases which obscure the very real constraints on state action.

What has been said is that human behavior, more specifically, compliance with norms, is not explicable solely in terms of avoidance of retaliation. This does not mean that retaliation is not a significant form of international interaction, for it does occur and, when occurring, need not take the form of war. Although less fascinating than war, retaliatory actions in several forms, including the use of force short of war,[80] warrant more systematic investigation, particularly to determine de-

[78] Barbara Tuchman, *The Guns of August* (New York: Dell, 1963), pp. 24-25.

[79] Julius Stone, *Quest for Survival* (Cambridge: Harvard University Press, 1961), p. 8.

[80] E.g., Walter Phillips Davison, *The Berlin Blockade: A Study in Cold War Politics* (Princeton: Princeton University Press, 1958). For a suggestion that a third party perform the retaliatory function, see Robert Gomer, "Some Thoughts on Arms Control," *Bulletin of Atomic Scientists* 17 (April, 1961): 133-37.

layed effects. Delayed effects can be political, economic, and legal, the last having both norm-building and rule degradation potential with no generalization or calculus of probability presently possible. The most that can be said with certainty is that one foundation stone of international law has been vengeance,[81] a foundation stone also of consequence to the stability of other societies.[82]

To reach a broadened view of sanctions, two approaches are possible. One is to subsume punishments and rewards under the rubric "sanctions" and to refer to positive and negative sanctions. Another and more complex approach is to distinguish the two and to employ the term "retribution," that is, like for like whether good or evil, to cover rewards and sanctions.[83] The former would be essentially an adaptation of the sociologists' usage; the latter would be more in harmony with traditional legal thought. The former might counteract a common tendency to narrow "retribution" to mean solely "vengeance" and to ignore the promise of reward contained in many laws; the latter would remove ambiguity from the term "sanction" by confining it to the negative side of the like-for-like spectrum.

[81] Jacques Lambert, *La vengeance privée et les fondements du droit international* (Paris: Sirey, 1936).

[82] William E. Lewis, "Feuding and Social Change in Morocco," *Journal of Conflict Resolution* 5 (1961): 43-54.

[83] Hans Kelsen, *Society and Nature: A Sociological Inquiry* (Chicago: University of Chicago Press, 1943), pp. 58-64; F. E. Williams, *Orokaiva Society* (London: Oxford, H. Milford, 1930), pp. 170, 317; W. Lloyd Warner, *A Black Civilization: A Study of an Australian Tribe*, rev. edn. (New York: Harper & Row, 1958; Torchbook edn., 1964), pp. 96-98, 134-35, 148-52, 450; R. F. Fortune, *Sorcerers of Dobu: The Social Anthropology of the Dobu Islanders of the Western Pacific* (New York: Dutton, 1932; paperback edn., 1963), pp. 200-10; Rafael Karsten, "Blood Revenge, War, and Victory Feasts Among the Jibaro Indians of Eastern Ecuador," *Bureau of American Ethnology Bulletin* 79 (1923): 11; M.E. Durham, *Some Tribal Origins, Laws, and Customs of the Balkans* (London: Allen & Unwin, 1928), pp. 162, 163, 170; Margaret Hasluck, *The Unwritten Law in Albania*, ed. J. H. Hutton (Cambridge, England: The University Press, 1954), pp. 219-60.

Since we cannot hope to eliminate the latter usage, a diagrammatic representation might help toward greater precision.

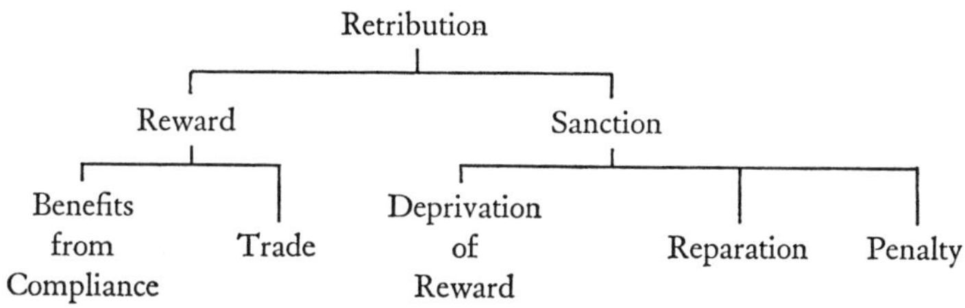

The inclusion of deprivation of reward among the sanctions means that, in terms of a scale, anything of zero return or less would be a sanction while anything on the plus side would be reward. The measurement would be relative, for docking a man's salary as a disciplinary measure would not necessarily mean a negative or zero salary. In this formulation, retribution is not restricted to law and, indeed, gives rise to the somewhat milder term, "reciprocity," which Malinowski and others saw as the central principle of life in primitive society.[84]

Furthermore, in terms of a communication model of law, stored legal messages announce consequences intended to follow certain precedent actions. The consequences could be positive sanctions or rewards. They could also be negative sanctions or, in the second formulation, simply sanctions. The law could then be regarded as including a threat of sanctions, even when promising rewards on the contingency that certain things be done or formalities complied with, which would have objectives such as the five identified by Arens and Lass-

[84] Bronislaw Malinowski, *Crime and Custom in Savage Society* (London: Routledge and Kegan Paul, 1926), chaps. IV, VIII, IX. See also A. W. Gouldner, "The Norm of Reciprocity: A Preliminary Statement," *American Sociological Review* 23 (1960): 161-78.

well, namely, deterrence, prevention, restoration, rehabilitation, and reconstruction.[85]

At the same time, assuming accurate transmission of the message, the problem of the credibility of the legal threat is raised. Transmission may not be free of static, including the noise resulting from ambiguity. But, if received, the message may yet not be credible. Pool suggests that threat is most likely to be effective when made quietly and long in advance and when it is always there as a sort of trip-mechanism.[86] If so, then nonenforcement would strain credibility. So, too, would the assumption that war may be indulged in response to a violation of a treaty, for example, even a violation in the form of a fifty-cent duty on aliens landing at American ports or some other rather trivial imposition.[87]

The noncredible threat could be expected to evoke not one of the four responses that Boulding enumerates, namely, submission, defiance, counterthreat, or an integrative response,[88] but a disregard that tends to undermine law. To the extent that disregard would constitute a precedent, the consequence could be that redundancy would operate to nullify a legal pre-

[85] Richard Arens and Harold D. Lasswell, *In Defense of Public Order: The Emerging Field of Sanction Law* (New York: Columbia University Press, 1961).

[86] Ithiel de Sola Pool, "Human Communication and Deterrence," Studies in Deterrence, No. 6, NOTS, China Lake, California (September, 1963), p. 45.

[87] For a classical example of such an absurdity in a basic case in the establishment of the United States claim of authority to abrogate treaties by means of subsequent legislation, see Justice Miller's opinion for the Supreme Court in the *Head Money Cases* (1884), 112 U.S. 580 at 589: "A treaty is primarily a compact between independent nations. It depends for the enforcement of its provisions on the interest and the honor of the governments which are parties to it. If these fail, its infraction becomes the subject of international negotiations and reclamations, so far as the injured party chooses to seek redress, which may in the end be enforced by actual war."

[88] Kenneth E. Boulding, "Towards A Pure Theory of Threat Systems," *American Economic Review* 53 (1963): 424-34.

scription. In other words, there appears to be a relationship between redundancy and credibility, particularly threat credibility, that requires exploration within the communications framework, if not also within that of learning theory, if scholars are to probe to the roots of international law.

Responsiveness

IN A CHAPTER on the "Evolution of Extended Conflicts" Eugène Dupréel notes that the characters of aggressor and defender intermingle as opposing forces tend to take the same forms and to resort to the same means in order to meet and neutralize each other. Efforts to balance the other side's actions, indulged because balance or imbalance is decisive, renders the moral issue of defender versus aggressor irrelevant to the outcome of extended conflicts.[89] Aside from being an explanation of why an originally just cause of war may fail to retain the element of justness on one side, Dupréel's approach has model-building potential for the current bipolar world. Jan F. Triska and David P. Finley, in an attempt to deal with responses disruptive to the existing system, have made use of a Dupréel theorem in applying the concept of response in kind to Soviet-American diplomatic relations.[90] In doing so, they get at such complexities of international affairs as failure to respond to disruptive innovations and misperceptions.

Challenge-response is one form of reciprocity. But when we employ the term "responsiveness," we are likely to think in terms of sensitivity to another's needs, dangers, and efforts to be friendly—a sensitivity that seeks to express itself on the plus side of the ledger. A question arises as to whether the route toward greater responsiveness lies through an increase in communication. Paul Smoker found an increase in Sino-

[89] Eugène Dupréel, *Sociologie générale* (Paris: Presses Universitaires de France, 1948).

[90] Jan F. Triska and David P. Finley, "Soviet-American Relations: A Multiple Symmetry Model," *Journal of Conflict Resolution* 9 (1965): 37-53.

Indian communications prior to the outbreak of hostilities in 1962—an increase similar to the European increase in communications just before the 1914 declarations of war. Smoker suggested that there is a breaking point at which sheer volume of communication *precipitates* crisis and that when decision-making machinery cannot evaluate messages quickly, it might be wise to avoid communication.[91]

Short of a possible breaking point, it would seem that responsiveness would benefit from communication. Special relations can help, and Bruce M. Russett's investigation of a phase of Anglo-American relations showed that personal, economic, and party ties increased responsiveness between members of the United States Senate and the British House of Commons.[92] Even more conducive to responsiveness is an agency which, while embedded in one government, has the task of dealing with one or more other states with regard for the foreign state's interests. Dean Pruitt's study of a geographic office in the Department of State indicates some of the persuasion methods that can be used to win over other government agencies to the support of what a foreign state believes it needs, while another of his studies suggests that mutual responsiveness is likely to give way to pure bargaining—that is, a situation in which concessions are made only when the other party has displayed the capacity and willingness to delay agreement and to carry out threats—whenever the relative bargaining strength of the parties comprising a dyad is changing.[93]

[91] Paul Smoker, "Sino-Indian Relations: A Study of Trade, Communication and Defense," *Journal of Peace Research* 2 (1964): 65-76.

[92] Bruce M. Russett, "International Communication and Legislative Behavior: The Senate and the House of Commons," *Journal of Conflict Resolution* 6 (1962): 291-307.

[93] Dean G. Pruitt, "Problem Solving in the Department of State," Monograph No. 2 (Denver: Social Science Foundation and Department of International Relations, University of Denver, 1964); and "Negotiations as A Form of Social Behavior," Studies of the Dynamics of Cooperation and Conflict, Technical Report No. 6, Office of Naval

The types of communications referred to in the preceding paragraph are not the types of communications stored in law books. They may, however, be productive of such legal communications in the form of international agreements. While not removing the threat latent in legal communications, they can assist in making such threats palatable. Whether they add to credibility may be another question, but their potential for doing so would lie, as Pool suggested, in their contribution to quietness in the presentation of threat and, presumably, in emphasis upon the reciprocal reward feature in an agreement. Thus, any assessment of the nature of international obligation must reach beyond the threat feature and attempt to determine the level of responsiveness or empathy among nations, taking care to account for the channels of communication that may be open to permit argument within one government on behalf of the views of another. In the effort to provide a full accounting of the invisible links that together constitute reciprocity, analysis of the effectiveness of such channels would profit from the application of concepts of communications theory like noise and redundancy.

Research (Buffalo: State University of New York, Department of Psychology, October 28, 1968), pp. 25-26.

Chapter V: Genesis and Evolution of International Legal Norms

Formal Sources

MUCH ATTENTION is given in the literature of international law to the formal sources of law, particularly to international agreements. To concentrate on formal sources may provide a service to the practicing lawyer whose professional demands may not require him to reach toward the roots of human behavior to understand why particular norms are what they are and why the legal system is what it is. Those who would probe into the depths indicated are keenly aware of the inadequacies of formal sources as explanations of legal evolution, for the formal sources are themselves the necessary objects to be explained. Indeed, the incapacity of formal sources to explain themselves is reflected in the old debate about whether formal sources are really sources or only evidence of international law.

Today the quantity of treaty law is such that legal scholars' attention tends to focus on this mass of explicit evidence of what international law happens to be. Less elusive than custom, international agreements provide handy substance for paraphrase, commentary, and scholarly interpretation. Furthermore, international agreements provide a relatively tangible basis for measurement by social scientists of the political, economic, and military relations of nations. For example, a comparison of the 1952 Paris treaty and the 1957 Rome treaties shows a lower degree of supranationalism in the latter than in the former. This is confirmed by what more recent interviews with elites and content analysis of leading newspapers have shown, namely, that in 1957 European integration reached a plateau on which it has remained.[1] Or analysis can

[1] Karl W. Deutsch, "Integration and Arms Control in the European Po-

be made of a country's treaties, as Triska and Slusser did for the Soviet Union, to ascertain which types of treaties are likely to have value and the grounds on which that country is likely to conform to its international agreements.[2] Still another approach was suggested by Peter H. Rohn to the 1965 Annual Meeting of the American Society of International Law, namely, the establishment of a treaty profile of the relations of states.[3] And it may be noted that among the measures of aggregate data employed by such investigators as Rudolph Rummel to try to ascertain the dimensions of states' foreign behavior are quantitative measures of treaties, military treaties, and multilateral treaties.[4]

But none of these approaches, legalistic or nonlegalistic, gets to the processes of the genesis and evolution of treaty law. A somewhat closer approximation to the evolution of norms occurs in legal studies concerned with the interpretation of existing international agreements by the parties, by national and international courts and arbitral tribunals, and by organ-

---

litical Environment," *American Political Science Review* 60 (1966): 354-65; Deutsch, "A Comparison of French and German Elites in the European Political Environment," in Deutsch, Lewis J. Edinger, Roy C. Macridis, and Richard L. Merritt, *France, Germany and the Western Alliance: A Study of Elite Attitudes on European Integration and World Politics* (New York: Scribner's, 1967), pp. 218-64, 298-300; J. Zvi Namenwirth and Thomas L. Brewer, "Elite Editorial Comment on the European and Atlantic Communities in Four Countries," in Philip J. Stone, Dexter C. Dunphy, Marshall S. Smith, and Daniel M. Ogilvie, *The General Inquirer: A Computer Approach to Content Analysis* (Cambridge: M.I.T. Press, 1966), pp. 401-27; Donald J. Puchala, "European Political Integration: Progress and Prospects," mimeographed (New Haven: Yale University, Political Science Research Library, 1966).

[2] J. F. Triska and Robert M. Slusser, *The Theory, Law and Policy of Soviet Treaties* (Stanford: Stanford University Press, 1962).

[3] Peter H. Rohn, "Institutionalism in the Law of Treaties: A Case of Combining Teaching and Research," *Proceedings, American Society of International Law, 1965*, pp. 93-98.

[4] Rudolph J. Rummel, "Some Dimensions in the Foreign Behavior of Nations," *Journal of Peace Research* 3 (1966): 201-24.

izations such as United Nations bodies. But here again, as with commentary on treaty texts, scholarly attention is focused primarily on output, not on input or on the processing of legal information within the system in conjunction with the input of other, nonlegal information.

To focus on input and on processes vital to the generation of norms, as well as to their change or revision over time, it is necessary to concentrate on what happened before international agreements took form and before revised interpretations were articulated. Diplomatic histories, including case studies of more nearly contemporary negotiations, are helpful in providing data that are discrete in character. But, given the different processing of data by individual scholars, diplomatic histories provide little basis for aggregation and comparison except through intuitive linkages.

Narrative continuity, not itself enough for generalization, may result from probing a specialized subject as deeply as the historical data permit. An older example of such a probe in depth and over time is T. W. Fulton's *Sovereignty of the Sea* (1910). A more recent specialized account is George Stambuk's volume on American military forces abroad, tracing the development from the territorial exclusiveness principle of *Schooner Exchange* v. *M'Fadden* (1812, 7 Cranch 116) to the modern status-of-forces agreements based on the assumption that foreign troops can be present for nonbelligerent purposes.[5] Stambuk takes note of the lack of doctrinal advance in the 19th century in the absence of situations stimulating the enunciation of new principles. But he also presents evidence that the law developed more rapidly on the basis of state actions and judicial distinctions before the NATO period than it has since the introduction of the NATO regime of status-of-

[5] George Stambuk, *American Military Forces Abroad: Their Impact on the Western State System* (Columbus: Ohio State University Press, 1963), esp. pp. 138-60, 163-66.

forces agreements.[6] The Stambuk approach employs traditional historical, legal, and political science methods to produce a unique study. It now demands companion studies to provide sufficient grounds for generalization concerning, among other things, rates of legal change. In the absence of systematized studies of diplomatic negotiations that are more than unique narratives, laboratory experiments in negotiating and bargaining behavior may provide more utilizable data for generalization about the genesis of norms, their evolution, and even their degradation under change and stress.

Indeed, the laboratory has permitted Cowan and Strickland to investigate, among other things, the fate of existing norms under conditions of isolation and the formation of new norms, despite certain defects in procedure that may or may not be capable of remedy in future experiments.[7] In a sense, it may be said that the laboratory even permits investigation of what precedes the negotiation stages. And it is to antecedent stages, including behavior that may not be deviant due to lack of a rule from which to deviate, that one must turn if the process of norm generation is to receive scientific exposition.

Much the same may be said about custom. Too frequently custom and case law are amalgamated to render the latter identical with the former. While it is proper that what constitutes custom should be embodied in case law on appropriate occasions, it is not proper to confound that which is the product of the behavior, say, of merchants or sailors with that which emanates from the minds of judges. Aside from the absurd-

[6] Cf. the experimental finding that in a small isolated group articulation of a rule derived from the practice of the subjects led to its abandonment in subsequent practice. Walter O. Weyrauch, "Law in Isolation: The Penthouse Astronauts," *Trans-action* 5 (June, 1968): 39-46.

[7] Thomas A. Cowan and Donald A. Strickland, "The Legal Structure of a Confined Microsociety (A Report on the Cases of Penthouse II and III)," Internal Working Paper No. 34 (Berkeley: Space Sciences Laboratory, Social Sciences Project, University of California, August, 1965).

ity that a rule is not law until it is violated and judgment is rendered,[8] the apparently unbreakable habit in most Western legal scholarship of confounding case law and custom casts a fog over the process of norm generation. This prevents even an accurate appraisal of the role of the courts vis-à-vis the behavior patterns of nonjudicial society.[9]

From what pattern has a person deviated when his deviation is not from something prescribed by legislator or court? Why do the paths of remedy lie sometimes in the direction of legislators (including treaty-makers and other diplomats) and sometimes in the direction of courts and arbitral tribunals? Is there any pattern in the choice of directions that may itself be said to be a behavioral rule of the system in question? Under what conditions, in addition to simple imitation, does deviation itself become the norm-changing, norm-creating action? One cannot trace the generation of a single norm, let alone develop sustainable generalizations, except by investigation over time of the deviant and conforming actions of those individuals, groups, and governments to whose conduct the norm refers.

Customary international law, the subject of so much dispute and disagreement, may best be understood as a process operating through time. It is thus essential to determine how customs originate, how they are maintained, and how they are altered. In a very basic sense, a custom is an observed regularity in conduct, the more or less spontaneous product of events that generates expectations about future conduct, thereby providing in today's thought a link between the past and future. It constitutes a regular, routine response to what are judged to be similar circumstances. In addition, it goes with-

[8] W. W. Buckland, "The Nature of Contractual Obligation," *Cambridge Law Journal* 8 (1944): 251.

[9] It may also be that the confounding of case law and custom may blind Western scholars to norm-generating forces present in non-Western societies.

out saying that custom does not constitute an iron yoke; customary law, like legislated law, can be and often is disobeyed.

In an ideal sense, an international custom is something done by most states. Yet we know that the ability of states to "legislate" through their own behavior is not equally distributed. Through power differentials or because of concentrated activity in a particular geographical region or functional area, a single state or group of states may function as a kind of opinion leader. The generally additive nature of customary lawmaking is modified to the extent that some countries are looked to as trend-setters.

Perhaps the central jurisprudential problem raised in the context of customary law is the problem of the ambiguity of actions. In short, what does it mean for a state to break a customary law? Since rules, whether customary or not, are guides to behavior, a deviant action constitutes a breach of the norm. But if customary international law is built incrementally out of a mix of private actions and foreign policy decisions, every act is potentially legislative, including every "deviant" act. To the outside observer of a broad period of time, a country's every act, together with its nationals' acts of eventually perceived international impact, either reinforces or undercuts existing behavior patterns. And the deviant act may easily be seen as the beginning of a new pattern of incremental "legislation."

Three factors lie behind the survival of customary rules. First, the rules function as predictors of the behavior of other states. Since all national political systems are ways of dealing with the problems of scarcity and resource allocation, some order in the international environment is essential. Customary rules serve this need for the reduction of randomness.

Second, in a broad, nontechnical sense, customs are precedents; they are past solutions to continuing problems. As such, they constitute what Thomas Schelling calls "focal-point solutions,"[10] features of the decision-maker's environment which appear unusually conspicuous. Despite the patently intangible character of customary norms, the visual metaphor remains valid. For internally held rules are as real a part of the statesman's view of the world as any concrete landmark. To the extent that a customary rule is perceived to be "natural" or "obvious," it will exert a dominant influence over decisions, quite apart from the convoluted question of whether there are sanctions to enforce it.

Third, deviant behavior is to some extent self-punishing. Customary rules grow out of interaction, out of mutual expectations, out of a network of reciprocity. They function because their operation benefits the participants, for example, in the matter of resource allocation mentioned above. The breach of a rule is not simply an act in the realm of ideas; it jeopardizes the concrete relationships between states and the benefits these relationships produce. Thus, it costs something to break a rule. A country may well choose to absorb the costs, but cannot expect deviance to be without consequences.

A rule persists both because it is deemed necessary and because it has become part of the political landscape. This tendency to survive means that a rule often continues as a factor in decision-making even after it has ceased to perform needed functions. In the absence of formal legislative machinery, how is it to be adapted to a changed situation? This is most commonly accomplished through the fiction, that is, through a transitional period in which a rule remains formally accepted but during which statesmen redefine its terms so as to alter its effect. As Maine recognized, the advantage of this arrangement is to maintain the appearance of stability while permitting changes in behavior.[11]

[10] Thomas C. Schelling, *The Strategy of Conflict* (New York: Oxford, 1963), chap. 4.

[11] Sir Henry Sumner Maine, *Ancient Law: Its Connections with the Early History of Society and Its Relation to Modern Ideas* (London: J. Murray, 1861), p. 25.

Just as a customary rule comes into being through the accumulation of common responses to the same problem, so such a rule changes in an incremental manner. Exceptions to it are made and the categories within it (e.g., "state," "territorial waters," "aggression") are stretched, so that new situations can be accommodated. If the fiction is successful, the accumulation of small changes will eventually reach the point where participants can face the necessity for comprehensive change and directly reformulate the rule. Or, if you will, the exceptions themselves are seen to be legislative acts contributing to the formation of a new rule.

One further problem of a theoretical nature remains, namely, the problem of time-lag. As we have seen, a rule can persist long after it is required; it is a solution to problems which no longer exist. This extended time-lag between past rule and present reality has been all too common in contemporary international law, even though the lag may not be nearly as great as for private law.[12] Yet it must also be observed that the total elimination of time-lag would produce even more disquieting results. If rules were totally responsive to behavior, they could serve no regulative function. The problem, then, is not one of eliminating the time-lag entirely, but of determining the *optimal* time-lag—short enough so that rules remain relevant, long enough to preserve continuity between past and present. In other words, law provides a range within which tolerable variations may occur. Efforts to reform, update, or modernize customary international law must consequently be directed at discovery of behavioral continuities, not at the fashionable inclusion of whatever happens to be current.

But the really unanswerable dilemma posed by the time-lag problem is in the area of social change. Optimal time-lag becomes genuinely possible not through deliberate reformist ef-

[12] Maxwell Cohen, "Basic Principles of International Law—A Revaluation," *Canadian Bar Review* 42 (1964): 449-62.

forts but simply because a society's processes of change operate at a moderate rate. At present no scheme for social engineering allows us to retard rapid social change—this is precisely the problem customary international law now faces. The ability, through technological means, to speed up social change has not proven reversible; until reversibility can be achieved, customary international law remains subject for its efficacy to largely uncontrollable secular trends.[13]

Related to the problems of time-lag and social change are the writings of publicists, some of whom call attention to problems and systemic changes while others argue that basically things remain the same or that impending changes should be resisted. Obviously, there is a time-lag, variable according to circumstances not yet systematically identified and classified, between the perception of problems and systemic changes, their verbalization, articulation of legislative and interpretative "solutions," and general international response. During this interval, how critical is the role of the publicist? Relatively little has been done to investigate how the normative statements of publicists enter international law, even though their writings have traditionally been cited as one of the sources of international law. At best there has been occasional effort, such as that of Chester Newland, to ascertain the extent to which tribunals resort to the guidance furnished by contributors to legal periodicals.[14] Reliance of courts upon certain publications provides only a first glimpse at the hypothesized influence of publicists. There should be dimensions both broader and deeper which may be susceptible to probing by diligent researchers.

[13] For a reexamination of the theory of social evolution, see Donald T. Campbell, "Variation and Selective Retention in Socio-Cultural Evolution," in H. R. Barringer, G. I. Blanksten, and R. W. Mack (eds.), *Social Change in Developing Areas* (Cambridge: Schenkman, 1965), pp. 289-308.

[14] Chester A. Newland, "Legal Periodicals and the United States Supreme Court," *Midwest Journal of Political Science* 3 (1959): 58-74.

In one direction the probe might be directed toward the international system and its structure for linking subsystems which contain differential lawmaking elements. If the output of legal processes is regarded as a special linguistic coding system, then a phase of communications theory can be brought into play; for one phase of communications theory suggests that linguistic coding systems are elicited by the structure of social systems.[15] In a simpler approach that would concentrate more on form than on content, one could perhaps restrict the view of the social structure to the "society of lawyers" in a particular system. But once one adds content to his concerns, the problem of coding is broadened and lawyers become but a segment of the society to be considered. Furthermore, societal structure alone may be an insufficient explanation of the transformation of publicists' normative statements into law. However much societal structure may help in explanation, the transformation referred to is dynamic, not static.

Borrowing again from communications theory, the concept of redundancy suggests another direction to be taken. Whether or not it be true that, like languages, life seeks an equilibrium of 50% redundancy, some balance is sought between the expected and the unexpected and between organization and disorganization. Value structures appear to be capable of intermeshing with redundancy patterns either as psychologically peripheral traits or as more central motives.[16] The intermeshing of values with redundancy patterns seems to happen when publicists' statements of normative quality have an impact on behavior. Redundancy patterns of consequence are of two types: (1) patterns occurring in the writings of publicists; (2)

[15] Basil Bernstein, "Elaborated and Restricted Codes: Their Social Origins and Some Consequences," in J. J. Gumpers and D. Hymes (eds.), "The Ethnology of Communication," *American Anthropologist* 6, no. 2 (Special Publication, 1966): 55-69.

[16] Benjamin N. Colby, "Behavioral Redundancy," *Behavioral Science* 3 (1958): 317-22.

patterns emerging from the unilateral acts of states. But we must trace the spread of norms in historical circumstances if there is to be illumination of the process of transformation from pious statement to legal quality. In the realm of international law, the investigation would be more difficult than, for example, in the case of labor law. By contrast with the latter, the process in international law is generally clandestine. It lacks the element of public advocacy that simplifies the tracing of the course from idea to wages and hours legislation.

When the output from publicists' statements is custom, determination of the moment of the transformation process' completion becomes a more elusive goal. A court does not always provide the researcher with the statement, as in the case of *The Scotia* (1871, 14 Wallace 170), that enough similar unilateral acts have occurred to permit the conclusion that an international custom has arisen. Few guides exist in the literature of international law concerning the cumulative effect of unilateral acts, even though the rapid development of a legal regime of the continental shelf has recently traveled the course from successive unilateral acts past custom to the status of treaty law. Discussions of unilateral acts have largely concerned the binding effects of unilateral declarations. Redundancy patterns have been ignored, particularly the redundancy patterns in unilateral actions not brought to the attention of the courts. One method of tracing such patterns, while also attempting to ascertain legal quality, would be to tabulate the reactions of states to specified acts by other states. To do so requires the assumption that reactive behavior can be a norm-generating force and is also at some point of time evidence of the consensus said to underlie all law—an obverse manifestation of the consensus declared positively for particular legal norms. This consensus may be regarded as a convergence of expectations, while the tabulation of reactions would be evidence of the rise and spread of expectations that states shall act in certain ways and that, if they do not, certain responses are proper.

Norm-Generating Forces

AMONG THE norm-generating forces or stimuli to which attention may be given are the following: (1) environmental influences, (2) situational influences, (3) conflict, (4) claims and demands, (5) actions of deviants, (6) activities of private persons, (7) past acts or precedents. How these factors are interrelated is a problem to be approached through systems analysis with particular attention to communications, information processing, and decision-making as affected by such things as perceptions and attitude structures.

Public policy is not included among the norm-generating forces listed because in content public policy tends to be an amalgam of the forces listed. At the same time public policy, including policy toward existing norms and legal systems, tends to be a filter assisting in the transformation of normative aspirations into legal norms. Furthermore, since laws represent a segment of public policy, the researcher seeking to identify norm-generating forces will also be searching for policy-generating forces.

Environmental and Situational Influences

ADDA BOZEMAN's historical study of the development of international relations to 1500 suggests that on at least some occasions when nations face the same hazards or the same environmental uncertainties, they will produce common norms.[17] In addition, there is experimental evidence that *ad hoc* rules of behavior have some impact upon escalation situations and threat patterns.[18] This experimental evidence may be parallel to

[17] Adda B. Bozeman, *Politics and Culture in International History* (Princeton: Princeton University Press, 1960), passim.

[18] N. Averch and M. M. Levin, "Simulation of Decision-Making in Crisis: Three Manual Gaming Experiments," RAND Memorandum RM-4202-PR (Santa Monica: RAND Corporation, August, 1964).

extrapolations from U.S.–Soviet relations of behavioral norms limiting violence to some level below total war.[19] Both the experimental and historical data relate to a threatening, uncertain environment in which the primary goal may be the negative one of averting calamity.

In a benign environment there appears to be a need for positive goals in order to produce cooperative, problem-solving behavior. At least the experiments of Muzafer Sherif indicate that in the boys camp situation that he studied the threat generated cooperation but the establishment of common goals for groups in a condition of interdependence was more helpful in generating standardized norms.[20] Whether this is also true in international affairs is uncertain, but at least some propositions can be formulated to test by reference to historical data.

The environmental change to which most attention has been accorded in recent years has been the attainment of statehood by numerous Asian and African polities. This change has introduced a measure of uncertainty. The Western imposition of a common political language has led to distortions of meanings and so, possibly, to a deterioration of once apparently secure Western values.[21] Much depends upon how far the West is prepared to go in adopting non-Western meanings for the sake of accommodation. In terms of time, this change follows upon two other persistent value-disrupting events, namely, the appearance of a Communist bloc of states after 1945 and the scientific and technological revolution of the 20th century.[22]

[19] See, e.g., M. M. Halperin, "The Limiting Process in the Korean War," *Political Science Quarterly* 78 (1963): 13-39; Amitai Etzioni, "On Self-Encapsulating Conflicts," *Journal of Conflict Resolution* 8 (1964): 242-55.

[20] Muzafer Sherif, et al., *Intergroup Cooperation and Conflict: The Robber's Cave Experiment* (Norman: University of Oklahoma Press, 1961).

[21] Bozeman, *Politics and Culture*, pp. 8-10, 497-98, 520-21.

[22] W. R. Schilling, "Science, Technology and Foreign Policy," *Journal of International Affairs* 13 (1959): 7-18. For an expression of con-

Among the changes that affect the environment are those produced by particular nations as a result of research and development programs. Some, because they affect combat and security capacities, represent threats to be countered by such formal norms as the treaty ban on nuclear testing in the atmosphere. Development of nuclear weapons, missiles and guidance systems, instruments of chemical and bacteriological warfare, and of reconnaissance aircraft and satellites represent scientific and technological threats to the international system and its units. Other research development activities, such as long-range communication systems, carry the promise of desired and peaceful improvement of the international system and the increased well-being of its units. Such developments, as well as those that threaten, carry a norm-generating potential; coordinated use of technology's products requires regulative guidelines.

Environmental change is something to which men and their organizations must respond. The response may be, but need not necessarily be, adaptation. It can be a response of ignoring or resisting change as expressed in the address of Francis I of Austria to the professors of the Gymnasium at Laibach in 1821: "Hold to the old, for it is good, and our ancestors found it to be good, so why should not we?"[23] In international affairs, the subjects being the lawmakers, adaptive responses can occur with a relatively short time-lag. However, as

---

cern over dictation of the rate of innovation by values and motives that run behind socio-economic development, see Ernst B. Haas, "Toward Controlling International Change—A Personal Plea," *World Politics* 17 (1964): 1-12. For concern over the failure of the West to think in terms of restraints rather than solely in terms of expansion, including expansion of production, see B. Landheer, "The Image of World Society and the Function of Armaments," *Peace Research Society (International), Papers,* Ghent Conference, 1964, vol. 2 (1965), pp. 232-241.

[23] Quoted by R. W. Seton-Watson in his Introduction to Karl Tschuppik, *Francis Joseph I: The Downfall of an Empire,* trans. C.J.S. Sprigge (New York: Harcourt, Brace, 1930), p. xiii.

is shown by the failure to adapt fishery conservation practices to modern technology, the time-lag in the adaptation of international law to technological innovation can be quite extended.[24] What some of these adaptations have been will be dealt with in subsequent sections of this and succeeding chapters. For the present it is enough to note that environmental changes are a norm-generating force,[25] even though what change occurs in law is a function of what change is perceived in the landscape and is passed through communication and attitudinal filters. Because these filters exist as products of socialization and specialized training, we doubt that legal skills, even though necessary, are sufficient to adapt international law to technological change or to the complex social change represented by the advent of new African and Asian states.

As far as situational influences are concerned, these are in part environmental. That is, they are environmental to the extent that they represent responses to perceived external conditions at a particular time.

Conflict, Claims, and Demands

CONFLICT, often popularly treated as the condition in which laws are set aside, is actually a producer of norms—if not immediately, at least in its aftermath. For conflict brings issues between the contending parties to the fore and provides con-

[24] Ralph W. Johnson, "Regulation of Commercial Salmon Fisheries: A Case of Confused Objectives," *Pacific Northwest Quarterly* 55 (1964): 141-45; Ralph Turvey, "Optimization and Suboptimization in Fishery Regulation," *American Economic Review* 54 (1964): 64-76; James Crutchfield, "The Marine Fisheries: A Problem in International Cooperation," Papers and Proceedings of the Seventy-sixth Annual Meeting of the American Economic Association, 1963, *American Economic Review* 54 (1964): 207-18; J. L. Hart, "Some Sociological Effects of Quota Control of Fisheries," *Canadian Fish Culturalist* 22 (1958): 17-19.

[25] Perhaps the best treatment of the interaction of the engineering and legal aspects of a technological change permitting the exploitation of once untouchable resources is M. W. Mouton, *The Continental Shelf* (The Hague: Nijhoff, 1952).

ditions for the articulation of norms designed both to resolve an ongoing conflict and to anticipate, if not avoid, recurrences. It also generates governing procedures for conducting conflict.

The work of Hohfeld and Corbin on legal terminology made use of the conflict element underlying law to stress the bilaterality of legal relationships.[26] They were primarily interested in developing a technique for untangling those relationships, but an unintended consequence was to open legal theory up to an interactional approach. Corbin's work contained the seeds of social science analysis:

> A statement that a legal relation exists betweeen A and B is a *prediction* as to what society, acting through its courts or executive agents, will do or not do for one and against the other.

Furthermore, all legal rules could be studied in terms of two-party relationships.

The Hohfeld-Corbin suggestion of linkages between conflict and law is of even greater interest now than it was half a century ago when it was formulated. These linkages should be regarded more as compatibilities than as incompatibilities, even though law presumably has as one of its functions the establishment and maintenance of order. Rather than being in opposition, law and conflict can go hand in hand. Order is a combination of cooperation and *managed* conflict, and law is an instrument for the attainment of both. In pursuit of these twin ends, a good deal of conflict is built into legal systems. The adversary process, involving the clash between advocates, is the prime example of the ritualization of conflict within legal institutions.[27] In primitive law, the feud has been seen to

[26] Arthur Corbin, "Legal Analysis and Terminology," *Yale Law Journal* 29 (1919): 163-73, esp. pp. 164f; Wesley Newcomb Hohfeld, *Fundamental Legal Conceptions as Applied in Judicial Reasoning* (New Haven: Yale University Press, 1919).

[27] Jerome Frank, *Courts on Trial* (New York: Atheneum, reprinted, 1963), pp. 80-102.

occasionally serve rather than subvert order, just as the "just war" has been viewed as supportive of international law.

In its everyday usage "conflict" denotes the condition par excellence of estrangement between the parties. Yet the bilateral approach Hohfeld and Corbin brought to law can be extended to conflict. Both law and conflict operate through webs of interaction that become interrelated, for example, when conflict is encapsulated within the judicial process (e.g., the adversary process). Even though we may speak figuratively of a "gulf" between contending parties, neither the attitude of hostility nor indulgence in violence per se removes conflict from the realm of interaction[28] or from an interrelationship with law.

Interaction is communication in the broadest sense,[29] and if we place conflict on a continuum ranging from total indifference to total involvement, we find that conflict is far closer to the latter than to the former. But the vast majority of conflicts fall short of total conflict. Many international conflicts involve parties with not only disputed interests but also shared interests, and it is on the basis of the latter that conflict resolution is usually effected.[30] The kinds of messages transmitted by hostile acts are not pleasant ones to hear, but for all that they remain messages, and the relationship between parties to a conflict is one of often intense mutual involvement.

Conflict, then, is one among many modes of interaction and, in theory, is capable of binding individuals and groups together as well as splitting them apart. In fact, conflict frequently possesses a socially useful function, so long as it is

[28] Raymond W. Mack and Richard C. Snyder, "The Analysis of Social Conflict—Toward an Overview and Synthesis," *Journal of Conflict Resolution* 1 (1957): 212-48.

[29] Bernard Berelson and Gary A. Steiner, *Human Behavior: An Inventory of Scientific Findings* (New York: Harcourt, Brace & World, 1964), p. 326.

[30] Schelling, *The Strategy of Conflict*, p. 5; Fred Charles Iklé, *How Nations Negotiate* (New York: Harper & Row, 1964), pp. 2-4, 31-32, 88, 118-21.

channeled into the correct forms and directions. Parliamentary systems that involve two or more parties are in a state of almost constant but moderate conflict. The clash of interests that characterizes legislative bodies generally falls within a circumscribed range of permissible intensity.

The distribution of conflict may actually serve to unify, rather than fragment, the body or society in which it occurs. Of course, if a number of conflicts continue to exist between the same groups, integration becomes impossible. But if different conflicts exist between different combinations of parties, the conflicts may well tie the society together. For example if A and B habitually find themselves opposed to C and D, the chances for the integration of the four into a single unit remains remote. But if a number of other conflicts cut across the AB-CD blocs, the likelihood of polarization is diminished (e.g., A-C, B-D, A-B, C-D, AC-BD, AD-BC). Enemies in one context are allies in another. What we may call cross-cutting, as opposed to parallel, conflicts serve to moderate, if they do not eliminate, disagreements. Since one shares common future interests with the party with whom one is currently in conflict, one hesitates to escalate to the level where a total breach becomes necessary. The frequently commented upon success of early 19th-century European diplomacy depended in part on just this flexibility of alliances. Since one usually fought a past and future ally, the prudent victor did not press his advantage.

Cross-cutting conflicts offer one example of the functional distribution of conflict. Another example, more germane to a legal discussion, involves the channeling of conflicts into acceptable forms. Thus, the courtroom with its clash of views becomes a microcosm of society, but the conflict, instead of erupting again in such a way as to threaten the society, is now enacted in a framework of ritualistic constraints. We are only now beginning to see the possibility for this kind of enactment on an international scale. Certainly the United Nations

Security Council during the Cuban Missile Crisis of October, 1962, served such a function. Indeed, there have been suggestions that a primary latent function of the United Nations is to provide an arena within which international conflicts can be transferred to the verbal level.[31] If true, this would account for the persistence of the practice of public debate, which on the surface provides nothing that is not already available through traditional diplomatic machinery. Legislative bodies, too, may persist in part because they offer a forum for the symbolic expression of conflict.

Hence, conflict does not disappear but merely moves from a societally dangerous level to a level where societal institutions can accommodate it. In this sense, conflict per se is not necessarily functional to the society in the way that cross-cutting conflicts in particular are. But since heterogeneous interests and scarce resources make conflicts endemic in almost any social setting, the transfer of conflicts to specific, bounded arenas at once legitimizes them and renders them relatively harmless. Judicial institutions, broadly construed, offer microcosms of society. Hence, conflict cannot spread wholesale through the society but, instead, is confined to a miniaturization of society. International organizations, whatever else they do, provide a microcosm of the international system.

The relationship between conflict and international law has been rendered particularly unclear by changes in the technology of warfare. The combination of nuclear deterrence and "brushfire wars" has effectively undercut the classical distinction between the "law of peace" and the "law of war." The blurring of a once clear line entails the revision of norms. But the inherent difficulty of customary systems is their inability to effectively assimilate rapid change. Hence, the normative system concerned with international conflict dates from

[31] William D. Coplin, *The Functions of International Law: An Introduction to the Role of International Law in the Contemporary World* (Chicago: Rand McNally, 1966), pp. 82-83, 94-95, 166.

a period when the conduct of war and, indeed, the very definition of war was far different than it is now. Under such circumstances the raw material of legal redefinition lies in the current practices of states as outlined in official statements and in the works of such non-lawyers as Herman Kahn, whose "ladder of escalation" represents the hierarchy of sanctions for the 1960's.[32]

Treating "conflict" as a generic term that embraces such varied manifestations as quarrels, court proceedings (especially, but not exclusively, under the adversary system), political contention, internal wars, and foreign wars, it is possible to employ an analytical structure that will permit identification of norm-generating effects at the several stages of the conflict process. Indeed, lawyers have developed a working analytical structure along this line.

In terms of the stage of conflict, certain rules arise appropriate to each stage. In the initial phase, rules develop to determine who can present what types of claims and demands, the manner of initial presentation of and response to claims and demands, and the available choices of arena in which to present particular types of claims and demands. In part, these rules result from state practices related to the structure of the international system and its subsystems; in part they arise from the deliberate formulation of rules by competent agents or agencies. Uncertainties exist, as in the classical effort to distinguish justiciable and nonjusticiable issues.

The stage of direct confrontation in a chosen arena gives rise to rules governing the conduct of conflict, e.g., the law of war or rules concerning arbitral procedure. It is at this stage that the *ius in bello* comes into play, while the *ius ad bellum* is relevant to the preceding stage. Rules about the use of force short of war (e.g., the rules about procedure and proportionality

[32] Herman Kahn, *On Escalation*, rev. edn. (Baltimore: Penguin, 1968), pp. 37-51.

enunciated in the *Naulilaa Case* of 1928)[33] are products of the confrontation stage.

At the close of the proceedings, violent or nonviolent, other rules come into play that relate to the decision-making formalities and the basis for decision, e.g., majority, unanimity, will of the conqueror, signature, and ratification. Postdecisional rules deal with the following: the manner of implementing the decision; transfer of the conflict to another arena, including presumably higher authority; rules, if any, concerning the hierarchical position of authorities; rules concerning the conflict of authorities and norms when incompatible outcomes result from conflicts in two or more arenas.

The above enumeration by stages and types of rules neither pretends to be complete nor rules out the possibility of rules overlapping stages, e.g., in the case of transfer to another arena. It is certainly not intended, by the aggregation of forms of conflict, to revive myths such as the old claim that war is a form of international adjudication. Rather, it suggests that the lawyers' carefully drawn classifications relating procedural norms to relevant stages of various international procedures are not by themselves a very incisive indication of norm-generating processes and stimuli. They provide a beginning—a fragmentary glimpse, often but not always anecdotal, of stimuli toward norm-generation.[34]

Perhaps the lawyer has done the most important part of his analytical task by presenting and classifying data on hand. Further use of the data on norm generation may be a task for social scientists. To date, with the possible exception of anthropologists, social scientists have not probed deeply into a number of international procedures to understand the reasons

[33] German-Portuguese Arbitral Tribunal, 8 *T.A.M.* 409, 422-423; 2 U.N. Reports 1019, 1027-28.

[34] Studies of international arbitration that reveal problems in cross-national pleading can provide data concerning stimulation. E.g., Kenneth S. Carlston, *The Process of International Arbitration* (New York: Columbia University Press, 1946), pp. 7-10.

why many technical norms of procedure exist. Consequently, they have not probed the generative process. Concern with the substantive output of the processes may have the effect of deflecting social scientists' attention from the technicalities of procedure.

In regard to claims and demands, it is sufficient here to note that Myres S. McDougal's works have had significant impact. Most importantly, his works present both a framework and its applications that permit scholars to relate legal procedures to public policy and so to political procedures and outputs. The only suggestion to be made here is that the greater scientific value of the McDougal approach probably lies in its focus on norm generation and the stimuli to it rather than on substantive output. Toward substantive output an attitude of neutrality is desirable if the full potential of the McDougal approach as an explanation of the norm-generating force of claims and demands is to be realized.

Impact of Deviance

DEVIANCE may be treated as having an impact on the law in two ways. First, deviance that is successful in producing a change in practice, whether or not sufficiently widespread and fundamental to be classified as revolution, is by its success a norm-generating or norm-evolving process. By the simple fact of a change of behavior, with or without benefit of formal lawmaking, a new norm comes into being or an old one is changed. In this case, the analytical problem is essentially twofold: (1) determination of the time when the new behavior can be said to have attained general normative effect, and (2) determination of the stimuli to deviate and the reasons for the particular reception accorded the stimuli by the deviants.

Second and more complex is the problem of the actor whose deviance does not attain normative status. Instead of the deviant's own conduct becoming the norm, the reaction to it becomes the standard embedded in the morality, the practices, or the law of the society, as in the case of the 19th-century development of international norms concerning insurgency,[35] for 19th-century insurgency does not represent deviance from an international norm-prohibiting rebellion. No such norm existed despite the Holy Alliance and despite the requirement that government treat regimes in power diplomatically. The deviance involved in Latin American insurgency related to established domestic political, economic, and social conditions. But international impact resulted and foreign governments' reactions took the form not of rules to aid in quelling insurgency but of rules on how to have dealings with insurgents. Lawmaking procedures may be set in action as much in response to this kind of deviance as in response to more formalized agitation by propagandists and interest groups that in the meanwhile may be conforming to unwanted laws rather than indulging deviant behavior.

Response to deviance may be largely intuitive, as may first impressions that certain behavior is expected and that a norm exists rather than just some *ad hoc* reactions. At some point intuition is buttressed by the statements of publicists and, more importantly, by the pronouncements of governmental decision-makers. Something more than intuition underlies the conclusion that a norm exists as a result of responses to deviance.

Statute books, treaty collections, court reports and reports of arbitrations, and legal commentaries record responses to deviance. Occasional records may set forth instances of deviant behavior but, except for uniform crime reporting in some countries, there is little systematic handling of such data. Unsystematic handling of data on responses to deviance can result from a number of circumstances, among them the following: the information required is from a period of little scholarly activity and poor record-keeping compared with the

[35] P. Calvert, "The 'Typical Latin-American Revolution,'" *International Affairs* 43 (1967): 85-95.

present; the events seemed too trivial, as in the cases where driving on the left was prescribed in horse and buggy days to prevent individuals from being accidentally struck by whips; the matter was so specialized, as in the case of numerous health hazards, that it received attention only in specialized tracts and treatises.

Yet, systematic assembly of available scattered data on the impact of deviance has the potential of bearing fruit not just by shedding light upon the law-generation process but also by demonstrating that social process variables may cluster together. The work of Rummel and Tanter on internal and international conflict, although not developing the significance of deviance, is suggestive of the utility of factor analysis to produce clusterings.[36] A manageable number of indicators would both permit parsimonious analysis and assist the formulation of propositions with significantly predictive power. Because of the need to work with scattered and incomplete data, the Rummel-Tanter technique may not be appropriate. But its objective can be a starting point when devising procedures suitable to the type of data on law-stimulating deviance that can be collected.

In a broader sense, the focus would be upon the social function of deviance rather than just on its lawmaking function. For example, let us assume that a viable system develops for holding national officials responsible to more than their own national segments of mankind, as a consequence of principles enunciated at Nuremberg. Paradoxically, Hitler's excesses, morally inexcusable as they were, would emerge as essential ingredients of the evolution of law and international politics in the same way that Charles I's and George III's taxation

[36] Rudolph J. Rummel, "Testing Some Possible Predictors of Conflict Behavior Within and Between Nations," *Peace Research Society (International), Papers,* Chicago Conference, 1963, vol. 1 (1964), pp. 79-111; Raymond Tanter, "Dimensions of Conflict Behavior Within and Between Nations, 1958-60," *Journal of Conflict Resolution* 10 (1966): 41-64.

without representation stimulated the development of Anglo-American political democracy and constitutionalism. They drew forth responses that created law.

A study by Katz, Libby, and Strodtbeck suggests that groups need deviant members and deviant roles. Based on an experiment with store employees, the investigators found that although there are group members whose status increases with conformity, there are others of lower status whose conformity does not result in commensurate rewards and, indeed, appears as a threat to the rank of members of higher status.[37] Without villains, where are heroes; without rabble, where is aristocracy? The actions of deviants, other than successful changes of practice and successful revolutions, produce responses that include lawmaking and social structuring. It is conceivable that society would not be society but an ant colony without deviants and deviant behavior, even when deviance is not formally institutionalized and excesses curbed in a manner represented by Her Majesty's loyal opposition.

Activities of Private Persons

PUBLIC authorities constitute a convenient focus that tends to obscure the law-generating quality of the acts of private persons, some of them deviants. Yet, it should be obvious that the simple effort of sailors to avoid collisions generated rules of the sea, that the undertakings of merchants to do business in far-off lands led to rules concerning the treatment of aliens, and that the enterprise of riverboat owners led to rules concerning freedom of navigation and even to the internationalization of some rivers. A political scientist has suggested that

[37] E. Katz, W. L. Libby, Jr., and F. L. Strodtbeck, "Status Mobility and Reaction to Deviance and Subsequent Conformity," *Sociometry* 27 (1964): 245-60. For an experiment that saw conformity increase with unfavorable reaction to deviants but decrease when the subjects were informed that other group members had reacted unfavorably, see V. L. Allen, "Conformity and the Role of the Deviant," *Journal of Personality* 33 (1965): 584-97.

much would be gained from studies of the judicial process that were centered on the litigants to determine what they seek, how they become involved in litigation, and how they evaluate the moral legitimacy of tribunals.[38] Actions in the day-to-day conduct of business are sometimes accompanied by deliberate law-creating efforts resulting from experience with inconveniences and with threats to continuation of an activity. These activities seem to be inconsequential to the legalistic study of customs except when there is no authoritative pronunciation by a court or arbitral tribunal to give assurance that a rule exists. Indeed, even in the case of treaty law it is possible that an historical study of the treaty may not look beyond intergovernmental negotiations, thereby missing prior significant but private generative activity.

Some examples may be mentioned. It is customary for treatises on international law to make reference to Grotius' argument for the freedom of the seas and to the mythical "battle of the books" between Grotius and Selden. Much more important to the development of freedom of the seas, to the establishment of a customary regime of territorial waters, and to the contention for the rule "free ships, free goods" were the activities of Dutch fishermen in the herring fishery, the enterprise of Netherlands shipbuilders in producing the then largest fishing and merchant fleets, and the defiance by Dutch shipping interests of the restrictive laws and policies concerning trading emanating from their own public authorities.[39]

[38] Matthew Holden, Jr., "Litigation and the Political Order," *Western Political Quarterly* 16 (1963): 771-81.

[39] D. W. Davies, *A Primer of Dutch Seventeenth Century Overseas Trade* (The Hague: Nijhoff, 1961), pp. 1-7, 23-27, 39; Violet Barbour, *Capitalism in Amsterdam in the 17th Century* (paperback edn., Ann Arbor: University of Michigan Press, 1963), pp. 19, 31-32, 35-42, 70, 105-108; G. N. Clark, *The Dutch Alliance and the War Against French Trade, 1688-1697* (Manchester: The University Press; London and New York: Longmans, Green, 1923), pp. 26, 31, 43, 45-55, 74-75; John Horner, *The Linen Trade of Europe During the Spinning Wheel Period* (Belfast: M'Caw, Stevenson & Orr, 1920), pp. 350, 359.

Private advocacy is represented by the efforts of 18th-century English advocates of tariff drawbacks for imported linen re-exported to American plantations. They contended for a statutory rule for seizure of foreign ships putting into English ports except under stress of weather or want of provisions.[40] Their arguments were far from the first to uphold exemptions from the rigor of local law when stress of weather brought an alien ship into port, but they serve to represent the kind of private agitation that contributes to the emergence of a rule of international law.

As long ago as 1923, G. N. Clark made the complaint, still lacking adequate response, that histories of international law provide insufficient accounts of the European commerce to which can be traced important developments in both private and public international law. That private individuals and organizations attempt to influence the content of international agreements affecting their activities seems almost self-evident.[41] The effort can extend even to the point of representation on a negotiating team. Influence attempts warrant closer study than they have been accorded.

One may not readily assume that interest groups would be the actual formulators of international agreements with governmental negotiation becoming essentially a formality to assure implementation of the accord reached by private persons. Yet just this sequence has occurred. The International Rubber Regulation Agreement of April, 1934, was just such an agreement. The story begins with the abortive efforts of private parties to achieve first self-regulation and subsequently governmental implementation. Private efforts began during World War I and produced no results until the 1930's. Success came after about a year's negotiations beginning in the

[40] Horner, *The Linen Trade*, p. 229.

[41] E.g., Alan D. Robinson, *Dutch Organized Agriculture in International Politics, 1945-1960* (The Hague: Nijhoff, 1961), pp. 92-105.

spring of 1933. Intergovernmental negotiation required only about two weeks' time in the spring of 1934.[42]

It may be noted that the route to rubber regulation, even though involving prominently the activities of private persons, did not proceed from custom to agreement. Such a progression might have occurred if a private international scheme of 1920 for control of production had attained a relatively satisfactory level of effectiveness. Skipping the stage of custom suggests a need to search for the sets of variables conducive to passage through the stage of custom and those inhibiting the genesis of custom, thereby requiring the early adoption of written rules if there is to be any regulation at all. In addition, we would want to know the sets of variables conducive to and impeding passage from the stage of custom to written law. Is the process patterned or is it random? Is it the same in the international arena as in the domestic? Are such patterns as might emerge common to all systems or unique to particular international and domestic systems?

Consideration of the activities of private persons should require a special focus upon one obvious group of private persons, namely, lawyers. A few books have appeared that examine the personalities, attitudes, approaches, and activities of lawyers, although not with concern for international law. Nevertheless, they do serve as indicators of the possible. Jerome E. Carlin's study of Chicago lawyers helps to identify the points at which dubious competence and dubious ethics enter into the legal process. Relying heavily on the concepts of Merton and Parsons, Hubert J. O'Gorman has studied the attitudes of a sample of New York City lawyers toward divorce practices. This study has been criticized for indulging a mis-

[42] For accounts that differ in emphasis according to the time of writing, see Charles R. Whittlesey, *Governmental Control of Crude Rubber: The Stevenson Plan* (Princeton: Princeton University Press, 1931); Sir Andrew McFadyean (ed.), *The History of Rubber Regulation, 1934-1943* (London: Allen & Unwin, 1944); K. E. Knorr, *World Rubber and Its Regulation* (Stanford: Stanford University Press, 1945).

conception of what lawyers are and for an alleged unfamiliarity with the legal literature concerning divorce and divorce procedure. The criticism, if correct, makes clear the need for substantive knowledge before engaging in attitude sampling or other social science research. A study of Wall Street lawyers by Erwin O. Smigel employed the interview technique but, among other things, failed to ascertain what Wall Street lawyers do as professionals in respect to the private sector of the world economy. Walter O. Weyrauch employed interviews in Germany as a beginning effort designed to determine whether and to what degree lawyers as a professional class have similar personalities and approaches.[43] His study has been criticized for violating some established principles of interviewing and sampling, but it must be remembered that randomness and neatness of structure are not easily attained outside the United States. The merit of Weyrauch's study derives from its effort to break a path.

In a continuation of his work on the European Communities, Stuart Scheingold conducted a program of systematic interviewing of attorneys during the winter of 1964-65. Attorneys often being the only link between the Communities and the businessmen, the kind of advice they offer clients and the directions in which they prod them are of great importance to European development. According to Scheingold, legal outputs provide supportive potential for the political system in the form of specific support from the winners, structural support from the socialized, and possible diffuse support from all parties. Consequently, he treats attorney's advice as legal outputs, not inputs as might be the case in relation to court procedures. This means that the attorney will be looked at in

[43] Jerome E. Carlin, *Lawyers on Their Own* (New Brunswick: Rutgers University Press, 1962); Hubert J. O'Gorman, *Lawyers and Matrimonial Cases* (New York: Free Press of Glencoe, 1963); Erwin O. Smigel, *The Wall Street Lawyer* (New York: Free Press of Glencoe, 1964); Walter O. Weyrauch, *The Personality of Lawyers* (New Haven: Yale University Press, 1964).

two ways, that is, as a producer of outputs and also as a reactor to outputs in the form of executive decisions and judicial rulings. Scheingold also sees it as appropriate to infer the attitudes of clients toward the legal subsystem from the attitudes of their attorneys in order to obtain a clue to the impact of the law on the members of the system.[44]

The five studies suggest possibilities that could be employed in respect to international law, given a combination of substantive and methodological competence. Besides the contribution made by lawyers in the form of briefs and oral presentations to courts, which may have either immediate or delayed effect,[45] their contributions to development of the law itself and to their nations' acceptance of international law are essentially unknown. Here is one of the areas in which simple information gathering is needed, and only a part of the needed information can be obtained from court records.

Precedent

THE PRINCIPLE of *stare decisis*, so firmly implanted in Anglo-American legal methodology, seems on the surface to render its adherents peculiarly ill-equipped for the vicissitudes of international law. And yet the concept of precedent ought to be central to international law. True, if precedent is limited only to court decisions, its utility is slight. But suppose one

[44] Stuart Scheingold, "Law of the New Europe: A Scheme for Political Analysis," mimeographed (Cambridge: Harvard University, Center for International Studies, September, 1965), pp. 21-23. Cf. André Donner, *The Role of the Lawyer in the European Communities* (Evanston: Northwestern University Press, 1968), where more stress is given to the judicial function.

[45] For example, the argument, irrelevant to the case being heard, of Robert Goodloe Harper in *The Amiable Isabella* (1821), 6 Wheaton 65, which is the only support in that case for Justice Miller's citation of *The Amiable Isabella* when holding the courts to be powerless in the face of a Congressional breach of treaty. *The Clinton Bridge* (1867), 1 Woolworth 155, in turn became one of the precedents cited by Miller in support of the decision in the *Head Money Cases* (1884), 112 U.S. 580.

were to construct a continuum ranging from legal systems totally contained by their codes to those whose norms arose totally from behavior. On such a continuum, Anglo-American law would surely lie closer to international law than would the civil law systems of Continental Europe. Both Common and International Law draw their breath from incremental change. In the former, change proceeds gracefully from the cumulative efforts of judicial craftsmen. In the latter, the subjects of the law are also its revisers, engaged, however unwittingly, in a constant up-dating process.

We know little enough of precedent in our own legal system. Refined to the point of art,[46] it has nevertheless escaped the scrutiny reserved for judicial policy-making. Instead, it has been treated simply as a tactic in the service of policy or as the occasion for the manifestation of virtuosity. What has been lacking is a clear notion of how and why precedent, rather than codification, is the option chosen. The evidence points to the inevitability of judicial discretion, exercised (as by appellate courts) through the manipulation of norms or (as by trial and code courts) through the manipulation of "facts." One would imagine that international tribunals, having foresworn precedent, would thus feel freer to exercise discretion; but the limitation on *stare decisis* has simply been symbolic of a whole set of political constraints.

In a customary system, it is hard to see how precedent can be altogether ruled out. Thomas Schelling speaks of "focal points" in any decisional situation, i.e., alternatives so much more conspicuous than the others that they are chosen by default.[47] What endows an alternative with such prominence? One important element is the fact of having been chosen in the past. The focal point must have some characteristic that "qual-

[46] Karl N. Llewellyn, *The Common Law Tradition: Deciding Appeals* (Boston: Little, Brown, 1960), pp. 62-120.

[47] Schelling, *The Strategy of Conflict*, pp. 21-80, 111-13.

itatively distinguishes it from surrounding alternatives."[48] And one such characteristic is transference from a successfully resolved dispute in the past. It is an insufficiently remarked-upon fact of life that, all other things being equal, things will be done as they have been done. In this sense, Kelsen's *Grundnorm* rests on a sound social-psychological foundation.

A customary system is one where, by definition, actors behave as they have in the past. Precedent, instead of inhering in a single institution (the courts), becomes the key to understanding the entire system. The majority of rules achieve legitimacy by usage rather than by identification with a single law-promulgating institution. Precedent may in time become diluted in international law as it has in domestic law. Treaties and codifications may come to supplant custom, as legislation achieved ascendency in English law.

Conformity is another fact of life.[49] The pull of the familiar or of the judgment of peers discourages innovation. Where channels for institutionalized change are lacking, such pressures are bound to be deeply felt. States which are nonconformers are generally those wrapped up in an abnormally cohesive ideology which shields them against consensus-producing forces. Frequently these ideologies are of a chiliastic nature and explicitly reject the existing international system. In the absence of millennial expectation, most states are content to accept international law as the routine judge of its actions because, as Brierly has put it, "the demands that it makes on states are generally not exacting . . . on the whole states find it convenient to observe it. . . ."[50]

Thus change in the legal system is endemic. Indeed, the

[48] *Ibid.*, p. 111.

[49] S. E. Asch, "Effects of Group Pressure Upon the Modification and Distortion of Judgments," in Eleanor E. Maccoby, et al. (eds.), *Readings in Social Psychology*, 3rd edn. (New York: Holt, Rinehart and Winston, 1958), pp. 174-83.

[50] J. L. Brierly, *The Law of Nations*, 6th edn., Sir Humphrey Waldock (ed.) (New York: Oxford University Press, 1963), pp. 71-72.

most telling criticism one could make of international law is that it does not change enough, always lagging behind behavior. Despite the reality of change, however, a counterpressure is always at work. Field has called it "the fiction of completeness." A normative system, he writes,

> . . . is normally thought of as if it were complete in its coverage, inasmuch as each person includes his own inferences as to dubious rules as part of his concept of the legal system.[51]

In international terms, each state fuses legal rules with its interpretation of those rules. The fiction of completeness has been strikingly observed in customary systems, because in these systems there is less likelihood than in municipal systems of there being an authoritative proclamation of *the* law. In primitive societies, the elders are taken to be the authoritative source, but it is empirically demonstrable that their "authoritative" interpretations conflict with each other.[52] The works of international law codifiers also preserve the image of completeness. The recognition by the Statute of the International Court of Justice that treatises form a legitimate source of law indicates the search for authority in an uncentralized environment.

The fiction, Maine suggested, is the earliest and simplest mechanism for legal adaptation. The fiction of completeness gives the appearance of coherence even where day-to-day flux belies it. The belief in stability becomes as much a part of the legal system as does the change which contradicts it. The fiction of completeness, as well as some other less encompassing fictions, smoothes over the inconsistencies that endemic change cannot help but produce.

[51] G. Lowell Field, "Law as an Objective Political Concept," *American Political Science Review* 43 (1949): 229-49.

[52] E.g., Laura Bohannan, "A Genealogical Charter," *Africa* 22 (1952): 301-15.

Brierly's observation concerning the low level of international legal demands is as perceptive as it is initially startling. International law has a high tolerance for conflict. Whether it is, in fact, any higher than the tolerance of municipal law systems is uncertain. The greater magnitude of international violations must be balanced against the greater scope of its jurisdiction. In any event, international law is a normative system of enormous plasticity and adaptability. It lies anchored in the past by its dependence on precedent in the broadest sense and, as man is a creature of habit, precedent serves as a remarkably effective means of securing obedience. But that is only half the coin, for the ever-changing nature of custom and the fictional safeguards against disorienting change allow the system to alter its shape through time without excessive challenges to its validity.

System Change and Legal Evolution

Much work needs to be done on changes in the law that take place concurrently with or as a consequence of basic changes in the international system. Problems encountered in the study of this phase of international change would not be identical with those related to change within an on-going system. For the phenomenon to be dealt with is not gradual change but mutation. In Morton Kaplan's conceptualization, a transformation of the characteristic behavior of a system results from an input that leads to a radical change in the relationships between the variables of the system or even in the identity of the variables.[53] Although Kaplan does not use the term "mutation" in his definition of a step-level function, the basic transformation to which he refers can be treated as a form of system change analogous to the biological mutation which entails an input producing radical transformation. The biological

[53] Morton A. Kaplan, *System and Process in International Politics* (New York: Wiley, 1957), p. 5.

transformation introduces an heritable variation, while the social transformation affects historical continuity.

While Kaplan was concerned about the input and the distinction between the step-level function and other inputs, the greater concern of the student of international law will be with outputs, that is, the extent of change in laws. If he were to identify the laws changed and to isolate them from the laws that were left unchanged, he would be in a position to ascertain just which legal norms warrant the designation "fundamental," because without their change there would have been no fundamental system change. Conceivably, a before-and-after comparison of the laws could be achieved and would yield important information on changes in goals; restructuring of relationships among subsystems; survival of some old goals, roles, and relationships; and the mutual impact of the old that survives and the new that is introduced upon each other and upon systemic processes.[54] Hopefully, a before-and-after comparison would not restrict itself to legal change but would be related to political, economic, and social research that would also help to pinpoint unrealized goals.

According to Hayward R. Alker, some important changes in the international system can be ascertained through a factor analysis of General Assembly roll-call votes, the indicator of change being the changing factor loadings of particular issues and regression coefficients for variables influencing conflict alignments.[55] While analysis of roll-call votes may as a rule indicate only minor system changes, continuation of such analysis from year to year could conceivably reveal trends and cumulative effects.

[54] On the problem of search for structural continuities existing independently of ideological flux and changes in weaponry, see George Liska, "Continuity and Change in International Systems," *World Politics* 16 (1963): 118-36.

[55] Hayward R. Alker, Jr., "Dimensions of Conflict in the General Assembly," *American Political Science Review* 58 (1964): 642-57.

Cumulative effect, particularly if amounting in its sum to significant positive feedback, may turn out to be the true step-level function rather than a single input at a particular moment. For instance, the United Nations has (1) had a centralizing impact on international decision-making, (2) exercised some management of armed forces voluntarily made available, (3) had some control over conflict between nations, and (4) been able to provide a measure of supervision of the execution of international agreements. But its gains in authority have been gradual, extending over too brief a period for a cumulative effect that with assurance could be regarded as a fundamental system change. To keep constant check, assuming that doing so were feasible and that meaningful indicators were selected, could provide trend information that might be used to forestall a subjectively undesirable systemic change or to mitigate its effects. Of course, trend information cannot stimulate the foresight conducive to forestalling or mitigation, if step-level functions are sudden inputs of irresistible magnitude rather than the product of cumulative inputs.

The existence of secondary effects renders difficult any effort to discern trends toward systemic change. Identifying secondary effects and disentangling them from basic trends could overwhelm a researcher with too many variables. It would be preferable to avoid the difficulties with which, for example, Mirko Lamer contended when he examined the world fertilizer economy to determine how changes in one sector of human activity can have widespread systemic effects.[56] A reflector of changes in significant variables is desirable and it may be that an indicator such as General Assembly roll-call votes will serve. Detailed excursions into offbeat areas and into the morass of detail are avoidable if and only if a set of indicators is shown to have the desired reflective quality and

[56] Mirko Lamer, *The World Fertilizer Economy* (Stanford: Stanford University Press, 1957).

also to perform with at least preliminary aggregative effect in respect to crucial variables.[57]

A fairly common assumption is that positive feedback has undesirable, destabilizing effects while negative feedback regulates and stabilizes. Under this assumption, the purpose of discerning systemic trends would be to insert countermeasures in order to avoid or minimize the effects of cumulative positive feedback. In other words, if, for example, what Roberto Lucifero intuitively suggested in a rather remarkable speech—namely, that the national state is but a phase in the evolution of international organization and is being overcome by presently operative processes,[58]—is undesirable, then countermeasures such as Soviet and Gaullist emphasis on sovereignty are in order. But if change is desired, then some form of controlled positive feedback should be sought.

John R. Platt, arguing that social institutions can be changed by an individual who amplifies his intelligence by a social chain reaction that produces an exponential increase in the reaction stimulated by a new idea, suggests that a beneficial runaway chain might have to be employed to combat a malignant runaway chain. Presumably, a beneficial runaway chain would be an adaptive mechanism not available when resistance to change exists at a level inhibiting adaptation. In respect to international belligerence, Platt suggests that insertion of a party structure to convert international tension into party tension might be desirable.[59] Apparently, "feedback tokens," possibly including money, would be needed for reinforcement.

[57] To employ a simple example, a steam pressure gauge conveys information not only about the condition of the water but also about the condition of the container and the fire.

[58] Roberto Lucifero, *Il ritorno di Cristoforo Colombo* (Rome: Tipografia del Senato, 1949).

[59] John R. Platt, "Social Chain Reaction," *Bulletin of Atomic Scientists* 17 (November, 1961): 365-69.

In the absence of careful study of what has happened in the past to effect system changes—bipolarization and alliance rigidity after 1870 is not explained simply in terms of the Franco-Prussian War and the Ems telegram—it may be doubted whether it is possible to distinguish with assurance beneficial and malignant runaway chains. Nor is identification and distinction of runaway chains a sufficient explanation of system change and control of positive feedback, for in addition a measure is needed of the international system's receptivity or absorptive capacity at given times in order to explain why particular chains could get started, let alone reach a runaway condition. The problem is comparable to that of explaining why Japan and not China became Asia's first modern industrial society.[60]

In regard to the law itself, an important question is whether international law changes with system change as do the behavioral rules suggested by Kaplan. Present concern is not about the correctness of Kaplan's suggested rules or their status as generalizations of what international law prescribes. Rather, it is about whether his suggestion that behavioral rules change when systems change is also applicable to international legal norms.

On the more particular war-peace level of change,[61] this problem troubles courts and foreign offices. It may be deduced that if war and the restoration of peace can produce changes in international norms (e.g., as in the case of the human rights approach superseding the minorities treaties approach of the

[60] Norman Jacobs, *The Origin of Modern Capitalism and East Asia* (Hong Kong: Hong Kong University Press, 1958); Thomas C. Smith, *Political Change and Industrial Development in Japan: Government Enterprise, 1868-1880* (Stanford: Stanford University Press, 1955), esp. pp. 3-4, 15, 21-23, 34-35; Karl Hax, *Japan: Wirtschaftsmacht des Fernen Ostens—Ein Beitrag zur Analyse des wirtschaftlichen Wachstums* (Cologne: Westdeutscher Verlag, 1961).

[61] A change from war to peace or vice versa is a change in the condition of a system. Step-level change or system mutation may or may not accompany such a change.

interwar years), then system mutation must have a similar effect. To date we do know that important changes in the international system, characterized by Kaplan as a change from a balance-of-power to a loose bipolar system, occurred. But in what ways was international law transformed to fit the world of 1945 and after instead of that of 1939 and before? Was it even transformed significantly, or does it still, dysfunctionally, reflect the pre-World War II international system? Even a comparison of textbooks of different periods might prove informative, provided the findings were tabulated and aggregated to present systematic evidence of apparently basic behavioral norms that might be compared with a similar structure drawn from nonlegalistic manifestations of international behavior.

Impact of Subsystem Changes

Subsystem changes can affect the international system in many ways. At one subsystem level, regional organization, much has been happening that has received the attention of lawyers and social scientists. At the state level, the impact of internal changes upon the international system has been accorded more attention by diplomatic and economic historians who have had to account for the rise to international influence of such states as Germany, Japan, the United States, and the Soviet Union.

In regard to impact on international law, de Valk, Erades, and others have been giving attention to the current and potential impact of regional organizations, particularly the Western European Communities.[62] Less has been said and certainly much less demonstrated on the impact of internal changes in

[62] W. de Valk, *La Signification de l'intégration européenne pour le développement du droit international moderne* (Leiden: Sijthoff, 1962); L. Erades, "International Law, European Community Law and Municipal Law of Member States," *International and Comparative Law Quarterly* 15 (1966): 117-32.

particular countries. Yet it is inconceivable that the *pax Britannica* did not have its influence on the law. The British lead in the development of the law of the sea is known in regard to such varied matters as prize law and distinctive lights for steam vessels. To what extent the rule of effective occupation represented British rather than a roughly equal influence of the several colonial powers is not clear. What impact on international law resulted from the 19th-century unification and industrialization of Germany? From the industrialization of Russia? Has the impact been only that stemming from reaction to deviance? In what ways has the internal development of Latin American countries, particularly Mexico, affected international law including the law of claims for mistreatment of aliens?[63]

If foreign policy decisions reflect a complex of internal and external constraints, then changes in the state-subsystems or state-units can be presumed to have impact on the international system. However, that such impact can occur does not mean that it necessarily does occur. Nor is it certain whether such impacts as may be traceable correlate with military and naval capability, culture, wealth, prestige, or newness, to mention but a few possible variables. The mere mention of Mexico or any other Latin American state suggests that national influence is not merely a function of armed forces' capability. Nor is newness a variable necessarily associated with culture. A non-Western culture is not a prerequisite for a bankrupt treasury, but it may be an inescapable accompaniment to a transformation from colony into state. Nor was there any-

[63] On the earlier situation in which support of existing regimes was the only route to inducing investment and economic growth and the subsequent bringing to the fore of new leadership groups, see David M. Pletcher, *Rails, Mines, and Progress: Seven American Promoters in Mexico, 1867-1911* (Ithaca: Cornell University Press, 1958); Raymond Vernon, *The Dilemma of Mexico's Development: The Roles of the Private and Public Sectors* (Cambridge: Harvard University Press, 1963), pp. 76-78, 120-22, 127-28.

thing particularly non-Western or culturally different in the United States' proclamation in 1793 of the doctrine of neutral duties or in the Dutch 17th-century advocacy of freedom of the seas. Newness per se, not restricted to a particular time or to the non-Western world, does not appear to have been investigated as a phenomenon[64] or for its impact—despite the perils inherent in the inexperience of leaders of new states as demonstrated in the pre-World War I Balkan tinderbox as well as on both earlier and later occasions—upon the international system and its law. In short, newness should be treated as independent of the cultural dimension which of itself warrants special attention for its norm-generative potential.

Cultural Factors and Value Similarities and Differences

An odd paradox surrounds the study of values in law. No one doubts for a moment that legal rules are value statements. Indeed, as pointed out earlier, the problem now seems to be to mount a "revisionist" attack on this belief, to draw out the non-normative content of rules. Notwithstanding the prevalent identification of legal rules with value statements, the *systematic* study of values has almost wholly bypassed law. It is in itself a recent field of study, insofar as it grounds itself in the behavioral sciences rather than in philosophy.

The current branches of value inquiry have neither touched

[64] An approach to an investigation of newness is made by Doreen Warriner (ed.), *Contrasts in Emerging Societies: Readings in the Social and Economic History of South-East Europe in the Nineteenth Century*, selected and trans. G. F. Cushing, E. D. Tappe, V. deS. Pinto, and Phillis Auty (London: Athlone Press, University of London, 1965). Also reflective of psychological factors related to newness and exaggerated by yearnings for Great Power status, not unlike what emanates from today's new states and from new regimes such as Red China, is M. Andrea Rapisardi-Mirabelli, *La Guerre Italo-Turque et le droit des gens*, reprint from *Revue de droit international et de législation comparée* (Brussels: Bureau de la Revue, 1913).

the law nor involved jurisprudential writers.[65] The conceptual foundations for such study have been typically rigorous, but one looks in vain for even a passing reference to lawyers or the law.[66] Values seem to be operative everywhere *but* in the law. Yet the greater the cultural heterogeneity of the area in which law is supposed to operate, the more relevant value concerns become. It is a tacit premise of legal theory that a legal system depends upon a value consensus and contributes to that consensus.

International law has been somewhat lax in considering the implications of cultural diversity for itself due to a peculiar set of historical circumstances. International law grew out of European values at a time when those values were being diffused globally through a kind of cultural imperialism.[67] Consequently, the reality of underlying cultural diversity did not make itself felt until the post–World War II dismantling of colonial empires made it evident that what was needed was not a culturally specific but a truly intercultural law. For that which is culturally specific may well create intercultural conflict rather than resolve it. Actually, systematically deviant behavior had cropped up earlier, particularly in the initially hostile attitude of the Soviet Union toward international law and traditional diplomacy.[68]

[65] Rollo Handy and Paul Kurtz, *A Current Appraisal of the Behavioral Sciences* (Great Barrington, Mass.: Behavioral Research Council, 1963), pp. 131-36.

[66] Philip E. Jacob, et al., "Values and Their Function in Decision-Making," *American Behavioral Scientist* 5 (Supplement, May, 1963). Law never explicitly enters this otherwise admirable outline, subtitled "Toward an Operational Definition for Use in Public Affairs Research." Even the section on "elite groups" omits lawyers from consideration.

[67] A view most vividly expressed in F.S.C. Northrop's analysis of the world dispersion of the contract principle, *Philosophical Anthropology and Practical Politics* (New York: Macmillan, 1960), pp. 323-27, and *The Complexity of Legal and Ethical Experience: Studies in the Method of Normative Subjects* (Boston: Little, Brown, 1959), pp. 299-300.

[68] For a provocative discussion of the question whether a deep interpenetration of Western and Russian values is possible, see Emanuel

If the universality of international law is in fact "make-believe,"[69] it behooves us to determine the nature of the fragmenting forces. The decline of Western power in the underdeveloped world removed what was frequently a veneer of European values. The ethnocentric identification of law per se with its Western manifestations cannot long survive when Western institutions confront indigenous legal forms. It remains true that, with varying degrees of success, Western conceptions of law were grafted onto native institutions. What must be recognized is that, surface similarities aside, non-Western concepts of law express different (although not always contradictory) social goals.[70] The traditionally monolithic concept of a globally relevant international law must give way to a transitional concept of cultural and legal pluralism. It is from the latter base, grounded in empirical reality, that the movement towards a realistic globalism must begin.

International law has always been bounded in space and time. Despite its clear links to Roman law, it is a post-feudal phenomenon. The accumulated rules, methodologies, and commentaries that make up its corpus started at that point in time when the feudal polity began to give way to the state. Nevertheless, it is also true that other times and other places produced a sophisticated level of international intercourse. In the West not only the Roman Empire but the earlier Greek city-state community constituted regulated, law-producing areas. The East attained a high degree of international order

---

Sarkisyanz, *Russland und der Messianismus des Orients—Sendungsbewusstsein und politischer Chiliasmus des Ostens* (Tübingen: J.C.B. Mohr, 1955).

[69] Myres S. McDougal and Harold D. Lasswell, "The Identification and Appraisal of Diverse Systems of Public Order," *American Journal of International Law* 53 (1959): 1-29.

[70] Cf. B. S. Chon, "From Indian Status to British Contract," *Journal of Economic History* 21 (1961): 613-28; F. Luchaire, "L'Apport européen dans l'élaboration des droits nationaux des pays en voie de développement," *Revue Administrative* 102-103 (1964-65): 565-81.

long before European penetration, e.g., ancient India and pre-Han China. We must, therefore, accept two kinds of international law for study: first, the familiar sort, sanctified by the usages of states and centered on the European value-area; second, an analytic concept of international order which will adequately describe those historical instances that fall outside the first (or concrete) concept.

In the face of this evidence, it is puzzling to report the lack of study in our time of the cultural diversity that precedes law. McDougal and Lasswell's "Diverse Systems of Public Order" comes closest. Nothing, however, approaches in scope Wigmore's world legal inventory of 1928.[71] The primary reason for this neglect, at least insofar as public international law is concerned, is the feeling that no necessary connection exists between legal-cultural pluralism and the international legal order. In any case, private international law was thought to be adequately dealing with these questions. It did adequately deal with them, from the practitioner's standpoint. Yet the division of labor between private and public international law, while productive in the short term, has had the unintended effect of separating public international law from relevant empirical data.

Private international law has all along had to accept the spectrum of state legal systems (and, inferentially, cultures), for its function was to resolve the conflicts divergence produced. Public international law, by contrast, is predicated upon uniformity, reinforced in the 19th century by the hope of Christianizing and civilizing the quaint peoples in far-off places—quite a contrast from Lord Stowell's recognition of the legal validity of the customs of non-European peoples.[72] Partly

[71] John Henry Wigmore, *A Panorama of the World's Legal Systems* (St. Paul: West, 1928). See also the perspectives sketched in McDougal, Lasswell, and W. Michael Reisman, "Theories About International Law," *Virginia Journal of International Law* 8 (1968): 188ff.

[72] *The Helena* (1801), 4 C. Rob. 6; *The Madonna Del Burso* (1802),

this has been due, as we have noted, to the genuine cultural homogeneity that prevailed during international law's formative period. But other factors entered in, too, most notably the inductive method. In a general way, legislated, promulgated law is deductive, moving from a general rule to instances of behavior. Customary law is, by contrast, inductive. General rules arise out of aggregated instances of behavior. The rules then apply to behavior, but in the way they are formed, there is a definite movement from the particular to the general.

One of the consequences of the inductive construction of legal rules is that those within the system look for what ties parts together rather than for what separates them. The legally relevant phenomena are those that conform to rules already established or those that, by tying in with other phenomena, give promise of producing some new generalization. Induction leads one to continuously search for likes and ignore unlikes. But induction, despite the claim it has upon our common-sense selves, has its philosophical drawbacks. As philosophers of science have noted, even the most ambitious collection of documenting instances will not assure against the subsequent appearance of a disconfirming instance.[73] Against every psychological pull, it must be admitted that there is no *logical* law of inertia. The mere existence of an inductively generated proposition is not sufficient to render it resistant to events. But too often it is precisely the psychological pull, rather than logical considerations, which has exerted itself upon public international law.

Inductively generated rules, once stated, have been assumed to possess global validity. They have been thought to have been validated by past instances which put them out of the reach of future events. Now that the homogeneous cultural

---

4 C. Rob. 172; *The Hurtige Hane* (1801), 3 C. Rob. 324; *The Fortune* (1801), 2 C. Rob. 92.

[73] Karl R. Popper, *The Logic of Scientific Discovery* (London: Hutchinson, 1959), p. 27.

veneer has fallen away from much of the world, the confirming instances of the past offer no proof for the present. The inherent weakness of induction has come to plague international law as it did the physical sciences. If induction is to continue in use—and the nature of customary systems makes that almost inevitable—then some recognition must follow of its limitations, the primary recognition being that international law attempts to function in a culturally polyglot world.

But could not cultural diversity be simply a surface phenomenon, interesting but legally of little concern? Cultures and values imply not simply the external world of diverse social and political institutions but diverse perceptions as well. What is involved are alternative means of conceiving of the world and what is important in it. F. S. C. Northrop has demonstrated that law is intimately tied to epistemology—to the way in which we know.[74] And there are many ways in which we know, many means by which different pictures of the world are confirmed. Each of these possesses different consequences for law. An international public law out of phase with the patterns of thought of some part of the world could hardly be readily accepted there.

The time will surely come when we have something like a "value map" of the world, such that the major value divisions are clear to us. That is a goal toward which the social sciences can best advance. The picture that may emerge will probably be the same kind that faces the central government of a federal, pluralistic state, except that international law lacks the machinery of diffusion, administration, and imposition that a state is presumed to possess.

The alternatives that are apt to present themselves are these: first, to accept a partition of international law into international law*s*, united by a smaller body of shared norms than now is assumed to exist, and aided by a public "conflict of law"

[74] F.S.C. Northrop, "The Epistemology of Legal Judgments," *Northwestern University Law Review* 58 (1964): 732-49.

specialty; second, to attempt through modern techniques of communication and diffusion of information to build up a common world legal culture cutting across regional divisions. Both may be needed, not just to gain respect for international law but also to give substance to the "general principles of law" for which search has gone on since the words were written into the Statute of the Permanent Court of International Justice without thought that they might embrace non-European principles.

Intercultural Law

THE PROBLEM of intercultural relations is now with us in a form unknown to Europeans at least since the heyday of Ottoman and earlier Arab power. Indeed, once the tide of conquest abated and systems of deference appeared in the form of consular courts and extraterritoriality, the resultant compromise between the principles of the personality and the territoriality of law were quite different from what is needed to meet today's circumstances. Degeneration of the Capitulations is symbolic of the more widespread degeneration of patterns of deference into the rule of the stronger and more mobile. In extreme form the rule of the stronger and more mobile took the form of imperialism and colonialism.

As has been suggested, there is much to be learned from the blending of European and non-Western law under the mantle of imperialist rule.[75] But in this greatly decolonized world much more of what is pertinent to cultural mingling as it relates to law is to be learned from the reception of Western law by those non-Western societies whose formal independence

[75] See, e.g., René Maunier, *The Sociology of Colonies: An Introduction to the Study of Race Contact*, ed. and trans. E. O. Lorimer, 2 vols. (London: Routledge and Kegan Paul, 1949), vol. 2; Joseph Schacht, *An Introduction to Islamic Law* (Oxford: Clarendon, 1964), chap. XIV; Anwar Ahmad Qadri, *Islamic Jurisprudence in the Modern World (A Reflection Upon Comparative Study of the Law)* (Bombay: N. M. Tripathi, 1963), chap. XV.

survived Western imperialism and from extensions of official law by new, modernizing states.[76] Both asserting independence and imposing official law are acts that entail a measure of identification with and even imitation (however subconscious) of the more powerful. The possibly common phenomenon of identification with the powerful might explain more about the development of international law in both its European and global phases than simple concentration upon the consequences of independence for much of Africa and Asia.[77]

It seems to be generally accepted among scholars that international law needs to shed its appearance of being foreign law and to take on the character of a truly intercultural law. The shallow version of this thesis would require change in the content of the rules so that they may reflect non-Western values. A more profound view cannot escape the realization that many and perhaps most international legal norms do not require transformation of substance in order to attain an intercultural quality of more than European scope. Indeed, there is evidence that seemingly desirable changes would prove undesirable for non-Western states that realize reasonable aspirations for national development.

What we have suggested in this section is that evidence from national law is at hand to permit inferences pertinent to international law. This evidence can illuminate the process by which existing legal norms can pass from the state of being foreign into the state of being truly intercultural. Foreign-

[76] See, e.g., Bülent Davran, "Die Rechtsstellung der Pflegekinder und die Rezeption des Schweizerischen Zivilgesetzbuches," *Annales de la Faculté de droit d'Istanbul* 3 (1954): 405-24; Marc Galanter, "Hindu Law and the Development of the Modern Indian Legal System," (Paper presented at the Annual Meeting of the American Political Science Association, September, 1964).

[77] For quite a suggestive article that also has potential relevance for explanation, possibly in terms of psychological distance, of the growth of blocs and the significance of bloc leadership, see Mark Mulder, "The Power Variable in Communication Experiments," *Human Relations* 13 (1960): 241-57.

ness, it may be recalled, is a state that may but need not necessarily be accompanied by imposition. From this it follows that the processes of the uncoerced reception of European law and the extension of official law, the latter perhaps embracing an unmeasured proportion of international law, should be instructive. Moreover, appropriate comparison with the forced process under imperial rule would aid the identification of indigenous processes of legitimation not of authorities or governments but of legal norms.

Chapter VI: International Procedures and Agents

Intermingling of Law and Bargaining

Over the years international law has developed a complex classification of the means by which disputes may be peacefully resolved: "mediation," "arbitration," "conciliation," "judicial settlement," "fact-finding," "good offices." While systems of classification can be helpful in sorting out differences, they also obscure likenesses. In a system with as many contingent roles and *ad hoc* situations as international law, there may be some profit in temporarily telescoping the categories of pacific settlement in order to see, first, whether there are any unifying factors and, second, whether there might not be other forms of classification that tell us more about how peaceful settlement works. By so telescoping the categories of peaceful settlement we remove the technical connotations of not only the classificatory terms but also the expression "peaceful settlement" itself. This avoids excluding likenesses that may also be found in applying norms by means of procedures other than those that would ordinarily be embraced in the rubric "peaceful settlement" and at the same time permit us to see those features of other procedures that enter into peaceful settlement.

We shall call this telescoped concept simply "mediation," with the caveat that it need not connote any of the characteristics of what is technically known as mediation. The concept has three principal elements. (1) It involves a movement from dyadic interaction to triadic interaction.[1] That is, what

[1] Vilhelm Aubert, "Conflict and Dissensus: Two Types of Conflict and of Conflict Resolution," *Journal of Conflict Resolution* 7 (1963): 26-42. For a useful review of the functions, tactics, resources, and capabilities of third parties, see Oran Young, *The Intermediaries: Third*

was originally a relationship between two persons—two belligerents—is converted into a three-person relationship, in which the belligerents are joined by some "third person" who comes between them. (2) It operates, at the lowest level, in a contingent fashion. It occurs when necessary and need not be associated with formal courts or compulsory procedures. (3) Finally, it exists independently of any means of coercion, although these may come to be associated with it. Such a mediator comes between the conflicting parties with the aim minimally of suggesting potential solutions or facilitating mutual concessions, or both.

Within this and similar frameworks a distinction is frequently made between "law" and "bargaining."[2] In the literature of international law a dichotomization is often made between "judicial settlement" and "mediation."[3] The law-bargaining division is made along the same lines. Legal conflicts, it is said, are "conflicts of value" while bargaining involves "conflicts of interest."[4] Such a conceptualization has its uses, but it also has two important defects. First, it sets outside the purview of the law those means of conflict resolution that occur informally and in noninstitutional settings. Since international relations, not being centralized, is replete with these *ad hoc* arrangements, it seems self-defeating to exclude them from the typology of legal processes. When that is done, there is very little left to deal with. Second, and more important, the dichotomy turns out on examination to be far less clear-cut than first imagined.

Bargaining itself, though it appears wholly rational, rests upon a normative assumption. Bargaining is used because

---

Parties in International Crises (Princeton: Princeton University Press, 1967), chaps. 1-3.

[2] Aubert "Conflict and Dissensus," pp. 30f.

[3] Charles de Visscher, *Theory and Reality in Public International Law* (Princeton: Princeton University Press, 1957), p. 335.

[4] Aubert, "Conflict and Dissensus," p. 31.

prior procedural norms have been accepted. The solution is not justified in terms of rules; but rules are essential if it is to be reached. The bargaining process is stylized and conventional, and its conventional elements cannot be taken for granted. Our separation of bargaining from law has been facilitated by peculiarities in the American legal system. Judgments of American courts are almost always of the winner-take-all variety. Court-imposed compromise is almost never seen,[5] a fact glaringly evident in automobile injury cases. The sharp contrast between the all-or-nothing verdicts handed down by courts and the flexibility of bilaterally arranged settlements appears to reinforce the differences between law and bargaining. In fact, however, there is no necessary reason why courts could not issue compromise verdicts. They do so in other municipal systems and we misrepresent the judicial process when we attribute the rigidities of American jurisprudence to the institution in general—perhaps even demand it as has been done in criticisms of arbitration.[6] In fact, there are genuine loci of bargaining in the American legal system, but they are at a low level of visibility. We see little of what goes on in the pre-trial conference or in discussions between prosecution and defense over the dropping and retention of charges.[7] But these bargaining acts play important roles and demonstrate that law and bargaining are inextricably interwoven.

International legal roles are frequently occupied on a contingent basis, i.e., as circumstances require; the incumbent of a legal role slips into another and more long-lived role when

[5] John E. Coons, "Approaches to Court Imposed Compromise—The Uses of Doubt and Reason," *Northwestern University Law Review* 58 (1964): 750-94.

[6] E.g., W. C. Dennis, "Compromise—The Great Defect of Arbitration," *Columbia Law Review* 11 (1911): 493-515.

[7] Maurice Rosenberg, "Court Congestion: Status, Causes, and Proposed Remedies," in Harry W. Jones, (ed.), *The Courts, the Public, and the Law Explosion* (Englewood Cliffs: Prentice-Hall, 1965), pp. 29-59.

the contingency has passed. This being the case, it seems self-defeating to define "law" so narrowly that these *ad hoc* activities cannot be assimilated to it. If bargaining itself is norm-governed, and if "law" and "bargaining" occur in the same institutional context, there is no compelling reason to segregate them.[8]

Some sort of mediation enters whether or not conflict resolution is affected through an imposed verdict or a mutually agreed upon compromise. Indeed, it may even be said that a kind of mediation takes place when conflict resolution occurs in what is outwardly a simple bilateral negotiation. Too often we have mistakenly equated the mediation *function* with judicial institutions. Just as we have broadened our concept of third-party settlement to embrace these circumstances, so we can now enlarge it further to include situations in which even the third person seems not to be present, i.e., "bargaining."

The apparent absence of the mediator need not necessarily imply the absence of mediation per se, if we are willing to redefine the third person.[9] There is manifold evidence in the history of international relations of outwardly bilateral negotiations in which neither party pressed its full advantage and in which both exercised restraint in defining and pursuing their objectives. There is even experimental evidence that, although resorted to only when another person was perceived to be unwilling to fulfill wants but was the only person able to do so, individuals with a capacity to threaten do so only after a moral appeal has proved ineffective.[10] The present relationship

[8] Several excellent examples of the intertwining of law and bargaining are presented in C. Neale Ronning, *Law and Politics in Inter-American Diplomacy* (New York: Wiley, 1963). For a treatment of legal and political analyses of international affairs as complementary, see Louis Henkin, *How Nations Behave: Law and Foreign Policy* (New York: Praeger for the Council on Foreign Relations, 1968).

[9] Michael Barkun, "Conflict Resolution Through Implicit Mediation," *Journal of Conflict Resolution* 8 (1964): 121-30.

[10] David R. Schmitt, "The Invocation of Moral Obligation," *Sociometry* 27 (1964): 299-310.

between the United States and the Soviet Union has often been described in this way. Yet a classical bargaining model could scarcely account for this kind of circumspection. Of the same type is the general ethos of restraint that suffused the balance-of-power system, in which maximum short-term gains were sacrificed in the interests of long-term stability.

It is characteristic of these situations that the participants sense that they are both members of some common community or system from which both derive advantages. Their membership in this community of interests makes certain demands upon them, the primary one being that they will do nothing that will jeopardize the survival of the community. For them these demands constitute norms; to the extent that the community is cohesive and solidly based, its members internalize these norms. The norms become part of the predispositions that the parties bring to any decisional situation. When common norms so influence the thinking of disputants as to decrease the level of demands that they make upon one another, the norms themselves become the third person. In an analytic sense the relationship has reached a triadic stage, for community norms have intervened between the purely selfish demands of the antagonists.

So conceptualized, few bilateral situations remain wholly bilateral or wholly bargains. The element of law so suffuses these instances of "implicit mediation" as to collapse any meaningful law-bargaining distinction. The national policy-maker may perceive the same environment in any of a number of ways, determined not only by the preponderance of evidence but also by institutional role constraints, cultural patterns, personal predispositions, and internalized norms. The policy-maker in a sense "carves out" of this plastic reality his own picture of events.[11]

[11] Richard C. Snyder, H. W. Bruck, and Burton Sapin, "Decision-Making as an Approach to the Study of International Politics," in Snyder, Bruck, and Sapin (eds.), *Foreign Policy Decision-Making*

Once we recognize the importance of the cognitive element in decision-making, it is easy to see the role of intangibles. Law need not always be associated with palpable sanctions to make its presence felt. When it enters into the complex calculus of national decision-making simply as information concerning the substance of decision, it is just as much a factor in human behavior as when it acts through threat of negative sanctions.

International law, so poor in the implements of enforcement, possesses a rich and widely diffused set of ideas. The international community of law-trained decision-makers, many in high policy positions, provides a geographical continuity even in the absence of tightly structured institutions. The diffusion of norms, a common literature, and specific approaches to problem-solving permeating this professional group allow for coordination at a previously ignored level of visibility. Adam Smith's metaphor of the invisible hand has had its abuses but has had its uses as well. There *are* self-regulating systems; individual decisions *can* mesh even though each decision remains discrete and independent. Distaste for the values which self-regulation may have brought to the fore in the economic arena ought not to obscure its relevance to international law.

Diffusion of the substance and skills of international law allows decision-makers in independent political systems to concert their actions. An international law subculture transcending political boundaries allows states to make useful and verifiable predictions of the behavior of others. By introducing an

---

(New York: Free Press of Glencoe, 1962), pp. 14-185. See also Dean G. Pruitt, "Definition of the Situation as a Determinant of International Action," in Herbert C. Kelman (ed.), *International Behavior: A Social-Psychological Analysis* (New York: Holt, Rinehart and Winston, 1965), pp. 391-432. On definition of the situation at the outbreak of the Korean War, see Glenn D. Paige, *The Korean Decision [June 24-30, 1950]* (New York: Free Press, 1968), pp. 96-100, 130-34, 147, 169-79, 244-52, 258-61, 294-95.

element of predictability into the flux of international relations, international law allows states to allocate their resources rationally and to act with some assurance of the responses their actions will engender in others.

Agents of Diplomatic Intercourse

THE AGENTS of international intercourse have multiplied to include many more functionaries than the traditional ambassador and consul. No one has called this development more forcefully to scholars' attention than Michael H. Cardozo.[12] Unfortunately, the field is not well-trodden by social scientists or lawyers. Some hortatory literature can be found.[13] Special situations, such as the use of scientists as negotiators at Geneva in 1958, have caught the attention of several scholars, perhaps because novelty was associated with the dramatic issue of nuclear disarmament in the atmosphere of East-West confrontation.[14] But less spectacular events and functions receive at most sporadic attention. Much more attention is given to national foreign aid policies than to international system developments that may attain life independent of national policies. Yet, if international society is in the process of development through the growth of functional cooperation, then it would seem that more attention could be concentrated on

[12] Michael H. Cardozo, *Diplomats in International Cooperation: Stepchildren of the Foreign Service* (Ithaca: Cornell University Press, 1962). See also Clifton E. Wilson, "The Information Agent Abroad: New Dimension in International Law," *Journalism Quarterly* 42 (1965): 243-52.

[13] E.g., Vincent M. Barnett, Jr., "Changing Problems of U.S. Representation Abroad," *Public Administration* 17 (1957): 20-31.

[14] Harold Karan Jacobson and Eric Stein, *Diplomats, Scientists, and Politicians: The United States and the Nuclear Test Ban Negotiations* (Ann Arbor: University of Michigan Press, 1966), esp. chaps. III, VI; Robert Gilpin, *American Scientists and Nuclear Weapons Policy* (Princeton: Princeton University Press, 1962); Donald A. Strickland, "Scientists as Negotiators: The 1958 Geneva Conference of Experts," *Midwest Journal of Political Science* 18 (1964): 372-84.

developing international communications networks and on the growth of international functional elites.

With relatively little done on networks and elites in such functional areas as agriculture, finance, and science, we can do little but exhort and note that the situation is somewhat similar in regard to private activity. For example, one of us asked a student to look into the possibility of ascertaining the reality of some scientists' assertion that, because of their international activities and their use of a common, nonpolitical language, the scientists are pioneers in the establishment of an international society. Unfortunately, even such basic data as who belongs to what organizations, who attends meetings of such organizations, who are officers, and what is done besides just meeting for a few days is poorly kept, scattered, and requires a tedious task of collection. So-called analyses of developments are little more than pious statements and assumptions lacking empirical support. It would appear that the first task is to collect and classify basic data, and that this data should not confine itself to private persons and their activities but should also include much more and better organized information on agricultural attachés, cultural attachés, special functional missions, and the like, so that we can obtain better measures of international societal development in both its public and private sectors.

In regard to the traditional diplomat, certain directions of investigation other than the well-known approaches of Satow, Nicolson, and others have been suggested by recent studies. Suzanne Keller has dealt with diplomatic communication in terms not of conscious operational codes but of social factors of which the diplomat is unaware and over which he has no control. The social group from which the diplomat comes is taken as a primary object of study. Diplomatic communications themselves can be dealt with in respect to (1) technical knowledge of the symbols used by others for the purpose of establishing cognitive contact and (2) emotional reaction to what is said or written and agreement on the feelings that symbols are expected to evoke.[15]

In the direction of focus on the role of the national, Stewart E. Perry treats the national role as a mobilizing factor that coordinates the efforts of one society against another and can indulge almost any personality pattern. Although offering only a brief, suggestive explanation, Perry characterizes official representation of one's country as the most rigid definition of the national role, the most difficult to modify, and the least understood by the non-national.[16] Diplomacy and the law of diplomacy, particularly that part of the law that circumscribes the diplomat's activities in the receiving country, can be explained in depth through focus upon the diplomat's social group and the constraints of the national role. The bargaining process and, more narrowly, the negotiating process that engages the diplomat in at least some of his functions is vital to the adaptation of international law to situational and other variables. By making the humans who perform part of the bargaining process the object of inquiry with reference to their social roots and acquired roles, an explanation avoids the trap of claiming that it is adequate when limiting itself to overt substance and procedures.

Bargaining and Negotiation

In an earlier section, reference was made to bargaining as a feature of the judicial process. More obvious is the relationship of bargaining and negotiation to the international agreement-making process. In fact, bargaining and negotiation are the basic processes in the making of agreements. In the literature of international law relatively little attention is accorded these processes, for the focus has been upon the legal effects,

[15] Suzanne Keller, "Diplomacy and Communications," *Public Opinion Quarterly* 20 (1956): 176-82.

[16] Stewart E. Perry, "Notes on the Role of the National: A Social-Psychological Concept for the Study of International Relations," *Journal of Conflict Resolution* 1 (1957): 346-63.

the formalities and norms relevant to determination of competence to become party to an international agreement, the powers of the negotiators, and similar matters.[17] However, focus upon the bargaining and negotiating processes, without screening from view the norms and formalities that are operative at the several stages of negotiations, is what permits the discovery of explanations for both legal prescriptions and nonlegal formalities surrounding bargaining.[18]

Of the several economists, sociologists, and social psychologists who have contributed to the study of bargaining and negotiations, the most important contributor to theory has been Thomas C. Schelling whose treatise on *The Strategy of Conflict* clarified the differences between tacit bargaining, in which communication is incomplete or impossible, and explicit bargaining. When negotiations are a part of the bargaining process and entail face-to-face confrontation, other elements are still a part of the process. In confrontations such as the Cuban crisis it is evident that not only the President's speech but also the silent language, exemplified by naval action and the threat carried by troop movements, made it clear who was held responsible and what corrective action was expected.

The conflict element is central to Schelling and to the application of Schelling's ideas to international affairs by Fred C. Iklé.[19] Whether they must properly be included in analyzing all bargaining situations is somewhat questionable. Perhaps the requirement of conflict derives from an essentially Hobbesian view of human nature. Or it may be that headline events such as labor-management conflict, East-West con-

[17] E.g., J. Mervyn Jones, *Full Powers and Ratification* (Cambridge, England: The University Press, 1946); Hans Blix, *Treaty-Making Power* (London: Stevens, 1960).

[18] Wesley L. Gould, "Laboratory, Law, and Anecdote: Negotiations and the Integration of Data," *World Politics* 18 (1965): 95, 101-103.

[19] Fred Charles Iklé, *How Nations Negotiate* (New York, Evanston, and London: Harper & Row, 1964).

flict, and racial conflict drive problem-solving situations from the mind.[20] That problem-solving situations exist and entail integrative bargaining of a somewhat different nature than the bargaining occurring in predominantly conflict situations is suggested by Richard E. Walton and Robert B. McKersie.[21] Each case requires classification on the basis of both the presence and the intensity of the conflict element if the outcome is to be an analysis of bargaining and negotiation that covers all known manifestations. Such an approach would at the least avoid so broad a definition of conflict as to render the term useless as a classifier of international situations.

The outcomes of negotiations—and hence, their effects in international law—may be dependent upon the situation prevailing at the time of negotiation as well as the type of issue or problem. Such situation-related outcomes as extension of an existing arrangement, normalization of relations, redistribution, innovation, or side effects such as propaganda, deterrence, maintaining contacts, and influencing third states may, separately or in combination, serve as reasons for negotiating. Clearly, the outcome, particularly when side effects are the primary objective, need not be agreement. No agreement or continued negotiations are both possible outcomes. And even agreement may not settle issues at stake but merely make provision for subsequent settlement by a third party as a means of saving face.

Determination of objectives and analysis of tactics in specific bargaining situations can be rendered somewhat more certain by the application of social science techniques. For

20 A survey of an earlier period, 1941-53, found 68 abstracted psychological articles dealing with peace and 1,048 dealing with war. Joseph B. Cooper, "Psychological Literature on the Prevention of War," *Bulletin of the Research Exchange on the Prevention of War* 3 (January, 1955): 2-15.

21 Richard E. Walton and Robert B. McKersie, *A Behavioral Theory of Labor Negotiations: An Analysis of a Social Interaction System* (New York: McGraw-Hill, 1965).

example, Lloyd Jensen resorted to content analysis of the verbatim records of the disarmament negotiations from 1946 to 1960. Jensen's concentration upon the negotiation records was facilitated by his use of an index based on substantive concessions and retractions made by the two parties and by a second index based on the level of agreement reached at various times. It proved possible to extract an operational code of five rules relevant to disarmament negotiations. In view of what it indicates about the effects of different levels of tension, confidence in deterrence, and feelings of insecurity were disarmament to result, Jensen's study provides insights into the propensities to negotiate and to agree in this particular issue area.[22]

Case studies such as Jensen's form one set of data, important to the law-making and law-maintaining processes on the international level, that provide the meat for generalizations concerning international negotiations. Bryant Wedge and Cyril Muromcew undertook the examination of another verbatim record, that of the Eighteen-Nation Disarmament Conference, and studied it systematically from a communications viewpoint to display radical contrasts in Soviet and American reasoning, related negotiating styles, and apparent misperceptions.[23] Friedheim's studies of the Law of the Sea Conferences of 1958 and 1960 provide important insights into the impact of non-Western states on a process previously almost a Euro-American monopoly. Bechhoefer has indicated one route from bilateral U.S.–U.S.S.R. exchanges, through in-

[22] Lloyd Jensen, "Postwar Disarmament Negotiations: A Study in American-Soviet Bargaining Behavior," Ph.D. diss., University of Michigan, 1963 (Ann Arbor: University Microfilms 63-6910). For the parts published, see "Soviet-American Bargaining Behavior in the Postwar Disarmament Negotiations," *Journal of Conflict Resolution* 7 (1963): 522-41; "Military Capabilities and Bargaining Behavior," *ibid.* 9 (1965): 155-63.

[23] Bryant Wedge and Cyril Muromcew, "Psychological Factors in Soviet Disarmament Negotiation," *Journal of Conflict Resolution* 9 (1965): 18-36.

formal eight-state discussions and a twelve-state meeting, to the conference of 1956 that produced the Statute of the International Atomic Energy Agency. Both David H. Zook, Jr., and Bryce Wood have, in their treatment of the Chaco war, indicated how negotiating positions can shift in accordance with apparent and actual military situations and even end in a face-saving agreement of a sham arbitration *ex aequae et bono* with the award predetermined, something that occurs far more frequently in domestic labor-management arbitrations.[24] Sham arbitration of the Chaco dispute carried to an extreme the third party function of relieving the sense of inadequacy inherent in the making of concessions.[25]

Case studies are restricted undertakings that require integration not only with other case studies but also with studies by participants such as Arthur Lall who has not only published works dealing with particular negotiations and particular negotiating nations but also produced a wider ranging study in which he articulates a number of more general operational rules.[26] In addition, as the broader studies by Walton

[24] Robert L. Friedheim, "The Politics of the Sea: A Study of Law-Making by Conference," Ph.D. diss., University of Washington, 1962 (Ann Arbor: University Microfilms 62-6590); and "The 'Satisfied' and 'Dissatisfied' States Negotiate International Law: A Case Study," *World Politics* 18 (1965): 20-41; Bernard G. Bechhoefer, "Negotiating the Statute of the International Atomic Energy Agency," *International Organization* 13 (1959): 38-59; David H. Zook, Jr., *The Conduct of the Chaco War* (New York: Bookman Associates, 1960); Bryce Wood, *The United States and Latin American Wars, 1932-1942* (New York: Columbia University Press, 1966), pp. 149-58. On sham arbitrations in labor management relations, see Paul R. Hays, *Labor Arbitration—A Dissenting View* (New Haven: Yale University Press, 1966), pp. 62-63; Martin Mayer, *The Lawyers* (New York: Dell, 1968), pp. 365-67.

[25] Dean G. Pruitt and Douglas F. Johnson, "Mediation as an Aid to Face Saving in Negotiation," Studies of the Dynamics of Cooperation and Conflict, Technical Report No. 7, Office of Naval Research (Buffalo: State University of New York, Department of Psychology, January 10, 1969), pp. 14, 19.

[26] Arthur Lall, "Negotiating Disarmament—The Eighteen Nation Disarmament Conference: The First Two Years, 1962-1964," Cornell

and McKersie, Schelling, and Iklé demonstrate, the negotiating and broader bargaining processes are subject to study along a broader spectrum of activities than just those of international politics. Much can be learned from studies of labor negotiations, international business negotiations,[27] and negotiations between metropolitan governmental units that, in their independence of one another, must engage in tactics akin to diplomacy.[28] Unfortunately, what is not so well known and should be incorporated into studies of bargaining behavior is, as has been noted earlier, the bargaining at the pre-trial conference and in discussions between prosecution and defense over the retention or dropping of charges. Such an inclusion is desirable as a step in developing and testing cross-level hypotheses that would be relevant to legal proceedings as well as to economic and political negotiations.

Experiments in Bargaining

Bargaining experiments may or may not provide adequate tests of models derived from real world observations and may or may not generate propositions relevant to real world bargaining situations. The bargaining experiment is less an analogue to the wind-tunnel experiment, later to be verified by test flights, than a substitute source of information permitting the observation and recording of messages. The probability is

---

Research Papers in International Studies, no. 2 (Ithaca: Center for International Studies, Cornell University, 1964); *How Communist China Negotiates* (New York: Columbia University Press, 1968); *Modern International Negotiation: Principles and Practice* (New York: Columbia University Press, 1966).

[27] E.g., the instances reported in Richard D. Robinson, *Cases in International Business* (New York: Holt, Rinehart and Winston, 1962).

[28] E.g., Matthew Holden, Jr., "The Governance of the Metropolis as a Problem in Diplomacy," *Journal of Politics* 26 (1964): 627-47, which contains a proposal for testing the Haas, Kaplan, and Deutsch models of international processes by reference to strategies of metropolitan consensus formation.

high that what is observed and recorded is a consequence of the structure of the game and not a miniature replication of international or other simulated processes.[29] Hypotheses generated in the game may have relevance only to that particular game itself. Yet, certain features of games and of simulations employing human subjects are comparable to those of international relations, above all, to the interpersonal and small group situations that do exist in international intercourse. It may be that even if validation studies show that the world has not been reflected and its processes accurately displayed, important segments of those processes have been displayed to experimenters. The basic problem may become that of locating where the same things that occurred in the laboratory also happen in actual negotiations.

Can it be that what has been displayed in the form of small group behavior occurs not in international but in intraorganizational bargaining prior to or concurrently with international bargaining? Is what happens in interpersonal games comparable to occurrences in interviews between foreign ministers and ambassadors or in less formal interpersonal discussions particularly at international organizations? Does what is learned in the laboratory about the impact of personality confirm what diplomats' memoirs suggest? If it is realized that political gaming is young enough to permit only limited conclusions,[30] that much restructuring is possible, and that even

[29] Richard W. Chadwick, "Developments in a Partial Theory of International Behavior: A Test and Extension of Inter-Nation Simulation Theory (with) Supplement: Technical Notes," Ph.D. diss., Northwestern University, 1966 (Ann Arbor: University Microfilms 66-13, 964); Paul Smoker, "Analyses of Conflict Behaviours in an International Processes Simulation and an International System 1955-60," mimeographed (Evanston: Northwestern University, August, 1968).

[30] It has recently been suggested that in order to arrive at an adequate bargaining theory, it is necessary to go beyond game theory which is treated as necessary but insufficient. Martin Shubik, "On the Study of Disarmament and Escalation," *Journal of Conflict Resolution* 12 (1968): 83-101.

now some promising results are being obtained, then it lies within hope that many gaps in our knowledge of the negotiation process, the function of norms in channeling the process, and the impact of the process itself upon both procedural and substantive norms may yet be filled.

Bargaining Models

MODELS of the bargaining process may stress the conflict element mentioned in reference to Schelling. Emphasis on conflict may take the form of stress on strategies and upon capacities to inflict damage.[31] Or stress may be placed on utilities and their modification as the Iklé-Leites model does. Its attempt to account for bargaining by two parties or two alliances in respect to a single issue stresses minimum dispositions, estimates of the opponent's minimum dispositions, estimated probable outcomes, and sham bargaining ranges.[32]

Somewhat more interesting, because of the author's belief that models lying between the purely normative and the purely descriptive offer potential gains of considerable consequence, is Otomar J. Bartos' description of a mathematical model of negotiation based on the Von Neumann-Morgenstern theory of utility and the Bush-Mosteller stochastic model of learning. This particular model includes reference to the third-party process, which can enter into negotiations and judicial or quasi-judicial procedures. The third-party role was thought to be subject to a "recency effect" that would have tactical significance for negotiators. The "recency effect" refers to the circumstance that the later a proposal is introduced in a negotiating session, the greater its influence on the final decision. This

[31] E.g., Paul Diesing, "Bargaining Strategy and Union-Management Relations," *Journal of Conflict Resolution* 5 (1961): 369-78.

[32] Fred Charles Iklé and Nathan Leites, "Political Negotiation as a Process of Modifying Utilities," *Journal of Conflict Resolution* 6 (1962): 12-28.

occurrence was observed when conducting experiments with 35 groups of five subjects each.[33]

A problem with most bargaining models is that they tend to focus on very narrow facets of the process and are somewhat more suitable to the range of possibilities of norm-event interaction in the laboratory setting than to the broader range of international bargaining possibilities. Narrow focus is quite appropriate to the isolation of particular phenomena for study of their interrelationships. However, as has been suggested in respect to Schelling's more broadly applicable theory, stress upon the conflict element can of itself limit the situations to which a model may be relevant. For this reason, greater promise seems to lie in the effort of Walton and McKersie to build an integrated theory based upon four models, namely, distributive bargaining, integrative bargaining, attitudinal structuring, and intraorganizational bargaining. Moreover, they indicate ways in which their theory appears to be applicable not only to their central interest in labor negotiations but also to civil rights and international negotiations.

What the Walton-McKersie approach suggests is a need for an integrating concept, neutral in the sense of fitting both conflict and problem-solving situations. A communications model might well suit the purpose and also provide a link with a systems approach. Aside from the fact that bargaining occurs only through verbal and nonverbal communications, a choice of strategies and tactics is a choice of what to communicate and when and how to do so.[34] How is noise, both channel noise and semantic ambiguity, to be dealt with? Misperceptions, including misperceptions of intent, of bargaining

[33] Otomar J. Bartos, "A Model of Negotiation and the Recency Effect," *Sociometry* 27 (1964): 311-26.

[34] See, e.g., E. H. Fedder, "Communication and American-Soviet Bargaining Behavior," *Background* 8 (1964): 105-20; Stuart C. Dodd, "Ten Semantic Tangles and the Threat of War," *Journalism Quarterly* 35 (1958): 170-76.

range, of commitments, of the norms governing procedure, of one's own and the other's capabilities, are all problems of sending, relaying, and receiving information. Even the third-party role, whether one of facilitation of communication or exercise of independent judgment, is the role of a sender and receiver of messages.[35] The recency effect discussed by Bartos is a communications effect. It is probably not a simple consequence of the late proposal but also related to the length of the negotiating period, to the amount and types of competing messages, and to the accuracy with which the third party receives messages prior to processing them. If the phenomena of verbal and nonverbal bargaining can be fitted into a broader communications model that takes account of the attitude structuring and other psychological aspects of information processing, then bargaining theory can become more than a rational ordering of strategies and tactics because it would then link bargaining behavior to more pervasive processes occurring within structured systems.

Negotiations Between Enemies

A word should be said about bargaining between enemies as an important phase of norm-generation affecting the stability and maintenance of an international system. In respect to Cold War enemies, there is a good deal of material of varying types and quality being produced. A good deal less is said about bargaining with Red China, including use of the communication channel in Poland, than about bargaining between the

[35] Recent experimental findings suggest that the third-party role has a different impact, and in some circumstances can lead to deterioration of the adversaries' performance as negotiators, when the third party functions as observer rather than negotiator. Didier van den Hove, *Étude de deux modes d'influence sociale dans la résolution d'un conflit d'intérêt: Médiation et observation—Recherche expérimentale exploratoire*, 2 vols. (Louvain: Université Catholique de Louvain, Faculté de Philosophie et Lettres, Institut de Psychologie et des Sciences de l'Éducation, 1968).

United States and the Soviet Union. In the latter case, the span of attention includes uses of limited war as a bargaining tool.[36] Studies have also been conducted on assurance between adversaries—assurance emerging as a compound of levels of trust and perceptions of relative power that in turn decompose into such factors as perceived capabilities, perceived competence, and perceived intentions.[37]

Relatively little attention is paid to bargaining and negotiations between the contending parties in time of war, even though such negotiations during hostilities have been important determinants of the nature of postwar worlds. Some studies deal with minor wars such as those of South America. The most important study of negotiations between World War II enemies is, of course, Paul Kecskemeti's *Strategic Surrender* (1958).[38] If one of the consequences of wars, particularly major wars, is a restructuring of the international system, then negotiations, successful or unsuccessful, between enemies require an analysis that seeks their contributions to the systemic and normative changes that emerge from the wars.

In a somewhat different vein is an article that treats the

[36] E.g., the articles by Herman Kahn, Morton A. Kaplan, and Thornton Read in Klaus Knorr, and Read (eds.), *Limited Strategic War* (New York: Praeger, 1962).

[37] Richard E. Walton, Wesley L. Gould, Donald A. Strickland, and Michael J. Driver, "Social and Psychological Aspects of Verification, Inspection and International Assurance: Final Report," United States Arms Control and Disarmament Agency (West Lafayette, Indiana: Purdue Research Foundation, January, 1969), p. 6; Driver, "American College Elite Opinion and International Assurance," Studies of the Social and Psychological Aspects of Verification, Inspection and International Assurance, Technical Report No. 4.1, United States Arms Control and Disarmament Agency (West Lafayette, Indiana: Purdue University, Herman C. Krannert Graduate School of Industrial Administration, October, 1968), p. 35.

[38] An earlier study, based on Nuremberg documents is Maxime Mourin, *Les tentatives de paix dans la Seconde Guerre Mondiale (1939-1945)* (Paris: Payot, 1949).

early stages of World War II as an example of restraint and tacit bargaining by which the German Government ineptly tried to limit the air war while the British sought to expand it.[39] If nothing else, this article suggests that even major wars can provide displays, even if less successful, of the tacit bargaining that has been a notable feature of the limited wars since 1945.

Violent Processes

WITHOUT attempting to revive apologies for and glorifications of war, we find ourselves unable to avoid the conclusion that war and other manifestations of violence have been and still are processes integral to both the maintenance and change of international systems. As much as we dislike the reality, we cannot escape the fact that over the centuries far too many people have depended upon violence and the threat of violence to meet some felt need either momentary or gnawing over an extended time. This means that not just the function of conflict but specifically that of violence requires systematic investigation.

Were the problem of violence and particularly that of war a relatively simple matter of economies that have become dependent on supplying the professional practitioners of violence, then reorientation to a disarmed world, were it to come into being, would be essentially a matter of hard-nosed planning and execution of plans to mitigate attendant hardships.[40] Unfortunately, war is not a problem so simple that one can re-

[39] G. Quester, "Bargaining and Bombing During World War II in Europe," *World Politics* 15 (1963): 417-39.

[40] On the economic aspects of arms expenditures and their curtailment, see e.g., Walter Isard and Eugene W. Schooler, "An Economic Analysis of Local and Regional Impacts of Reduction of Military Expenditures," *Peace Research Society (International), Papers,* Chicago Conference, 1963, vol. 1 (1964), pp. 15-44; Emile Benoit and Harold Lubell, "World Defense Expenditures," *Journal of Peace Research* 3 (1966): 97-113; Benoit (ed.), *Disarmament and World Economic Interdependence* (Oslo: Universitetsforlaget, 1966).

direct conflict into non-violent channels simply through the relief of frustrations. However relevant the frustration-aggression thesis may be to interpersonal relations, intergroup relations are not rendered violent merely through a transfer of personal frustrations to higher levels, including international relations.[41] For one thing, despite efforts to alleviate frustration, there would still remain the more difficult problem of dealing with frustration-seeking behavior.

Findings related to the psychology of the individual and his tendencies toward violence are dead ends as explanations of international affairs unless they can be related to the functions of violence not just in but on behalf of international systems. Some guidelines may be provided by what is known about violence and its removal in domestic systems. On Choiseul Island the imposition of peace by the British destroyed much of the indigenous culture in which social and political leadership had been dependent on conflict. Self-interest replaced kinship obligations, societies became leaderless, and only a partial reordering of social life on the basis of contact with European institutions, not on Choiseulese foundations, has been achieved.[42] Closer to home it must be recalled that the spread of the narcotics habit coincided with an undertaking to repress gangs and gang violence in Harlem.

Information concerning what was removed from a society when violence was removed provides a clue to systemic functions performed by violence. At the international level there

[41] See, e.g., Leonard Berkowitz, *Aggression: A Social Psychological Analysis* (New York: McGraw-Hill, 1962); Aubrey J. Yates, *Frustration and Conflict* (New York: Wiley, 1962). The basic work that stimulated a great deal of research is John Dollard, et al., *Frustration and Aggression* (New Haven: Yale University Press, 1939).

[42] Harold W. Scheffler, "The Social Consequences of Peace on Choiseul Island," *Ethnology* 3 (1964): 398-403. See also, on conflict among Brazilian Indians, Robert F. Murphy, "Intergroup Hostility and Social Cohesion," *American Anthropologist* 59 (1957): 1018-35. Cf. H. L. Nieburg, "Uses of Violence," *Journal of Conflict Resolution* 7 (1963): 43-54.

has been no such displacement except the elimination of the private wars of knights and barons that were quasi-international due to the ineffectiveness of authority nominally superior under the feudal contract. Today, there exists the possibility that the balance of terror has displaced major war as an international process and substituted minor wars with limited escalation possibilities, subversion, and increased espionage to fill the systemic vacuum.

Even without a clear-cut example of an international suppression of violence, the slim possibility that a substitute for major war has been found indicates the presence of a systemic as well as a psychological function of violence. What functions violence performs and whether they are indispensable are problems to be attacked both from the direction of what is known about the consequences of the repression of violence within societies and from the direction of the analysis of international systems and their processes. The need to determine the functions of war was recognized by apologists for war despite their misleading doctrines based on insufficient knowledge, methodological inadequacies, and in many cases an infusion of romanticism.

Even though they do not by themselves explain the sources of disequilibrium and related functional problems in the disequilibrated system, applications of equilibrium theory to the problem of aggression represent a systems approach to the study of international violence.[43] Kaplan's rules for system behavior are similar and embrace both possible instrumental and possible system functions of war. Moreover, such studies as have been made of preventive war and of collective intervention deal with another basic phase of the problem.[44] What can

[43] E.g., Johan Galtung, "A Structural Theory of Aggression," *Journal of Peace Research* 2 (1964): 95-119.

[44] E.g., Karl Ernst Jeismann, *Das Problem des Präventivkrieges im europäischen Staatensystem mit besonderem Blick auf die Bismarckzeit* (Freiburg and Munich: Karl Alber, [1957]).

be learned about the systemic functions of international violence presumably could be of eventual significance to the development of a law concerning aggression.

Also of significance to the maintenance and functioning of a system are its rituals. In respect to conflict generally and combat specifically, rituals have been established, among them the pre-modern rules of chivalry and primitive warfare.[45] The laws of modern warfare fall into the same category and should not be lightly dismissed as legalistic idealism.

If one of the things that can be accomplished by means of law is a reduction of surprise and the accompanying embarrassment incapacitating office-holders for role performance,[46] then the rituals accompanying the outbreak, conduct, and termination of hostilities are quite important to the proper functioning of a system. Negative reactions to the Japanese attack without warning at Port Arthur in 1904 and at Pearl Harbor in 1941 and to German excesses in two World Wars are symptomatic. Something more than the mere violation of sensibilities or cherished values surely must be discernible in the responses that included the proceedings at Nuremberg and Tokyo. The responses, the elaboration of customary and written rules concerning hostilities, the emergence of such rules at various stages of societal development—all say something about needs of the human being and the systems in which he has lived, systems that have hardly been touched by the extant literature on the laws of war.

In making reference to surprise and embarrassment we have suggested only one possible line of investigation. Another direction would attempt a deep probe of what results from the

[45] E.g., Maurice Leenhardt, "Notes d'ethnologie Néo-Calédonienne," *Université de Paris, Travaux et Mémoires de l'Institut d'Ethnologie* 8 (1930): 46. Several examples of rituals are provided by the readings in Paul Bohannan (ed.), *Law and Warfare: Studies in the Anthropology of Conflict* (Garden City: Natural History Press, 1967).

[46] E. Gross and G. P. Stone, "Embarrassment and the Analysis of Role Requirements," *American Journal of Sociology* 70 (1964): 1-15.

disruption or abandonment of ritual or, perhaps, the lack of its development.[47] Obviously, such a probe would have to deal with the problems of information, its transmission, and entropy. In addition, it would touch upon the problem of differences between the ritualization of war and that of law enforcement—including the controlled, formalized actions of police—together with the probabilities of transforming the former into the latter.

[47] Paul Smoker, making reference to an article by J. Maynard Smith, takes note of the surrender ceremonies of birds that are better developed and more obvious than those of humans. "Fear in the Arms Race: A Mathematical Study," *Journal of Peace Research* 1 (1964): 61-62.

Chapter VII: Some Regulatory Problems of the Contemporary World

PRECEDING chapters have dealt with international law as a functional subsystem of the international system. Communication, and integrative, adaptive, and socializing functions have received attention, as have more specific matters such as the role of law in the foreign policy decision-making process, international procedures including bargaining and negotiations, the genesis and evolution of international legal norms, the protection of the units of the international system, and international societal development. The tenor of the preceding commentary has been that focus on the content of international norms and on procedural formalities reveals little about the nature and functions of international law and about processes, including the legal process, that survive structural changes. For this reason we have maintained that, although knowledge of the operative norms and procedures is essential, a scientific approach, aimed at extending knowledge and avoiding lapse into value-based argumentation, requires application of the most advanced social science concepts and techniques.

To what extent generalization is to be allowed to discard the information derivable from the specificity of international legal rules and their interpretations depends upon the nature of each problem investigated. Certainly, one cannot support a statement that the international legal system is changing in certain ways unless one has sufficient information to demonstrate specific changes over a determinate span of time. To do so requires familiarity with the norms related to particular areas of human activity subjected to investigation.

Even so, it may be doubted whether simple recapitulation of written and customary international laws and changes in them can do more than provide symptomatic evidence of the state of the international system and its components or the workings of the legal ingredient in international processes. To find the actual relationships between symptoms and processes is essential to social diagnosis that is to be more useful than a reference to the workings of evil political spirits. Probes in depth into areas of human activity either already covered or susceptible to coverage by international legal norms become more significant to the degree that they incorporate psychological, sociological, economic, and similar data. Even the more settled areas of international law are subject to more rigorous explanation, possibly even in formulations manifesting predictive power.

Division and Control of Space

A TRADITIONAL and primary concern embodied in international legal norms has been the two-dimensional division and control of space. So central has been this concern, together with corollary jurisdictional issues, that traditional international law has been aptly defined as the science of territorial jurisdiction.[1] Obviously and quite simply, until recently the earth's surface has been man's abode, the arena for his conflicts, the spatial component of his polities, and the scene of his productive, trading, and social activities. The surface has been the reference zone for extensions of control to the subsoil, continental shelf, coastal fisheries, and the limits of the atmosphere. Technicalities related to title, acquisition, and loss of territory, as well as political arguments in support of territorial claims, symbolize the significance of surface areas to human pursuits. Assertions of exclusiveness of jurisdiction similarly signify the importance of territory.

Publicity recently accorded Robert Ardrey's *The Territorial Imperative* (1966) at least serves as a reminder that the ter-

[1] Thomas A. Walker, *The Science of International Law* (London: Clay and Sons, 1893), pp. 44, 91.

ritorial problem may be something more than a matter of grounds for good title, procedures of acquisition and loss, and assertion of claims. Premature generalization concerning territoriality derived from data on the behavior of slime mold, dog, bird, and human can be dangerously misleading. At the same time, what can be learned about manifestations of territoriality among dogs[2] and other animals emphasizes the enduring characteristics of a phenomenon appearing among biological and social entities of different compositions and structures.

At the levels of the human being and human organizations there is also a wide range of manifestations of territoriality. Spatial points of reference in the Arab world do not display the fine, although often diffused, gradations that are to be found in the American system of reference points.[3] Nor is space similarly organized, used, claimed, or defended by human groups ranging from band to modern state.[4] Differences in reference points, of themselves or in combination with other differences, give rise to the suspicion that they may bear a significant relationship to the images produced by territorial demarcations among different peoples. Apparently, East Arabian frontier problems are traceable in part to a lack of concepts of territorial and political sovereignty of the European sort. The lack is not simply a matter of nonexposure to European ideas. It is also related to the nomadic way of life that, except in the cases of some symbiotic Bedouin economies, combines

[2] E.g., Konrad Z. Lorenz, *Man Meets Dog* (Cambridge: Houghton Mifflin, 1955).

[3] Edward T. Hall, *The Silent Language* (Garden City: Doubleday, 1959), chap. 10.

[4] See, e.g., C. Daryll Forde, *Habitat, Economy and Society: A Geographical Introduction to Ethnology*, 5th edn., paperback (New York: Dutton: 1963), pp. 12, 26-27, 33-34, 92-93, 333-34, 361-62, 373-75, 406-407; P. H. Gulliver, "Land Shortage, Social Change, and Social Conflict in East Africa," *Journal of Conflict Resolution* 5 (1961): 16-26; L. Paladin, "Il territorio degli enti autonomi," *Rivista trimestrale di diritto pubblico* 11 (1961): 607-90.

wandering over a fairly well-defined territory overstepped with risk, and occupation of more narrowly defined sites for a considerable period of each year.[5] In the circumstance of differing images and points of reference, rules of international law concerning territorial title, claims, acquisition, and loss represent an attempt to engraft substantive and procedural uniformity upon diversity, hopefully to mitigate the undesired effects of the latter.

Even though international law is relatively settled in respect to territory, conflicts over land are still with us. Territorial conflicts suggest that the international law of territory is effective when it provides the collectivities with which individuals identify something equivalent to protection of their psychic space. The interwar minorities treaties, the old regime of extraterritoriality, and extraterritoriality's modern equivalent in the form of the tourist resort may provide some refuge from anti-Yankee sentiment or from culture shock. They constitute evidence of a felt need of the self to withdraw not just from others but from culturally alien others.

Psychic space refers to an area or limit within which individuals will not permit others to make decisions and concerning which they are not open to persuasion. Central to the psychic space to be preserved are interests so closely bound to the individual's well-being, survival, and self-maintenance that manipulation, infringement, or deprivation is not tolerated. Instinctive avoidance of codification of rules to preserve psychic space may be displayed even though an observer may be able to discern and record relevant rules manifest in behavior patterns.[6]

[5] J. B. Kelly, "Sovereignty and Jurisdiction in Eastern Arabia," *International Affairs* 34 (1958): 16-24; C. Daryll Forde, *Habitat, Economy and Society*, pp. 406-407.

[6] Thomas A. Cowan and Donald A. Strickland, "The Legal Structure of a Confined Microsociety (A Report on the Cases of Penthouse II and III)," Internal Working Paper No. 34 (Berkeley: Space Sciences

While the symptoms of inaccessibility, regression, and ego-loss include hysteria and panic, perhaps that which is most relevant to the phenomena of the legal definition of territory is withdrawal. Experiments with confined microsocieties at the University of California's Space Sciences Laboratory produced group phenomena similar to those displayed by the basically closed society of the medieval village, by Tokugawa Japan, and also by some contemporary states. When the investigators approached the subjects with decision-making tasks, they found the subjects identifying strongly with each other and rejecting outside irritants. Moreover, aversion to decisions that would reactivate internal conflicts produced a tendency toward "cocooning," that is, toward passive isolation by withdrawal and sleeping.[7] Even more important were two defenses against possible or anticipated invasion that accounted for 59% of the time of one experiment. These defenses, in a situation in which physical isolation was virtually impossible, were group passivity and isolated or independent activity. Withdrawal in the latter case was active withdrawal indicative of the restriction of the meaning of psychic space to group situations providing opportunity for an appreciation of the ingenuity displayed in maintaining independence.[8]

Great as is the gulf between a laboratory microsociety and the state exposed to the international environment, there is reason to investigate whether there may be links between the individual's maintenance of psychic space and the territorial

---

Laboratory, Social Sciences Project, University of California, August, 1965), pp. 9, 72.

[7] *Ibid.*, p. 73.

[8] Martin Stow, "The Sociological and Psychological Structure of a Confined Microsociety," in Cowan and Strickland, *ibid.*, pp. 165-66. Similarly, after the Mongols were expelled, Chinese culture displayed a tendency to adhere to traditional models and to resist foreign influences until the late 19th century. Kenneth Scott Latourette, *The Chinese: Their History and Culture*, 2nd edn., 2 vols. in one (New York: Macmillan, 1934), 1: 278.

principles that receive expression in the technicalities of international law. If socialization of the individual produces identification with ever larger groups expressed not only in terms of organizations such as a state or tribe but also in terms of spatial reference points, then the law of territory reflects the maintenance of psychic space "writ large" by those capable of producing relevant rules. Capability would not mean simply power but, among other things, the possession of workable concepts such as Europe's reservoir of Roman Law concerning property.

The above-mentioned experiment suggests explanations of the past legal protection of independence, extraterritoriality, and minorities regimes. But the confinement experiment also contains a suggestion relevant to the future of a changing world. The suggestion is that in a group situation maintenance of psychic independence and countering anticipated invasion thereof is more easily done through interaction than through passivity.[9] Assuming this to be the case, and also assuming, with greater breadth than Herz's concentration on the military aspects,[10] that the territorial state no longer presents the barriers to penetration that it once did, then it may well be that the law of territory will require adjustment not to promote withdrawal but to promote the kinds of interaction that are conducive to the maintenance of psychic space in a nonisolated condition. The Berlin Wall and Bamboo Curtain notwithstanding, effective attainment of such an interactive result would require the adjustment of national as well as international law. Lack of such mutual legal adjustment to an interactive world would risk, among other things, institutionalizing conflict-laden fears, including fears of inadequacy afflicting the politically ambitious.

[9] Cowan and Strickland, "Legal Structure of a Confined Microsociety," p. 165.

[10] John H. Herz, "Rise and Demise of the Territorial State," *World Politics* 9 (1957): 473-93.

Some Regulatory Problems

Peacetime Espionage

WIDESPREAD employment of espionage in recent decades gives rise to fears that traditional methods of conducting international affairs and defending territory are inadequate. At the same time there has been no replacement of the national state as the effective guardian of the existence and territorial integrity of the national components of the international system. Penetrability and permeability that can reach to the wellsprings of domestic politics have produced what amounts to an institutionalization of peacetime espionage by aerial reconnaissance and by highly sophisticated forms of such traditional means as counterespionage, subversion, and defenses against political subversion.

The record of expulsions of diplomatic personnel since the coming to power of the Communists, Nazis, and Fascists shows little change from the old situation in respect to heads of diplomatic missions; but it shows an unprecedented rate of expulsion, particularly since 1945, of lesser diplomatic personnel, largely for espionage or subversive activities.[11] This record suggests (1) that interdependence and vulnerability in the face of modern technology have increased at a more rapid rate than trust among nations and (2) that nationally operated inspection systems have become entrenched components of the international communications system. Indeed, among certain national components there appears to be an inverse relationship between interdependence and vulnerability on the one hand and trust on the other hand that also has the effect of preventing national inspection from being superseded by internationally operated inspection.[12] In consequence, there

[11] Alvin Kruse, "Offenses by Diplomats Against Receiving States," (Paper, Northwestern University, 1965).

[12] On the felt need for information about an adversary whose competence is perceived to be high, thereby increasing worries and depressing trust, see Richard E. Walton, Wesley L. Gould, Donald A. Strickland, and Michael J. Driver, "Social and Psychological Aspects

is a well-developed game of inspect and counterinspect, expel and counter-expel, that is conducted within recognizable limits. These in the main leave intact the procedures and norms relevant to the conduct of traditional diplomatic intercourse, particularly by heads of missions.

Whether the emerged practices can be treated as rules of customary international law and, if so, to what extent traditional abhorrence of espionage has been modified as an ingredient of law has yet to receive thorough examination. Perhaps the simplest related question is one raised by the Cuban missile crisis of 1962, namely, can national territory any longer be properly, let alone safely, regarded as inviolate to prying eyes? Does the preservation of the international system and its components now take precedence in a manner that legitimizes inspection by other states engaging in espionage and overflight in lieu of international inspection?

Frontier Zones and Boundaries

In general, the depth study of frontier zones and boundaries has been left to geographers. International lawyers have tended to content themselves with exposition of the formal requirements of demarcation and the like as set forth in formal instruments. Supplementation of this basic interest tends to be limited to such matters, among others, as customs regulation, admission of aliens, and succession problems when boundary changes occur. An exception to the usual restrictive approach

---

of Verification, Inspection and International Assurance: Final Report," United States Arms Control and Disarmament Agency (West Lafayette, Indiana: Purdue Research Foundation, January, 1969), pp. 8, 23-24, 28-29, 46, 47-48; Walton, "A System of Attitudes Related to International Assurance: Theoretical Framework and Review," Studies of the Social and Psychological Aspects of Verification, Inspection and International Assurance, Technical Report No. 1, United States Arms Control and Disarmament Agency (West Lafayette, Indiana: Purdue University, Herman C. Krannert Graduate School of Industrial Administration, September, 1968), pp. 14, 26-28, 39-40.

of lawyers is Paul de Lapradelle's *La frontière: Etude de droit international* (1928) which is still the best study of frontiers and a basic guide for geographers as well as for lawyers. Lapradelle's trizonal approach, judiciously blending traditional international law approaches, legal data, and the methods, concepts, and findings of other disciplines, treats boundaries within the context of borderlands subject to special political, legal, and economic regulations and administrative regimes.

Comprehensive consideration of boundary problems in various parts of the globe as expounded, e.g., in J.R.V. Prescott's *The Geography of Frontiers and Boundaries* (1965), leads to the question of whether the formal rules for boundary demarcation and administration do not conceal more problems than they solve. For example, even so well-settled a boundary as that between France and Switzerland in the Jura does not represent the realities of population movements, land lease and purchase in respect to agriculture and forestry, or the relationship of the frontier to the watchmaking industry. Actually, written guarantees have proved meaningless compared with customs regulations and the comparative values of the French and the Swiss franc which, since the 1880's, have served to place the economic boundary west of the political boundary.[13] Similarly, the real boundary in the Franco-Belgian borderland appears to be a function of the value of the French franc and the level of textile production.[14]

Given such differences between real and political boundaries in quite settled sections of Europe, one may question whether legal generalizations concerning boundaries and frontiers can be derived to fit European circumstances, let alone zones populated by nomads. An examination of the Turco-Persian

[13] Susanne Daveau, *Les régions frontalières de la montagne Jurassienne—Étude de géographie humaine* ([Trévoux]: Imprimerie de Trévoux, Pattissier, 1959).

[14] R. Sevrin, "Les échanges de population à la frontière entre la France et la Tournaisis," *Annales de géographie* 58 (1949): 237-44.

boundary settlement reveals that the effort to impose a European settlement, even with the aid of intervention over seven decades, produced difficulties traceable to the nomadic habits of frontier tribes, conflict between European and Oriental ideas and methods, and Moslem sectarian incompatibilities.[15] Even when a boundary has been demarcated, the strict boundary regime may not be readily established by the respective states nor may the habits of nomads be readily curbed in the aftermath of an abrogation of treaty rights to seek pasture and water for herds.[16]

In other words, whether peopled by nomads or industrialized populations, frontier zones develop characteristics not readily classifiable under the rubrics of traditional international law. It might be more realistic to think in terms of economic landscapes rather than political boundaries,[17] even though merely thinking about them alone will not eradicate incongruities. But the concept of economic landscapes may aid in molding the law in a manner that takes better account not just of nomads but also of the products of high energy social systems that take such forms as the Canadian-American energy system in the Pacific Northwest.[18] High-energy technology seems to produce regional diffusion of that technology

[15] Maurice Harari, "The Turco-Persian Boundary Question: A Case Study in the Politics of Boundary-Making in the Near and Middle East," Ph.D. diss., Columbia University, 1958 (Ann Arbor: University Microfilms 58-3226).

[16] On the Ethiopia-Somalia dispute and Ethiopian abrogation of the Anglo-Ethiopian Agreement of 1954, see J.R.V. Prescott, *The Geography of Frontiers and Boundaries* (London: Hutchinson University Library, 1965), pp. 139-44.

[17] See August Losch, *The Economics of Location* (New Haven: Yale University Press, 1954), pp. 192-210.

[18] See Wesley L. Gould, "Metals, Oil and Natural Gas: Some Problems of Canadian-American Co-operation," in David R. Deener (ed.), *Canada–United States Treaty Relations* (Durham: Duke University Press, 1963), pp. 168, 175-76; Leonard M. Cantor, "The Columbia River Power Project and the Pacific Northwest-Southwest Intertie," *Journal of Geography* 65 (1966): 20-28.

and the values that sustain it,[19] with spatial limitations largely functions of economic feasibility and culturally different viewpoints concerning natural resources, their values, and their uses.[20] While not presently stressed, the limits imposed upon economic regions by cultural differences are not to be underestimated.

One other economic response to national boundaries warrants attention. Given the circumstance that natural resource distribution does not correspond to the political distribution of peoples, pursuit of nationally advantageous resource policies may not be conducive to rational and equitable exploitation of the resources. When import-export and related national controls prevent market determination of resource distribution patterns, responses to deflections at boundaries are to be expected. One response has been the nonterritorial or, perhaps more accurately, semiterritorial firm operating transnationally but organized to mesh with the territorial jurisdictions of those political units that can both authorize and impede its operations. A good deal of attention has been given in recent years to the problems of the legal regulation of such firms and to the requirements to be met if they are to do business in particular countries. Greater depth would be obtained by the application of organization theory and by the development of quasi-spatial geographic concepts such as Robert B. McNee's "company region,"[21] more functional than

[19] Fred Cottrell, *Energy and Society: The Relation Between Energy, Social Change, and Economic Development* (New York: McGraw-Hill, 1955), p. 301.

[20] Alexander Spoehr, "Cultural Differences in the Interpretation of Natural Resources," in W. L. Thomas, Jr. (ed.), *Man's Role in Changing the Face of the Earth* (Chicago: University of Chicago Press, 1956), pp. 93-101.

[21] See Robert B. McNee, "Functional Geography of the Firm, with an Illustrative Case from the Petroleum Industry," *Economic Geography* 34 (1958): 321-37; "Centrifugal-Centripetal Forces in International Petroleum Company Regions," *Annals, Association of American Geographers* 51 (1961): 124-38.

areal in nature. For area enters essentially as a legacy from another day when economic organizations and economic regions were more readily contained within what were then developed political units. In regard to the semiterritorial company, the factor of area presents the problem reconciling the protection of the local populace, through the exercise of territorial jurisdiction, with the requirements of effective company operations.

Territorial Waters and Contiguous Zones

ALTHOUGH a great deal of attention has been given in recent years to the issues concerning the breadth of territorial waters and contiguous zones, there remains a good deal of work to be done to provide an empirical grounding for intuitively sensed correlations. For example, the special interest of the maritime nations has long been recognized. It was the concurrence of these nations, not of others, with regulations first employed by the British that weighed significantly with Justice Strong when he concluded that there was an international rule requiring steam vessels to display lights different from those carried by sailing vessels.[22] But one finds little scholarly correlation between national positions on the breadth of territorial waters and contiguous zones and data on the sizes and types of merchant and fishing fleets, the type of sea-borne commerce (e.g., cabotage or international) in which particular states are engaged, or the lobbying done at national capitals by particular interests.

To what extent have special interests been able to affect the composition of delegations to conferences on the sea and territorial waters? What interest groups in landlocked states are particularly anxious to secure access to the sea and which, if any, are indifferent?[23] To what extent was the argument ad-

[22] *The Scotia* (1871) 14 Wallace 170.

[23] On the problem of access to the sea, see Norman J. G. Pounds, "A Free and Secure Access to the Sea," *Annals, Association of American Geographers* 49 (1959): 256-68.

vanced by the United States at Geneva, namely, that broader territorial waters would lengthen routes and increase shipping costs, essentially rhetoric or perhaps a bargaining ploy constructed by omitting reference to the right of innocent passage?[24] What political organizations, whether parties or pressure groups, have demanded the extension of territorial waters or, as in Iceland, of fisheries limits and perhaps contiguous zones for protection against other activities such as smuggling?[25] Are the political groups who demand extension of water boundaries motivated largely by economic interests or by nationalistic sentiment?

Finally, one can ask a question not unrelated to the Chicago diversion issue and of obvious relevance to such undertakings as the Dutch Delta-Plan for sealing off arms of the North Sea. What interests are vulnerable and what responsibilities might fall upon a state if, through its waterfront construction or its attempts to reclaim land in areas of significant tidal flow, damage were to result in other states?[26] In circumstances in which such damage appears possible, what political processes are activated by whom in order to establish the international communication necessary to gain assurance that the

[24] Mary Carmel Fusiek, "How an Increase in Territorial Waters Would Increase Shipping Rates" (Paper, Purdue University, 1963). An attempt to canvass shipping line officials about the rate increase brought one reply from J. V. Guthrie, Vice President of the Cottman Company of Baltimore, to the effect that the extent of territorial waters has no effect on shipping rates, together with a response from the Acting Judge Advocate General of the Navy that rates would depend upon the honoring of the right of innocent passage and the nature of the regulations imposed on ships transiting territorial seas.

[25] On the role of Icelandic political parties and pressure groups in the political process that extended fishery limits from four to twelve miles, see Morris Davis, *Iceland Extends Its Fisheries Limits: A Political Analysis* (Oslo: Universitetsforlaget, 1963).

[26] E.g., A. C. Redfield, "The Analysis of Tidal Phenomena in Narrow Emboyments," *Papers in Physical Oceanography and Meteorology*, vol. 10, no. 4 (Massachusetts Institute of Technology and Woods Hole Oceanographic Institution, July, 1950).

potential damage does not occur? As may be seen from the last question, the natural scientist as well as the social scientist can provide the lawyer with data essential to an informed approach to current and potential issues related to territorial and adjacent waters. To the natural scientist one must also turn for information concerning the potentially recoverable resources of the continental shelf and the ocean bottom.[27]

Islands and Archipelagoes

THAT CLAIMS of title to islands or a group of islands may bring up the problem of the relationship between law and power is seen in the differences between Japan and the Soviet Union over the Kuriles and Sakhalin. Can the Soviet Union rely on the San Francisco Treaty to which the Soviet Union was not a party or upon the Yalta Agreement to which Japan was not a party?[28] Whatever the answers, such issues cannot be attacked without reference to profound questions of political as well as legal theory. Moreover, to deal with such issues at either the practitioner's or the theoretician's level begs for a calculation of the probabilities both of the law's chances of overriding national power and of the latent power of one nation being persuasive against the latent power of another. And if, in the outcome, the verdict were to go to the stronger national power or to the national power that through past action now possesses the islands in question, is there an impact upon the law that changes its substance or is the case one of uncorrected deviance? Does acquiescence by other states symbolize approval or powerlessness?

Somewhat similar issues arise in relation to the waters

[27] An excellent discussion of the potentially recoverable mineral resources, especially manganese nodules, at the bottom of the sea can be found in John L. Mero, *The Mineral Resources of the Sea* (Amsterdam, London, and New York: Elsevier, 1965), chaps. IV, VI, VII.

[28] L. Halkin-Destrée, "Le differend territorial nippo-soviétique: Les îles Kouriles et Sakhaline," *Chronique de politique etrangère* 18 (1965): 293-328.

embraced by archipelagoes. Is the carrying trade among the islands that make up such archipelagoes as the Philippines and Indonesia so dominant a portion of the commerce using those waters as to warrant the hitherto unprecedented regime sought at Geneva? Whether the regime contended for, particularly by Indonesia, were ever to be obtained or not, is the law that emerges a reflection of politics, economics, naval power, or the sheer impracticality of attempting to exercise jurisdiction over so vast an ocean area? So little has been written about the archipelago problem that one can only say that any tools that are brought to bear upon it should be enlightening to both lawyers and political scientists.

International Rivers and Lakes

INTERNATIONAL river problems have been productive of a rather substantial literature to which lawyers, social scientists, and natural scientists have contributed. A great portion of that literature deals with such problems as freedom of navigation, pollution, irrigation and power systems, and special regimes for particular rivers. Some effort has been made to determine whether a relationship exists between river usage and territorial change, with attention given even to navigation data for primitive tribes.[29]

More recently, attention has been given to the developments of river basins such as the lower Mekong.[30] Attention to entire basins represents a recognition both that river problems extend beyond the navigation issue and that there may be reasons, practical if not also moral and even legal, for aiding less wealthy nations to develop their river systems. Recognition that river problems extend beyond navigation has produced a

[29] Raoul Naroll, "Waterways and Territorial Change," Final Report to Project Michelson, U. S. Naval Ordnance Test Station, China Lake, California (Northwestern University, n.d.).

[30] E.g., C. Hart Schaaf and Russell H. Fifield, *The Lower Mekong: Challenge and Cooperation in Southeast Asia* (Princeton: D. Van Nostrand, 1963).

call not for a law of nations based on national sovereignty but for a law of a functional community.[31] Upon this point, more will be said in relation to energy fuels and energy systems. Problems of river basin development have turned attention to the possibilities for cost-sharing in international river development.[32] The problem of river development, including such health factors as the supply of drinking water and sanitary precautions, is an area that may raise acute issues related on the one hand to politicization of the technical and on the other hand to making politically possible that which is scientifically necessary. So far the law that has emerged and can be expected to undergo additional change could be labeled a social composite of the technical and political elements of river development.

Much the same can be said for lakes. Unfortunately, it has to be said largely by analogy with rivers, for there is so little legal literature about lakes and their special problems as to give rise to the suspicion that many writers regard lakes as merely wide places in rivers. For example, to our knowledge the only comprehensive studies of the international law of the Great Lakes to date are those by Don C. Piper and Charles Bédard.[33] Yet the problems of the pollution, particularly of Lake Erie, and diversion of waters are of great importance to the international megalopolis that extends from the north shore of Lake Ontario to the west shore of Lake Michigan. In this case the object of study is an international social and economic sys-

[31] J. J. Lador-Lederer, "Vom Wasserweg zur internationalen Gemeinschaft," *Friedens-Warte* 53 (1956): 225-44.

[32] E.g., Mark M. Regan, "Sharing Financial Responsibility of River Basin Development," in Stephen C. Smith and Emery N. Castle (eds.), *Economics and Public Policy in Water Resource Development* (Ames: Iowa State University Press, 1964), pp. 209-21.

[33] Don C. Piper, *The International Law of the Great Lakes: A Study of Canadian-United States Cooperation* (Durham: Duke University Press, 1967); Charles Bédard, *Le Régime juridique des Grands Lacs de l'Amérique du Nord et du Saint-Laurent* (Quebec: Les Presses de l'Université Laval, 1966).

tem, based upon a high energy system of continental significance, that operates largely through a bargaining process between two states and among a multiplicity of governmental and economic subsystems.[34] The Great Lakes are, unquestionably, unique in being both an inland waterway system and an artery for transoceanic commerce. The law that is relevant to them, whether international or domestic, provides an excellent opportunity for an examination of what the interplay of national and local sentiment and social and economic forces can produce in the absence of either latent or actual military threat.

Air Space and Outer Space

WHATEVER the speculations concerning the proper law for outer space and moon colonies and however accurate those speculations might be, we may expect that the outcomes will reflect both earthbound happenings and adaptation to the exigencies of outer space. Relative bargaining skills and fears for national security will affect the substance of the law that emerges.[35] Growth of the law of the air has been influenced by the interests of national airlines and by such considerations as the extension of neutrality, and thus of national sovereignty, to the air space.[36] As obvious as these considerations

[34] On the disruption of the unity of the St. Lawrence watershed by cession of the Ohio country to the United States and on Canadian efforts to restore the unity of the watershed, see Roy I. Wolfe, "Transportation and Politics: The Example of Canada," *Annals, Association of American Geographers* 52 (1962): 176-90.

[35] Wesley L. Gould, with the assistance of William Klecka and Charles Weyant, "The *New York Times* and the Development of Assurance Between Adversary Nations: Six Case Studies, 1961-1963," Studies of the Social and Psychological Aspects of Verification, Inspection and International Assurance, Technical Report No. 2, United States Arms Control and Disarmament Agency, (West Lafayette, Indiana: Purdue Research Foundation, December, 1968), Case No. 5, "Outer Space Cooperation," pp. 234-53, 268-69, 274, 276-77.

[36] John Cobb Cooper, *The Right to Fly* (New York: Holt, 1947), pp. 17-26, 42.

may seem, to reiterate them is to introduce a reminder of the relevance not only of earthbound events to the laws of the air and outer space but also of those laws to occurrences on the earth's surface.

Today the presence of a host of new states as international actors underlines the interrelationship of earth and space. For their presence has served to emphasize, beyond what the space race between the two primary Cold War contenders has done, the importance of the air and outer space to the acquisition of earthly prestige. Hans Heymann, Jr., has called attention to the potential economic and political consequences of the use by new and underdeveloped states of foreign economic assistance to create government-owned international prestige airlines.[37] Independently or in association with economic advantages, the air space is usable by new states to gain prestige, or at least to feel that they are gaining it.

Outer space is, of course, beyond the means of new states and the prestige factor is only that enjoyed by the two space-exploring nations among the populace and elites of the new states.[38] But it is not beyond the capacities of new states to seek a voice in the control of outer space just as they have sought a voice in the control of the seas and the air space beyond what experience through use might in an earlier day have allowed them. To an insignificant degree United Nations mechanisms provide nonusers and users with opportunities for self-expression.

Actually, the problem is broader than transportation on the seas, in the air, and in space and so calls for study on a

[37] Hans Heymann, Jr., "Civil Aviation and U.S. Foreign Aid: Purposes, Pitfalls, and Problems for U.S. Policy," RAND Report R-424-RC (Santa Monica: RAND Corporation, January, 1964).

[38] Changes in the prestige levels of the U.S. and the U.S.S.R. in non-Western countries are probed by Donald A. Strickland, "New States, Prestige, and the Space Age: Some Probable Connections," mimeographed (Berkeley: Space Sciences Laboratory, University of California, May, 1964).

broader scale than heretofore. Influence by nonusers and insignificant users upon the form and content of norms signifies an alteration in the procedures of norm generation and change. To the extent that custom is produced by the activities of the users of a route, a device, or a technique—above all, by the principal, more frequent, or more prestigious users—introduction of the larger number of nonusers into the norm generation and norm-changing procedure and the requiring of their consent marks an important step away from the least complex method of lawmaking.[39] What the cost is in the form of impositions by inexperience, perhaps even less experience than that of a customer, is as yet little measured and perhaps little understood, even though often sensed. We have anecdotal but not collected and categorized evidence of the impact of the inexperienced on lawmaking.

Man's early efforts to explore outer space and, next, to reach the moon have given rise to a considerable literature on the nature of space activities and the law that may regulate it. Necessarily, the literature is essentially both speculative and based upon analogy. Analogy serves anticipation, especially in respect to behavioral standards, by providing an anchor in what has gone before.[40] As McDougal, Lasswell, and Vlasic

[39] A compromise arrangement was employed in 1955 for negotiation of a Statute for the International Atomic Energy Agency. The first negotiating group of seven Western states was broadened to twelve, including Brazil, India, Czechoslovakia, and the U.S.S.R., and the draft was submitted to a world conference. That the conference made only slight modifications has been attributed to confidence that the broadened committee had examined issues in depth and without restriction to Western viewpoints. Arthur Lall, *Modern International Negotiation: Principles and Practice* (New York and London: Columbia University Press, 1966), pp. 346-47.

[40] On the need for anticipation and the costs of past failures to anticipate in terms of social consequences and regulatory needs arising from scientific and technological innovations-to-be, see Harold D. Lasswell, "The Political Science of Science," *American Political Science Review* 50 (1956): 961-79. The best known high caliber resort to analogy is Phillip C. Jessup and Howard J. Taubenfeld, *Controls for*

point out, "the participants in earth-space social process quite obviously already have at their disposal for the resolution of conflicting claims about the enjoyment of space and its resources precisely the same process of authoritative decision which they have established for resolution of their conflicting claims about their more terrestrial activities."[41] The authors of the prodigious *Law and Public Order in Space* then proceed to indicate the possibilities that may be derived from the present earthbound law, e.g., in regard to claims relating to the acquisition and enjoyment of resources.

An important feature of the McDougal-Lasswell-Vlasic study is its reliance not only upon legal and scientific literature but also upon some pertinent social science literature, particularly that on the economic impact of space programs. Perhaps because of its focus on international public order,[42] *Law and Public Order in Space* does not get beyond certain technological considerations related to the maintenance of such future microsocieties as the crews and passengers of space ships, the personnel of manned space stations, and moon colonies. Quite relevant to the problems to be faced in the near future are the studies and memoirs concerning polar expeditions, submarine voyages particularly in the age of the long-range nuclear submarine, the isolation of military and civilian personnel at weather and scientific outposts, mountaineering expeditions, mutinies, and other groups of men under stress. In

---

Outer Space and the Antarctic Analogy (New York: Columbia University Press, 1959).

[41] Myres S. McDougal, Harold D. Lasswell, and Ivan A. Vlasic, *Law and Public Order in Space* (New Haven and London: Yale University Press, 1963), p. 94. For a discussion of the manned space station in terms of an overall national space effort, see John M. Coulter and Benjamin J. Loret, "Manned Orbiting Space Stations," *Air University Review* 16 (May-June, 1965): 33-41.

[42] E.g., McDougal, Lasswell, and Vlasic, *Law and Public Order in Space*, p. 657, where a section on events on board spacecraft deals only with the probability that states will claim exclusive competence to establish discipline and prevent disorders.

addition, we now have the reports of group isolation experiments such as those, under the auspices of the National Aeronautics and Space Agency, that have produced the Cowan-Strickland and Weyrauch reports on the generation and degradation of rules. Future experiments can be expected to add significantly to our capacity to anticipate problems and needs for regulation during the coming launchings of multimembered spaceship crews and establishment of satellite and moon stations.

From the point of view of developing the law to be effective in space and on celestial bodies particularly in circumstances of loss of communication with earth, social-psychological aspects may be of greater consequence even to international affairs than technological factors, logistic matters,[43] or even the politico-legal relations among high-level earthly decision-makers. A lunar encounter between Soviet and American crews, with one or both out of communication with their home authorities, may bear resemblances to the encounter of Marchand and Kitchener at Fashoda or that of the rival parties on the day the Matterhorn was first climbed.

Communications, Propaganda, and International Information Flow

Testimony to the concern of international lawyers with problems of international mass communications is found in studies by Hilding Eek, John B. Whitton, B. S. Murty and George A. Codding.[44] Recent articles have dealt with pirate broad-

[43] For the use of a mathematical model to test the logistic possibility of a program culminating in construction of a lunar-based observatory, see R. J. Freeman, R. C. Moore, and G. F. Schilling, "Logistic Implications of an Astronomical Observatory on the Moon," RAND Memorandum RM-4916-PR (Santa Monica: RAND Corporation, February, 1966).

[44] Hilding Eek, *Freedom of Information as a Project of International Legislation: A Study of International Law in the Making* (Uppsala: Lundequistska bokhandeln, 1953); John B. Whitton and Arthur Larson, *Propaganda: Towards Disarmament in the War of Words* (Dobbs

casting and the recent attention given to satellite communication systems.[45] Much of the literature reflects an underpinning of our democratic ideology: the freedom of information, a freedom subject to the abuse of distortion and propagandizing. It also reflects a desire to eliminate the agitation to international violence and subversion that has become a constant feature of 20th-century communications by newspaper, magazine, radio, television, and mail.

One knotty problem is whether one can hermetically seal states from officially unwanted propaganda and the unwanted advertising of pirate broadcasting. Another problem is whether one can prevent purely domestic arousal of hatred of foreigners and their states. Can either problem be attacked while at the same time attempting to maintain freedom of information?

It may be questioned whether or not much of the thought concerning dangerous or malignant messages and impediments to the transmission of benign messages is directed only at symptoms and symptomatic relief. As long as men can formulate opinions, write and draw, and speak, they can propagandize. In fact, even those most concerned to impede trans-

---

Ferry: Oceana for the World Rule of Law Center, 1964); B. S. Murty, *Propaganda and World Public Order: The Legal Regulation of the Ideological Instrument of Coercion* (New Haven and London: Yale University Press, 1968); George A. Codding, *The International Telecommunication Union: An Experiment in International Cooperation* (Leiden: E. J. Brill, 1952); and *The Universal Postal Union: Coordinator of International Mails* (New York: New York University Press, 1964).

[45] E.g., M. L. Schwartz, "Foreign Participation in Communication Satellite Systems: The Implications of the Federal Communications Act," RAND Report RM-2971-NASA (Santa Monica: RAND Corporation, December, 1961); L. L. Johnson, "Some Implications of New Communications Technologies for National Security in the 1970's," RAND Report P-3639 (Santa Monica: RAND Corporation, September, 1967); H. F. van Panhuys and Menno J. van Emde Boas, "Legal Aspects of Pirate Broadcasting," *American Journal of International Law* 60 (1966): 303-41.

mission of dangerous messages want freedom to transmit their own opinions. As if this problem of individual psychology and antithetical goals did not induce enough complexity, there are the additional difficulties introduced by the preference of so many people to be propagandized so that uncertainties are reduced and regurgitation can replace thought. At hand are skills for use by the political manipulator—skills available at a price or through conviction. The combination of party, pressure group, and government activity have produced a propagandizing profession as dependent on propaganda for a living as are advertising agencies.[46]

Given only those psychological and sociological dimensions of the problem just suggested, it seems reasonable to ask whether the very fruitful points of scholarly thrust are those propaganda outputs that may stimulate violence, the responsibility for them, and legal principles potentially establishing liabilities. Perhaps the area of mass media and propaganda is one in which the scholar of international law should abjure the direct attack in favor of an oblique march, directed toward the sociological dimensions of mass communications systems. Or the approach might be made by way of more distant but pertinent social and psychological factors contributing to the production of undesirable propaganda.

It may be doubted that there is such a thing as an international mass communications system. Rather, as the existence of military blocs and national news agencies indicates, there are many systems in operation. Don R. Browne has questioned whether international broadcasting is even a system of mass communications in view of technical difficulties, listeners' general lack of interest in short-wave reception, and the uncertainty of foreign-based medium-wave operations dependent upon treaty relations that are themselves susceptible to political repercussions. Because most listeners hear only digests

[46] See e.g., M. Choukas, *Propaganda Comes of Age* (Washington: Public Affairs Press, 1965).

of those monitored foreign broadcasts that domestic newscasters select, Browne questions whether international broadcasting is even an example of unimpeded communication between the sender and the mass of receivers.[47]

Much the same may be said about the newspapers. Bernard C. Cohen has reminded us that an International Press Institute study of 93 American newspapers from October, 1952, to January, 1953, showed an average of 4.4 columns a day devoted to foreign dateline news. Another study cited by Cohen showed that five newspapers circulating in Madison, Wisconsin, presented during one week in April, 1960, the following totals for foreign news: *New York Times*, 185 columns; *Milwaukee Journal,* 88 columns; *Chicago Tribune*, 80 columns; *Wisconsin State Journal*, 34 columns; *Capital Times* (Madison), 20 columns (no Sunday edition).[48]

In part the small amount of foreign news published in the United States is traceable to "gatekeeping" that cuts the volume of news drastically as it flows from overseas through trunk wires and state circuits to local newspapers.[49] At the local level in the United States there appears to be considerable

[47] Don R. Browne, "The Limits of the Limitless Medium—International Broadcasting," *Journalism Quarterly* 42 (1965): 82-86, 164. See also W. Phillips Davison, *International Political Communication* (New York: Praeger for the Council on Foreign Relations, 1965), pp. 51-55; Harwood L. Childs and John B. Whitton, *Propaganda by Short Wave* (Princeton: Princeton University Press, 1942), pp. 305ff. On such techniques as inciting inflammatory statements, staging events, etc., see Daniel J. Boorstin, *The Image: A Guide to Pseudo-Events in America* (New York: Harper and Row, 1964).

[48] Bernard C. Cohen, *The Press and Foreign Policy* (Princeton: Princeton University Press, 1963), pp. 115-18. For a comparative study of dailies in seventeen nations, see Jacques Kayser, *One Week's News: Comparative Study of Seventeen Major Dailies for a Seven-Day Period* (Paris: UNESCO, 1953).

[49] Scott M. Cutlip, "Content and Flow of AP News—From Trunk to TTS to Reader," *Journalism Quarterly* 31 (1954): 434-46; John T. McNelly, "Intermediary Communicators in the International Flow of News," *Journalism Quarterly* 36 (1959): 23-26.

variation in news values and editing practices. Some studies report a fair measure of selectivity among stories while others report standardization of content and careless editing.[50] In part, there is good editorial reason for giving greater space to matters close to readers' personal and daily affairs.[51] The failure of the flooding of Cincinnati for six months with information in a multitude of forms to increase awareness of United Nations purposes may have been due to a general lack of felt need for more information.[52] A two-year experiment by Radio Stuttgart failed to produce a statistically significant change in listeners' awareness of what the Bundesrat is.[53]

It may be that a certain level of information must already have been attained, particularly by heavy interpersonal communicators, before more information is sought. Such, at least in respect to expert agencies supplying information, is indicated to have been the case in respect to information about the Detroit community fall-out shelter idea, but with the somewhat depressing additional finding that less impact was had upon message-seekers than on the general public.[54] The Detroit data appears to be related to the finding that listeners to foreign radio broadcasts are primarily students, educators, government officials, and professional newsmen. Could it be that

[50] See e.g., John L. Hulteng, "Testing Judgments in News Selection," *Journalism Quarterly* 36 (1959): 348-50; Guido H. Stempel, III, "Uniformity of Wire Content of Six Michigan Dailies," *Journalism Quarterly* 36 (1959): 45-48; Walter Gieber, "Across the Desk: A Study of 16 Telegraph Editors," *Journalism Quarterly* 33 (1956): 423-32; Warren Breed, "Newspaper 'Opinion Leaders' and Processes of Standardization," *Journalism Quarterly* 32 (1955): 277-84.

[51] Davison, *International Political Communication*, p. 52.

[52] *Ibid.*, pp. 28-29, 51-52; Shirley A. Star and Helen MacGill Hughes, "Report on an Educational Campaign: The Cincinnati Plan for the United Nations," *American Journal of Sociology* 55 (1950): 389-400.

[53] Elizabeth Noelle-Neumann, "Mass Communication Media and Public Opinion," *Journalism Quarterly* 36 (1959): 406-407.

[54] Verling C. Troldahl, Robert Van Dam, and George B. Robeck, "Public Affairs Information-Seeking from Expert Institutionalized Sources," *Journalism Quarterly* 42 (1965): 403-12.

what is sought is information buttressing an already established position based upon previously received messages, including the nonverbal messages of experience?[55] Or must account also be taken of source credibility and the relevance of a message to its receivers' personal affairs?

Given the circumstances indicated, the combined effort to impede the spread of dangerous propaganda while also assuring a free flow of information cannot proceed effectively by means of regulations directed primarily at the outputs of mass media. Perhaps a better approach is to start from a broader problem, namely, that of producing the prerequisites for more effective international law, for making international law known, and for producing support of and responsible demand for changes in international law.[56] What might be needed, whether in respect to rendering international law in general more effective or to controlling and restraining propaganda, is to insert into thoroughly studied communications systems those inputs that appear to have the best chances of preparing recipients for later advocacy.

The communication task is much more complex than the simple eloquence, hyperbole, and repetition which were once thought to account for the effectiveness of war-mongering and both subversive and defamatory propaganda. To fear dangerous propaganda or to be shocked by its apparent effectiveness is not enough. For dangerous propaganda, like acceptable propaganda, can also fail to manipulate people. Account,

[55] In a sense, what is involved is individual and group information processing not unlike the Soviet processing of news from the *New York Times*, the *Washington Post*, and a few other American newspapers to provide secret daily news summaries for the highest members of the Soviet hierarchy, less complete summaries for lower officials, and a still less objective file for the press. Davison, *International Political Communication*, p. 99; Theodore E. Kruglak, *The Two Faces of Tass* (Minneapolis: University of Minnesota Press, 1962), pp. 44, 93-94.

[56] James Mill, *Law of Nations*, pp. 5, 7-8, 32-33, in *Essays on Government, Jurisprudence, Liberty of the Press, and Law of Nations*, written for the *Supplement to the Encyclopaedia Britannica* (London, n.d.).

therefore, must be taken of the failures of eloquence, extremes, and repetition, as well as the failures of other propaganda techniques. To do so takes not only research but also efforts to change attitude patterns, the ranking of values in action situations, and the several steps in the flow of communications. Otherwise, advocacy of the legal repression of dangerous propaganda is a long-shot gamble that responsive and influential minds will produce both verbal formulation of the desired norms and that effective response to them will be reached.

Mob Violence

TURNING briefly to that collective recipient of provocative stimuli, the mob or crowd, it may be noted that we are not concerned just with an essentially domestic political and social force such as the lynch mob or the Parisians behind their barricades. Mobs also serve as instruments of foreign policy and as instruments of political communication. The mob has been the subject of a number of studies since Gustave LeBon's not too reliable examination of *The Crowd* (1896). Studies such as Rudé's tended to examine the behavior of mobs at specified historical periods, while principles of social psychology have been applied to specific situations by such writers as Hadley Cantril.[57]

For the international lawyer, the mob and mob violence have been of only occasional concern. The Don Pacifico affair, attacks on American citizens by Mexican and Panamanian mobs, the lynching of some Italians in New Orleans, and in-

[57] George Rudé, *The Crowd in History: A Study of Popular Disturbances in France and England, 1730-1848* (New York: Wiley, 1964); Hadley Cantril, *The Psychology of Social Movements* (New York: Wiley; London: Chapman & Hall, 1941). For a relevant application of sociological insights about collectivities in general, see Neil J. Smelser, *Theory of Collective Behavior* (New York: Free Press, 1962). See also Henry L. Mason, *Mass Demonstrations Against Foreign Regimes: A Study of Five Crises*, Tulane Studies in Political Science, vol. 10 (New Orleans: Tulane University, 1966).

juries suffered by aliens during riots at Kalgoorlie, Western Australia, have given rise to international claims and even to assertions that federal governments were not responsible for the failure of state authorities to provide adequate protection.[58] These cases, rather infrequent, dealt with the question of state responsibility for injury to aliens and so, indirectly, to the aliens' states.

Inviolability of legations, envoys, and their residences has been recognized since the early modern practice of *franchise du quartier*, the protection even carrying over into time of war.[59] In such cases responsibility would be for direct injury to a state. Although the more distant past has seen such incidents as attacks on diplomats' residences and even assassination of diplomats, it is only in the post–World War II period that the demonstration outside an embassy, consulate, or information agency or the mob attack upon it has become a tool of political manipulation. The use of the crowd directly against a state requires careful investigation not just with regard to the normative element. For a relevant law concerning mob action should be grounded on social-psychological findings about mobs and upon what is known about the making, organization, and manipulation of crowds. A realistic law, whether international or municipal, will take account of the crowd manager. Moreover, as Professor Lasswell reminds us, crowd formation can cross national boundaries to threaten the security of two or more governments and social systems.[60] This complication emphasizes the need for something more than just laws directed toward the repression of and liability for mob violence against the legitimately employed property or personnel of foreign states. Such laws can at most be but one

[58] Wesley L. Gould, *An Introduction to International Law* (New York: Harper, 1957), pp. 528-29.

[59] *Ibid.*, pp. 269-70.

[60] Harold D. Lasswell, "The Impact of Crowd Psychology upon International Law," *Philippine International Law Journal* 1 (1962): 293-309.

phase of crowd control that might include, as Lasswell suggests, both an international approach toward an effective free forum and an effort toward vindication of inclusive rather than exclusive claims.

Chapter VIII: Humanitarian and Economic Affairs

Treatment of Aliens

One of the paradoxes of the contemporary world is that with increased travel, with increased international business activity and with an abundance of new and revolutionary states there has been a marked falling off in resort to claims tribunals dealing with injuries to aliens. Does this mean that strong states are no longer able to bully the weak? Are Western states doing penance for past wrongs? Are aliens no longer rare and unusual creatures? Have some of the patterns of inter-ethnic relations that developed under colonialism proved both satisfactory and durable? Have some of the early experiences of independence revealed the indispensability of the technically-accomplished alien? Are many of the disputes that might have led to diplomatic intervention and settlement by claims tribunals now dealt with by commercial arbitration? Do local courts now treat aliens fairly?

Frequently, discussion of 19th- and early 20th-century Latin American claims arbitrations stresses the capability of Great Powers to impose their will on the weak. By opposing power and consent and attributing legitimating capacities only to the latter, such discussions disparage the legal quality of the rules enunciated by claims tribunals. Yet, decline in resort to claims procedures should raise the question of whether actual behavior toward aliens by many states is now more nearly in harmony with standards enunciated by the claims tribunals than in earlier decades. Conceivably, not just internal changes in underdeveloped countries or international system changes affecting Great Power behavior toward weak states but also a learning or socialization process accounts for the decline in resort to claims tribunals. Simplistic explanations ignore the function of learning in the lawmaking process. Moreover, the true dimensions of the problem of treatment of aliens are not comprehended by a focus on the treatment of Europeans and North Americans by non-Western and Latin American regimes.

Expanded dimensions of the alien problem now call for its treatment in more comprehensive terms than the older issues of exhaustion of local remedies, denial of justice, adequacy of police protection, and, in general, the so-called "minimum standard." Are the Chinese and Hindus settled in Southeast Asian countries accorded anything resembling the minimum treatment that Europeans demanded?[1] In the light of a history that has placed Cambodians in Vietnam and Vietnamese in Cambodia, what is the lot of each of these peoples in the territory of the other?[2] Do minimum standards apply to nomads whose periodic entry into a state's territory forms the basis for claims threatening its territorial integrity? Is there a relationship between ratings on the Bogardus Social Distance Scale and detectable variations in the treatment accorded aliens from different countries? To what extent would the influx of a large number of aliens, whether Europeans or non-Europeans, be perceived as a moral danger to be averted?[3] What relationships can be found that link the fear of moral danger from a large influx of aliens, opposition to governmental and intergovernmental efforts to prevent and to correct abuses of aliens, and differing capacities to absorb aliens of various stocks that threaten to make the mass immigrant a man with-

[1] E.g., D. P. Mozingo, "Sino-Indonesian Relations: An Overview, 1955-1965," RAND Memorandum RM-4641-PR (Santa Monica: RAND Corporation, July, 1965), pp. 22-29.

[2] Bernard K. Gordon, *The Dimensions of Conflict in Southeast Asia* (Englewood Cliffs: Prentice-Hall, 1966), pp. 43-48, 56-57.

[3] See S. P. Adenarayan, "A Study of Racial Attitudes in India," *Journal of Social Psychology* 45 (1957): 211-16. A Soviet party publication has expressed fears that cultural exchanges would permit alien ideological concepts to be spread in the Soviet Union. *New York Times*, June 6, 1962, p. 8.

out a country?[4] Does a border closing alleviate the problem of an alien presence sufficiently to offset counterproductive effects on other aspects of the national system?[5] Efforts to answer these and related questions, along with regard for the law of responsibility for injuries to aliens and treaty arrangements concerning population movements,[6] should provide a foundation in sociological, psychological, and political data for a realistic appraisal of the law as it has developed to date.

Minorities

PERHAPS no humanitarian issue that has affected the content of the international law of the 20th century has proved more of a conundrum than that of minorities and their rights. As Inis Claude has so clearly pointed out, the League of Nations approach had the effect of raising hostilities and frustrations for states protecting minorities while also providing "kin" states with a temptation to promote irredentist and subversive movements.[7] What appears to have resulted was a form of mutual scapegoating and some hostility catharsis, although it must be noted that research on such facets of the frustration-aggression thesis has still left great uncertainties at the individual level.[8] Much remains to be done before satisfactorily

[4] C. P. Kindleberger, "Mass Migration Then and Now," *Foreign Affairs* 43 (1965): 647-58; A. Bharati, "Problems of the Asian Minorities in East Africa," *Pakistan Horizon* 17 (1964): 342-49.

[5] Jean Rouch, "Migration au Ghana," *Journal de la Société des Africanistes* 36 (1956): 1-95; I. William Zartman, *International Relations in the New Africa* (Englewood Cliffs: Prentice-Hall, 1966), pp. 111-12, 140.

[6] Carter Goodrich, "Possibilities and Limits of International Control of Migration," in Milbank Memorial Fund, *Postwar Problems of Migration: Papers Presented at the Round Table on Population Problems, October 29-30, 1946* (New York, 1947), pp. 74-81.

[7] Inis L. Claude, Jr., *National Minorities: An International Problem* (Cambridge: Harvard University Press, 1955).

[8] E.g., Leonard Berkowitz and James A. Green, "The Stimulus Qualities of the Scapegoat," *Journal of Abnormal and Social Psychology* 64 (1962): 293-301; Berkowitz, Green, and Jacqueline B. Macauley, "Hos-

formulated and tested hypotheses about individual behavior can be amalgamated with what is known about propaganda and other communications patterns in order to explain group behavior toward minorities. The communications patterns must include those among the minorities themselves if we are to explain why they are not in the same position as opinion-based minorities that in democratic political systems can become the governments of tomorrow.[9]

Not the opinion-based minority but the minority produced by an unchanging or a very slowly changeable factor has been the intended beneficiary of an appeal to a positive law higher than the law of the state. Attempts to benefit minorities that cannot be changed virtually overnight can be directed at both democratic and authoritarian forms of government. In this sense, they are not discriminatory as an attempt to protect opinion-based minorities would be, for such an effort would necessarily be directed only against authoritarian regimes. Both types of regime can oppress permanent minorities. Such minorities could become governments only through the use of force against majorities. Were they to do so, they would themselves become targets of the treaty rules intended to prevent oppression.

Even the more universal human rights approach, expressing a "melting pot" concept, thrusts at both types of political regime and requires the consent of each. American fears of a human rights treaty and French hesitance about the Rome Convention for the Protection of Human Rights and Fundamental Freedoms are indicative of democracy's lack of immunity.

In the period of the League of Nations system it was the

---

tility Catharsis as the Reduction of Emotional Tension," *Psychiatry* 25 (1962): 23-31.

[9] See the observation on this point by W. Ivor Jennings, *The British Constitution* (Cambridge, England: The University Press, 1942), pp. 32-34.

minorities of Central Europe that engaged attention. To the extent that the present human rights approach has seemed applicable (even if unenforceable) in the popular American mind, its relevance has been to Stalin's Russia and its forced labor camps. What seems to have escaped general notice is the whole of the broad problem that embraces such minorities as whites in former colonial countries, Hindus and Pakistani in East Africa, non-European Jews in Israel, Armenians and Jews in Iran, Arabs and Eurasians in Indonesia, various national minorities in Communist China, and, of course, the Indians, French Canadians, and other minorities of the Western Hemisphere. It is noteworthy that there has been a basic reluctance to pull together all the data produced by specialists on race relations, cultural encounters, comparative politics, and international relations and law that is pertinent to minorities, as well as potentially related findings in the areas of individual and social psychology and in communications research. For example, whether in respect to the direction of mobs, the treatment of individuals in prisons and concentration camps, or governmental directives to make war, there are frightening implications in a Yale University experiment in which a surprising number of adult subjects carried out the directives of an anonymous experimenter to subdue a fifty-year-old man and subject him to painful electric shocks.[10] To synthesize what is available might well arm the doers of good in the human rights domain with something more substantial than moral principles and essentially agitative organizational techniques. As David Danelski has pointed out, what is needed is a jurisprudence anchored in human behavior and presenting empirically verifiable hypotheses.[11] For the inter-

[10] Stanley Milgram, "Some Considerations of Obedience and Disobedience to Authority," *Human Relations* 18 (1965): 56-76.

[11] David J. Danelski, "A Behavioral Conception of Human Rights" (Paper presented at the Annual Meeting of the American Political Science Association, September, 1964).

national lawyer the relevant human behavior is that of many minorities and many majorities, behavior that introduces a cultural complexity into the effort to find a common international standard of proper intergroup relations.

Refugees, Population Exchanges, and Forced Migrations

ONLY brief attention will be accorded the problem of refugees and those of migrations and population exchanges. The specialized literature on these subjects was largely generated by the momentous displacements of the two World Wars and their aftermaths. This problem is interrelated with others such as the treatment of aliens and minorities, hunger, population control, and capacities to absorb other stocks and cultures, as well as with such legal matters as compensation (e.g., for abandoned Arab property), nationality, and the right of a government to demand and obtain repatriation of its nations.

Two facets of these problems will be mentioned. In regard to refugees, greater attention might well be paid to their attitudes. In some cases this has been done, e.g., by Fred C. Bruhns in regard to Arab refugees from Palestine.[12] One of his findings, important for any politico-legal approach to the problem, was that objection to resettlement outside Israel stemmed from the inability to take clan, village, friends, and religious leaders with them. Thus, under certain compromise conditions, these Arabs of a decade ago could have accepted Israel's existence.

One problem related to population control is a suboptimal relationship of people to arable land, hence to food supply. This need suggests that internationally organized migration might become a feature of future decades. Yet to argue for the organized movement of people from overpopulated areas to sparsely populated regions of Africa, Australia, and Latin

[12] Fred C. Bruhns, "A Study of Arab Refugee Attitudes," *Middle East Journal* 9 (1955): 130-38.

America, as, for example, Sripati Chandrasekhar has done, would be to arouse fears.[13] In 1968 East Africa, disturbed by the presence of Hindu and Pakistani traders,[14] created legislation that produced a sudden migration to England that quickly produced immigration barriers. Clearly, migration as an aspect of population control is an area in which political reformer and legal reformer need to join hands with medical, agricultural, and technological expert to anticipate problems and to try to prepare the ground for necessary actions before immediate pressures render emotional issues acute.

International Medical and Sanitation Law

Of the literature of international law only a very small part of rather recent vintage has been devoted to medical law. In addition to the more administratively oriented studies of narcotics control, almost all of that literature is devoted to the law on military medicine that is found in or derived from treaties dealing with the sick and wounded in time of war.[15] As massive and concentrated as is the care of the wartime sick and wounded, it is but a small part of the medical problems with which international jurisprudence might well concern itself. As matters stand, for the less spectacular aspects of international public health measures one must turn chiefly to the medical literature for enlightenment.

One aspect of international regulation makes inoculation against yellow fever compulsory for all travelers entering the

[13] Sripati Chandrasekhar, *Hungry People and Empty Lands: An Essay on Population Problems and International Tensions* (New York: Macmillan, 1955).

[14] Indira Rothermund, *Die politische und wirtschaftliche Rolle der asiatischen Minderheit in Ostafrika—Kenya, Tanganyika, Sansibar, Uganda* (Berlin, Heidelberg, and New York: Springer, 1965).

[15] The problem of nuclear radiation is dealt with essentially in terms of the protection of workers and populations. See, e.g., Enrico Jacchia, *Atome et sécurité: Le Risque des radiations à l'âge nucléaire* (Paris: Dalloz, 1965).

internationally agreed yellow fever belt.[16] But it should not be thought that the assertion of inoculation or vaccination on the World Health Organization's yellow form of itself assures effective regulation. International searches for the passengers discharged from an airplane or ship after a fellow traveler, in some cases carrying a forged or otherwise improper vaccination certificate, contracted small pox, together with outbreaks of epidemics traced to arrivals of infected passengers (e.g., Great Britain in early 1962),[17] remind us that international medical law depends for its effectiveness upon local laws and habits, upon both legal and nonlegal forms of implementation. Objections that still persist to the pricking and puncturing attendant upon inoculation or vaccination—a form of tyranny in some eyes—impose a need for assurance that local physicians have not accepted a small consideration for attesting on the WHO form that vaccination has occurred when it has not.[18] In a pilot study conducted by the Division of Foreign Quarantine, of the United States Public Health Service, at fourteen international airports, the quarantine station at the then Idlewild Airport reported on a sample of 10% of the incoming flights from October 24 to November 2, 1960. Among other things, it was found that 1% of the arriving passengers failed to present a valid smallpox vaccination certificate and

[16] L. Dudley Stamp, *The Geography of Life and Death* (Ithaca: Cornell University Press, 1964; paperback edn., 1965), p. 44.

[17] *New York Times*, October 8, 1960, p. 8; October 12, 1960, p. 30; January 12, 1962, p. 2; January 13, 1962, p. 46; January 14, 1962, p. 2; January 16, 1962, p. 4; January 17, 1962, p. 3; February 25, 1962, p. 65; September 1, 1963, p. 5; September 3, 1963, p. 11; January 17, 1964, p. 14; October 11, 1965, p. 51; March 29, 1967, p. 3.

[18] This statement is based on information volunteered on various occasions by Asian students who have lived with one of us. On objections to health measures as an interference with freedom, see T. V. Smith, "The Ideological Strength and Weakness of the American Position," *Annals of the American Academy of Political and Social Science* 278 (1951): 38-46, esp. 39-40.

that 6.5% required surveillance as possible threats to the health of American citizens.[19]

But it is not only with travelers that international medical law is concerned. For example, consideration has been given to the possibility of synchronized efforts to eradicate smallpox. Doing so would require international agreements to ensure worldwide sharing and timing of national efforts through legal mechanisms, as well as through mechanisms now provided by the World Health Organization and by the World Health Assembly.[20] Some suggestions have been made for improving drug safety controls by requiring a common reporting system to forestall crystallization of national differences in observation and recording. Protection of populations and workers from nuclear radiation has already produced legal arrangements including those of the European Communities.[21] Although primarily with reference to its free circulation during war and the protection of zones for its storage, attention has been called to the need for an international arrangement for blood and its derivatives that would include elimination of discrimination and pressures on physicians concerning who shall receive transfusions.[22] Consideration of public health by the Council of Europe and the conclusion of agreements in that field have covered such matters as identification of blood groups, pharmaceutical problems, camping hygiene, sanitary control of food products, and re-

[19] Mildred L. McKinnon and Louis C. Redmund Smith, "Quarantine Inspection of International Air Travelers," *Public Health Reports* 77 (1962): 65-69.

[20] Harald Frederiksen, "Strategy and Tactics for Smallpox Eradication," *ibid.*, pp. 617-22.

[21] D. J. Finney, "An International Drug Safety Program," *Journal of New Drugs* 3 (1963): 262-65; Jacchia, *Atome et sécurité.*

[22] Paul Moreau, "Le Problème du sang sur le plan international," *Annales de droit international médical*, no. 3 (December, 1958), pp. 28-36.

habilitation and reemployment of invalids.[23] What perhaps cannot be done through legal means or international effort other than education is to eliminate diametrically opposed types of treatment such as the diets reportedly prescribed by Dutch and American doctors for colitis patients and by Italian and American doctors for pregnant women.

Attempts to assure the application of approved international standards and analytical practices in order that potable water be made available to all peoples has received much less public attention in the United States than the pollution issue.[24] Yet they are parts of the same problem. The pollution aspect extends beyond the problem of drinking water to that of recreational use without damage to health and to protection of fish and birds. Of course, protecting fish and birds from the consequences of pollution of water by sewage, oil, and industrial wastes such as those from pulp mills is an undertaking extending to salt water as well as to fresh water.[25] The wrecking of the *Torrey Canyon* and the escape of crude oil from a

[23] H. Pfeffermann and H. Wiebringhaus, "Les activités du Conseil de l'Europe dans le domaine de la santé publique," *Annales de droit international médical*, no. 11 (December, 1964), pp. 46-62.

[24] *International Standards for Drinking Water*, 2nd edn. (Geneva: World Health Organization; New York: Columbia University Press, 1963).

[25] M. Katz and A. Gaufin, "The Effects of Sewage Pollution on the Fish Population of a Midwestern Stream," *Transactions of the American Fisheries Society, 1952*, 82 (1953): 156-65; Katz, W. M. Van Horn, and J. B. Anderson, "The Effect of Kraft Pulp Mill Wastes on Some Aquatic Organisms," *Transactions of the American Fisheries Society, 1949*, 79 (1950): 55-63; M. F. Mörzer Bruyns, "Stookolievogels op de Nederlandse kust," *Levende Natuur* 62 (1959): 172-78, which includes discussion of the probabilities of reducing the number of bird victims of oil pollution through implementation of the convention on pollution. Threatened effects on aquatic life through ocean disposal of radioactive wastes appears less likely now that ground burial seems safe as well as less costly. Floyd W. Wilcox "The Role of the Government and Private Enterprise in Radioactive Waste Disposal," *Journal of Environmental Health* 27 (1965): 818-23.

well being drilled off Santa Barbara early in 1969 have dramatized the problem. But fresh water is the more pressing matter because of its multiple uses, including those for industry.[26]

What has been done on local levels to coordinate agencies both to abate pollution and to improve water supplies[27] requires attention if more international public health problems are to be attacked and if the nascent international medical law is to be molded into an effective instrument for establishing standards and obligations. Such standards need to be related to the requirements for preservation of the ecological system in which the human population must live if it survives its present stage of rapid growth, adapts to crowding, preserves a varied landscape of mixed productive and unproductive areas, avoids eutrophication of the oceans that apparently maintain the highly aerobic terrestrial environment, and develops both governmental and intergovernmental systems-analysis capabilities with effective mechanisms for action when there is "too much of a good thing" to maintain the needed environmental quality.[28] What we are suggesting is a somewhat different perspective with more concern for the collective self

[26] John A. Logan, "The International Municipal Water Supply Problem: A Health and Economic Appraisal," *American Journal of Tropical Medicine and Hygiene* 9 (1960): 469-76; R. O. Sylvester, "Some Influences of Multi-Purpose Water Usage on Water Quality," *Proceedings of the International Union for Conservation of Natural and Water Resources* (Brussels, 1959).

[27] See, e.g., G. M. Fair, "Pollution Abatement in the Ruhr District," *Journal* [of the] *Water Pollution Control Federation* 4 (1962): 749-66; Allen V. Kneese, "Water Quality Management by Regional Authorities in the Ruhr Area," in Marshall I. Goldman (ed.), *Controlling Pollution: The Economics of a Cleaner America* (Englewood Cliffs: Prentice-Hall, 1967).

[28] Eugene P. Odum, "The Strategy of Ecosystem Development," *Science* 164 (1969): 262-69; Alfred C. Redfield, "The Biological Control of Chemical Factors in the Environment," *American Scientist* 46 (1958): 205-21. On the need for legal and moral means of mutually agreed-on coercion in the absence of a technical solution to the problem of pollution by overpopulation, see Garrett Hardin, "The Tragedy of the Commons," *Science* 162 (1968): 1243-48.

than can be found, for example, in legal considerations of liability for damage caused to downstream states through pollution of international rivers.[29] Much the same may be said about air pollution for the basic problem is to promote concern by states for the health of their own citizens. Unless such concern is displayed, consideration of possible liability for international nuisances and injuries is peripheral.

Food

RELATED both to public health and to population control are problems of assuring an adequate and sanitary food supply. In regard to agriculture, fisheries, and whaling, both economy of operation and conservation are basic issues. But the operational meanings of economy and conservation may differ. Windmills may be an appropriate innovation to promote Pakistan's agricultural development but hardly for an advanced country. For long distance fishing fleets, although not necessarily for whaling fleets, more modern equipment might assist in promoting conservation and, if the surplus fishermen can be accommodated elsewhere in their countries' economies, put the industry on a sounder economic basis.[30]

[29] E.g., the paper by J. Hans Fischerhof and that by E. J. Manner in Wolfgang Christ et al., *Aspects of Water Pollution Control: A Selection of Papers from the Conference on Water Pollution Problems in Europe, Geneva, 1961*, Public Health Papers, no. 13 (Geneva: World Health Organization, 1962), pp. 53-73, 75-87.

[30] J. L. Hart, "Some Sociological Effects of Quota Control of Fisheries," *Canadian Fish Culturalist* 22 (1958): 17-19; Anthony D. Scott, "Food and the World Fisheries Situation," in Marion Clawson (ed.) *Natural Resources and International Development* (Baltimore: Johns Hopkins Press for Resources for the Future, 1964), pp. 127-51; Scott McVay, "The Last of the Great Whales," *Scientific American* 215 (August, 1965): 13-21. It is said that if modern methods were used, 27 thousand of the approximately 30 thousand Canadian and American salmon hunters would be unnecessary to retain present catch levels. Ralph W. Johnson, "Regulation of Commercial Salmon Fisheries: A Case of Confused Objectives," *Pacific Northwest Quarterly* 55 (1964): 141-45. See also R.G.S. Bidwell, "Decline of the Lobster," letter in *Science* 158 (1967): 1136-37.

Cultural factors enter into the problem of regulation where free fishing in deep sea fisheries leads to overfishing. Optimal utilization of North Pacific fisheries is not the same thing for Canadians and Americans as for Japanese and Russians. What Americans and others displaying North European tastes will eat limits the number of species that can be marketed profitably. Other peoples' tastes are not so limited and the opportunity to market a wider variety of species provides an additional incentive for the use of highly efficient equipment and even for the Japanese thesis that not abstention but the development of new resources should be the governing principle of regulation.[31] But for peoples whose tastes are for only certain fish, regulation means regulation of those species even if doing so would limit the catch of other species.[32] Fisheries regulation is a problem yet to be pursued in terms of its economic facets and the total world food situation.

From another point of view more closely related to medical law and public health, a problem exists in the diversity of national standards applicable to fresh and processed foods. Fish and fishery products are an example of a food for which it would be advantageous to have effective international standards as a safeguard against food poisoning.[33]

Population Control

THE TOUCHY subject of population control is one that arises out of imbalances in the accomplishments of modern science. One obvious imbalance is that between medical and agricul-

[31] The Japanese view is set forth in Hiroshi Kasahara, *Fisheries of the North Pacific Ocean*, H. R. MacMillan Lectures in Fisheries, 2 vols. (Vancouver: University of British Columbia, 1961, 1964).

[32] James Crutchfield, "The Marine Fisheries: A Problem in International Cooperation," Papers and Proceedings of the Seventy-sixth Annual Meeting of the American Economic Association (1963), *American Economic Review* 54 (1964): 207-18.

[33] J. Liston and J. M. Shewan, "A Review of Food Poisoning Caused by Fish and Fishery Products," *Journal of Applied Bacteriology* 18 (1955): 522 ff.

tural science and their applications to the world's several soil, climate, and cultural regions.[34] Another imbalance in many parts of the world is that between the rate of advance in disease control and the rate of conversion to high energy utilization. As Fred Cottrell has suggested, the population of the world's low energy regions is now beyond the point where the rate of accumulation of energy converters that sufficed for early Western development would suffice to produce the level of per capita productivity at which Western birth rates declined. Decrease in fertility for reasons other than those identifiable during Western industrial development appears to be necessary if population growth is not to outstrip the accumulation of converters.[35] No doubt lack of capital contributes to the slow accumulation of converters to date. But it is noticeable that some states have also seen the need for birth control along with economic development, even though in the low energy high population countries birth control, affecting the only productive factor over which the low energy farmer has control, has not yet been a marked success.[36]

What uses can be made of international law to deal with the population problem? Probably no direct uses are possible. It has been suggested that a principle may be emerging that would treat self-replacement as the right of an individual but would regard exceeding self-replacement as an aggression against society and against mankind as a whole.[37] Inter-

[34] See e.g., Warren H. Leonard, "World Population in Relation to Potential Food Supply," *Scientific Monthly* 85 (1957): 113-25.

[35] Fred Cottrell, *Energy and Society: The Relation Between Energy, Social Change, and Economic Development* (New York: McGraw-Hill, 1955), p. 168. See also Odum, "The Strategy of Ecosystem Development," p. 263.

[36] Katherine and A.F.K. Organski, *Population and World Power* (New York: Knopf, 1961), pp. 126, 150-51; Cottrell, *Energy and Society*, pp. 36-38, 117-19, 168-69. A measure of restrained optimism is expressed by the demographer, Frank W. Notestein, "The Population Crisis: Reasons for Hope," *Foreign Affairs* 46 (1967): 167-80.

[37] S. N. Afriat, "People and Populations," *World Politics* 17 (1965): 431-39.

national law can hardly impose that principle or even one more palatable to those of us whose strong affection for children and adults is reflected in our concern about overpopulation and for the welfare of individuals.

Indirectly, much may be done by use of international law provided that a systems approach is used and the potential systemic effects of normative and procedural inputs are traced as far as possible. One legitimate concern of the law is with occurrences that are aggravated by population pressure. Protection of the units of the international system, whether by guarantee of territorial integrity, international supervision of migration with procedures for the protection of potential recipients of migrants,[38] or continued reservation to states of the capacity to determine immigration quotas, could serve to reassure East African governments that see their territories as targets for the growing populations across the Indian Ocean. Another approach is through such normative inputs as investment guarantees and the creation of devices for international capital mobilization so that the rate of accumulation of energy converters in current low energy societies can be progressively increased and perhaps planned with better than either dogmatic or hit-and-miss rationality. In other words, more than is generally recognized in international law studies or studies of the population explosion, various segments of international law have as yet an only vaguely charted impact on the population problem by way of other variables.

Aliens in Business

Much has been written about the right of establishment, particularly in Western Europe. But we would like to suggest that the overall picture relating the various national and international legal provisions about the several types of alien businessmen to their functions and influence in the community

[38] On planned migration, see William Peterson, *The Politics of Population*, Anchor edition (Garden City: Doubleday, 1965), pp. 301-22.

has yet to be developed even to the extent that studies of particular communities would admit. There is a great deal of difference between the representative of a large American or German concern and a Hindu money-lender or a Lebanese tradesman. There is also quite a difference when the foreign elements control perhaps 70% of the economy instead of a share more nearly proportionate to their numbers.

To what extent movements to nationalize foreign-owned property are a function of the extent of foreign control over an economy is, in general, not clear. Intuitively, one would expect a relationship. But must extent of foreign ownership appear in combination with other variables and if so, what particular combinations? Are there sets of variables productive of nationalization even though foreign ownership would be a negligible factor?

Over and above the large businesses that draw much attention, there are other relationships to which attention should be given. To what extent are national economies dependent upon the skills brought by foreigners and, perhaps, nourished there for generations? Today we are primarily aware of the aliens who have brought engineering and other technical skills to underdeveloped lands. But we should not forget the skills which Spanish Jews brought to the Netherlands and the Huguenots to German states. In so far as Honduras has industry, it is that of the Americans, Arabs, and Jews of San Pedro Sula, with one Tegucigalpa plant established by an individual from San Pedro.

How well do the possessors of skills relate to the community? Are there among some peoples generalized attitude structures more receptive to skilled aliens, or at least certain skilled aliens possessed of attitude structures tending to promote their assimilation, than are to be found elsewhere? Why are the Ibo the people who carried their enterprise in West Africa beyond the bounds of Nigeria and to what extent do West Africans' receptivities differ? The use of social distance scales and of other tests for stereotyping and prejudice[39] might prove useful in an assessment of the probabilities of the effective application of rights of establishment in particular countries. Such tests might also suggest directions that the relevant law should take as stereotypes and prejudices persist, grow stronger, or wane, as the case may be. It should not be forgotten that aliens are normally voteless, that the pressure groups that have influence upon the local laws relevant to their businesses and professions are made up of nationals who may view the aliens' skills as roadblocks to their own achievement, and that political parties are likely to be unconcerned about the welfare of individuals whose support they may not need. The result may be a reflection in government policies of disparities in political strength.[40] Such a circumstance is the reverse of that of the state and elite group overly dependent upon the foreigner's skills and, perhaps, his capital. Both situations may require international regulation to mitigate extreme consequences.

Social Security Abroad

ALTHOUGH the problem of social benefits for workers who have migrated from one of the European Communities countries to another has received some attention, to our knowledge there has been no study on a broader scale of what is being done by other countries to assure social security payments to aliens. In the case of the United States, disbursements are made to payees in other countries, among them Greece, Bulgaria, Jordan, and Cyprus. For such disbursements to take place, either a Foreign Service Officer or, as in Athens, a Social Security official gathers evidence (including that concerned

[39] E.g., L. N. Diab, "National Stereotypes and the Reference Group Concept," *Journal of Social Psychology* 57 (1962): 339-51; A.K.P. Singh and O. P. Upahyaya, "Eleven Ethnic Groups on a Social Distance Scale," *Journal of Social Psychology* 57 (1962): 49-54.

[40] R. D. Tomasek, "The Migrant Problem and Pressure Groups," *Journal of Politics* 23 (1961): 295-319.

with overpayments), may be involved in court proceedings, and may have to deal with such problems as those presented by unwanted "claims helpers" and their attempts to obtain fees, as for example in Cyprus.[41] We only call attention to a need to examine such virtually unknown aspects of relations among states if a full picture of the international system is to be made known.

Foreign Aid and Economic Development

At the first plenary meeting of the American Section of the International Association for Philosophy of Law and Social Philosophy in November, 1966, one of the issues raised was whether international legal and quasi-legal obligations were coming into being to secure for developing countries the capital needed for their modernization. A strong case was made that abundant possibilities exist for the development of such obligations.[42] Whether it is going too far to say that eco-

[41] James Howard, "Notes from Abroad," *Oasis* 10 (April, 1964): 12-14, 21, reporting in the Social Security employees' magazine on some aspects of this activity.

[42] James F. Doyle, "Egoism and Altruism in the Modernization of Developing Countries," (Paper presented at the First Plenary Session of Amintaphil, the American Section of the International Association for Philosophy of Law and Social Philosophy, St. Louis, November 28-30, 1966). See also the question of a possible duty of U.N. members in their own decision-making capacities to promote higher standards of living, full employment, and social and economic development, D. Owen, "The United Nations Expanded Programs of Technical Assistance—A Multilateral Approach," *Annals of the American Academy of Political and Social Science* 323 (1959): 25-32. For the suggestion that "a kind of standing international legal obligation now almost exists to require support for the destitute, the ill-fed and the socially retarded," see Maxwell Cohen, "From Diversity to Unity: International Law in a Bipolar World," *Proceedings of the American Society of International Law, 1959*, p. 106. For a discussion of the multilateral approach to foreign aid that has some overtones relevant to the question of whether there is an obligation, see A. A. Fatouros and R. N. Kelson, *Canada's Overseas Aid* (Toronto: Canadian Institute of International Affairs, 1964), pp. 33-44, 49-50, 79-80, 100.

nomic aid rendered under both national and international auspices is giving rise to such an obligation is difficult to say. Indeed, it is hard to say that a developing country could formally demand capital and its provision become mandatory. Requests can be looked into by appropriate agencies and, for economic or political reasons, be provided or withheld.

But whether what obtains can or cannot properly be called a legal obligation, or whether legal obligation arises on a mutual basis only after a contractual relationship has been entered into, there is no doubt that facilities for acquisition of finance capital are needed. Great Britain's prompt response to the opportunities offered by the steam engine was in part a consequence of her possession of an organized capital market. Other countries that tried to catch up with Great Britain did so through official initiative in encouraging or quickly organizing credit institutions and by popularizing credit instruments.[43] For the developing countries, which require capital without being able to present the financing of economic growth as a business proposition to well-organized capital markets of their own, resort must be had to the public and, for countries not gripped by ideological restraints, private sectors of foreign economies.

To recognize that such needs exist is not to assert that an obligation has arisen or is arising to meet the developing countries' needs for capital. Not unless more than transient, year-to-year justifications for establishing a relationship of supplier and receiver of capital were to become firmly grounded could it be said that legal obligations were firm. Should they arise out of an enduring interdependence, such legal obligations would be meaningfully described only in terms of that interdependence at least until they had attained an existence of their own because of mutual expectations arising from knowledge of the obligations. Whether the Cold-War-aid game

[43] Arum K. Datta Gupta, "Foreign Contribution in British Capital Market Development: A Note," *Indian Economic Journal* 10 (1962-63): 454-57.

gives rise either to the basic interdependence or to the expectations lending to legal instruments the quality of obligations in their own right is at best a still not too carefully investigated topic. A systematic investigation of the expectations of one or two pairs of nations and of the expectations in a dyad of nation and aid-giving international organization would throw light upon norm generation as it may or may not be occurring in this area of international economic activity.[44]

International Pipelines

The ever larger oil and natural gas pipeline systems have been quite neglected in the literature on international law and international relations. American and British writers tend to give more attention to transportation across the high seas and, to some extent, along international rivers particularly when such rivers provide extensions of ocean shipping. More traditional forms of land transportation, namely, railroad and highway, receive virtually no attention except in Europe.[45] In general, border problems are few. Those that do exist between the United States and its northern and southern neighbors do not impose the multilateral complexities that have beset Western and Central Europe's main arteries. Hence, with prior inattention to land transportation as an international phenomenon of basic daily concern, it is not surprising that the newer, relatively unseen growth of pipelines and electric grids should receive little attention except at moments of relatively spectacular occurrences, such as British Columbia's rejection of the first version of the Columbia River

[44] For the views of two economists in a recipient country, see V.K.R.V. Rao and Dharm Narain, *Foreign Aid and India's Economic Development* (Bombay, Calcutta, . . . London, and New York: Asia Publishing House, 1963).

[45] E.g., Paul Durand, *Les transports internationaux (ferroviaires et mixtes): Étude comparée des nouvelles conventions de Berne mises en application le 1er mars 1956* (Paris: Sirey, 1956); Pierre Vergnaud, *Les transports routier internationaux* (Paris: Librairie Générale de Droit et de Jurisprudence, 1960).

Treaty. Even Secretary of the Interior Stewart Udall could not generate as much reaction to the issue of imported Canadian crude oil as to his own personality and convictions.

With rare exceptions, pipelines are not subjected to treaty regimes even on a bilateral basis.[46] Pipelines are a form of transportation that helps to delineate both energy systems and emerging systems for the allocation of an undetermined number of resources. What developed as a cost-cutting method of transporting fluids over ever-increasing distances has now become also a means of transporting solids. In the form of slurries of the product and water, coal, phosphate rock (including lumps of six to nine inches' thickness), nickel-copper and copper concentrates, borax, limestone, clay, sand, gravel, and, before long, wood chips for pulp are among the products transported over distances up to 100 miles over more than 100 slurry pipelines in North America. An improvement requiring less power than the slurry is the transport of capsules and cylindrical or spherical masses of material in a carrier liquid of water or oil, oil being an additional payload. This means that agricultural products, canned goods, pure chemicals, machine parts, and other commodities that can be encapsulated are among the products that may be carried by the pipelines of the future. So, too, are also such products as aluminum, iron and steel, sulfur, beneficiated ores, potash, plastics, and other materials that can be extruded, cast, sintered, or otherwise formed into spheres or cylindrical slugs. Thus, in addition to present multipurpose uses of pipelines (whereby successive batches of different liquid products can be sent either with negligible mixing between batches or, if necessary, by separating them with an inflatable sphere), increased pipeline usage,

[46] The exception in Canadian-American relations was the uneconomic Canol Project of World War II, the facilities of which were disposed of between 1945 and 1960, *Executive Agreement Series*, nos. 386-89, 416; *Treaties and Other International Acts Series*, nos. 1565, 1695-97, 4631; J. S. White, "Oil and Canadian Geography," *Canadian Geographic Journal* 60 (1960): 147.

in some still undeterminable proportion international, is to be expected.[47]

To indicate the growing international dimensions of pipelines just in relation to crude oil, petroleum products, natural gas, and natural gas liquids, we may take brief note of the international linkages to date or in progress. In the Western Hemisphere, Canada and the United States, the United States and Mexico, and Bolivia and Chile are linked by either natural gas or petroleum pipelines or, in the case of Canada and the United States, by both. Pipeline transportation from Northern Argentina to Northern Chile has been planned. In Western Europe, France and Germany, Italy, Germany and Austria, and the Netherlands and a yet undetermined number of neighbors are linked or are being linked either for distribution from ports or from the Slochteren gas field and the North Sea. The Druzhba (Friendship) Pipeline runs from the Soviet Volga fields to East Germany, Hungary, Czechoslovakia, and Poland. In addition, there is an East European pipeline from Rumania to Hungary. To reach ports, crude oil is piped from Algeria to Tunis and from Iraq and Saudi Arabia to the Mediterranean. A natural gas pipeline crosses the Soviet-Afghan border and an oil pipeline links East Pakistan and India. Thus, even the remoter and less developed areas of the world are scenes of pipelining either for regional use or as parts of combined pipeline-ocean systems of transport to industrialized countries.[48]

Where pipelining is concerned, there is clearly need for both

[47] For a readable summary of pipeline development and techniques, see E. J. Jensen and H. S. Ellis, "Pipelines," *Scientific American* 216 (January, 1967): 62-72.

[48] Alfred M. Leeston and John A. Crichton, "The Natural Gas Industry in Foreign Countries," in Leeston, Crichton, and John C. Jacobs, *The Dynamic Natural Gas Industry: The Description of an American Industry from the Historical, Technical, Legal, Financial, and Economic Standpoints* (Norman: University of Oklahoma Press, 1963), pp. 337-84. See also the articles appearing from time to time in *Europe and Oil* and in the *Oil and Gas Journal.*

social scientists and lawyers to look ahead and to bring to bear all relevant social, political, economic, and legal data. In Western Europe the existence of three Communities and six states just in the inner core complicates the formulation and implementation of common energy and transport policies.[49] International organizations of larger membership than the six states of Little Europe provide alternatives even for the Six and add complexity to the development of policies and rules suitable to Western European needs. Some attention has been given to legal and policy problems of pipeline transport in Western Europe,[50] and it appears that the Western European system is the one most likely to stimulate an important body of literature on the several aspects of international pipelining. To the extent that there are studies of pipelining in more than just a single region, these seem to emanate chiefly from writers for industrial journals and from geographers, like those of the French "circulation" school and those dealing with markets, who may be concerned with pipelines as one form of transportation that also includes high tension wires and water supply systems among the world's land transport systems.[51]

To date each writer dealing with pipelines has done so from the standpoint of his own special discipline with the in-

[49] On this problem, see Jaroslav G. Polach, *Euratom: Its Background, Issues, and Economic Implications* (Dobbs Ferry: Oceana, 1964), pp. 116-23, 171-74; Edgar Salin, "Energie-politik europäischer Industriestaaten oder europäische Industriepolitik," *Kyklos* 14 (1961): 451-81.

[50] E.g., L. Kopelmanas, "Internationale Rechtsfragen des Energietransports durch Pipelines," in *Aktuelle Fragen des Energierechts* (Cologne: Institut für Energierecht, 1960), pp. 65ff.; R. Wägenbaur, "Mineralölfernleitungen in der Europäischen Wirtschaftsgemeinschaft," *Aussenwirtschaftsdienst des Betriebs-Beraters* 10 (July, 1964): 206ff.; B. van der Esch," Legal Aspects of a European Energy Policy," *Common Market Law Review* 2 (1964-65): 139-67.

[51] E.g., Paul Claval, *Géographie générale des marchés* (Paris: Les Belles Lettres, 1962); René Clozier, *Géographie de la circulation: L'Économie des transports terrestres (rail, route et eau)* (Paris: Genin, 1964).

ternational aspects of the legal problems involved perhaps receiving the least attention although reflecting the most knotty problems. Hopefully, since the discussion of the legal aspects with international perspective is a venture upon little trodden ground, traditional legal scholarship might bring itself to compromise by incorporating other approaches to produce socially, politically, and economically well-grounded analyses of a problem now upon us. For, just as the construction of pipelines has given rise to clashes of interest ever since 1863 when oil-hauling teamsters in Pennsylvania tore up the first two-mile pipeline from well to railroad, so the possibilities opened by such experiments as those on the fuel cell present threats to existing interests.

Allocation of Resources

PROBLEMS of transportation serve to remind us that resources have not been distributed with regard to political boundaries which, along with other man-made barriers, have disrupted economies, diverted the flows of goods and funds, divided watersheds such as that of the St. Lawrence–Great Lakes, and given rise to disputes that have been settled by both legal procedures and nonlegal means.[52] The effort to acquire and allocate resources in the face of the political impediments established by national governments has given rise to various devices. Among them have been the cartel and the "company region."[53] Maldistribution of minerals and other basic com-

[52] Roy I. Wolfe, *Transportation and Politics* (Princeton: D. Van Nostrand, 1963); and "Transportation and Politics: The Example of Canada," *Annals, Association of American Geographers* 52 (1962): 176-90.

[53] Alvin W. Wolfe, "The African Mineral Industry: Evolution of a Supranational Level of Integration," *Social Problems* 11 (1963): 153-64; M. A. Adelman, "The World Oil Outlook" in Clawson (ed.), *Natural Resources and International Development*, pp. 27-125; Robert B. McNee, "Centrifugal-Centripetal Forces in International Petroleum Company Regions," *Annals, Association of American Geographers* 51 (1961):

modities, compounded by imbalances in the possession of technological skills and by divergent uses of a particular resource, give rise to conflicts. Conflicts over resources range in intensity from the proportions of Hitler's belligerent effort to acquire the Ukrainian breadbasket to conflicts of private interests susceptible to political settlement on the basis of the political effectiveness of the interests concerned.[54] The international dimensions of the resource problem are perhaps best illustrated by a comparatively minor but significant development that entails cooperation across a Cold War boundary, namely, the development since 1960 of a system for providing Hong Kong with water supplies from Communist China.[55]

What has just been said is undoubtedly obvious. But it is not so obvious that an area so inviting to international legal regulation as allocation of resources has been looked at from a systemic perspective. Such a perspective permits analysts to visualize the older undesirable cartels as system responses to otherwise insurmountable man-made barriers. The systems perspective is more than just an analytic viewpoint. It is also a decision-making perspective but only if decision-makers want to foresee the long-range consequences of what they do. Confined to identification of the momentary rights and wrongs that often overwhelm decision-makers and confine their responses to reactions to stimuli, the systems perspective can add little to intuition. A stab at the systems approach was indulged

---

124-38; Herbert S. Klein, "The Creation of the Patiño Tin Empire," *Inter-American Economic Affairs* 19 (Autumn, 1964): 63-74.

[54] On the latter type of conflict, see Marion E. Marts and W.R.D. Sewell, "The Conflict Between Fish and Power Resources in the Pacific Northwest," *Annals, Association of American Geographers* 50 (1960): 42-50. On the problem of the long stagnation of raw material export economies and the conflicts between host and investor countries, see Jonathan V. Levin, *The Export Economies* (Cambridge: Harvard University Press, 1960).

[55] John Rose, "Hong Kong's Water-Supply Problem and China's Contribution to Its Solution," *Geographical Review* 56 (1966): 432-37.

when journalists expressed fears that the supply of apparently cheap Soviet oil to Western Europe would detach countries from their Western orientations. Although cloaked with pseudo-profundity, neither sporadic fears of this type nor their opposite in the form of cloud-walking anticipation of extraordinary system-wide benefits from a new policy or a new law represent a true systems approach helpful to decision-making. Such an approach must be founded on syntheses of several more particular approaches, among them ecology and regional economics, that help to delineate the relations among suprasystems, systems, and subsystems.

It is not hard to find examples in which resources were allocated not on the basis of an economic landscape crossing political boundaries but on the basis of the latter alone. In the Canadian-American relationship alone there have been a number of ill-advised incidents. For example, when in 1952 the Paley Commission held that projected Free World demands for nickel to 1975 would be difficult to meet, United States procurement jumped to such an extreme that even high-cost marginal ores were exploited. This palliative produced so great a surplus in Defense Production Act inventories by 1957 that contracts were cancelled in 1959. Thereupon, Canadian nickel producers had to try to recover markets lost to other metals and to find new uses for their product. Until recently, competition between Canadian and American producers of lead and zinc produced attempts to protect American companies against Canadian firms that paid higher labor costs per ton of crude ore but obtained a higher value of lead and zinc per ton together with recoverable gold, silver, and copper. Protection included a freight-rate structure acknowledged by the Interstate Commerce Commission to have been discriminatory. As another example, United States encouragement of exploration for domestic sources of uranium ore while also arranging in 1952 to purchase the Canadian output led not only to the discovery by 1957 that the United States had the world's largest supply but also to the rapid exploitation thereof. Cancellation of options in 1959, even though mitigated by a stretch-out arrangement, had as one consequence the conversion of the model town of Elliot Lake, Ontario, completed in 1956, into a virtual ghost town until new markets were found.[56]

Only decisions based on a systems perspective capable of visualizing economies instead of nations could have produced decisions more considerate of enterprises and workers in another country.[57] An approach to a comprehensive systems approach was promised in the spring of 1963. After a meeting between President John F. Kennedy and Prime Minister John Diefenbaker, announcements were made that a comprehensive continental resources management policy would be formulated. Unfortunately, changes in leadership in both countries aborted this promising undertaking.

Energy Fuels and International Energy Systems

As HAS been stressed in various preceding sections, economic landscapes are highly complex structures even in their boundary subsystems. The same holds true for their more specific functional systems, particularly energy systems. Complexity is a feature of both the low energy systems of countries now seeking economic development and the high energy systems of industrial and advanced agricultural countries and regions. Whatever the correlation between the drops in national birth rates after a certain measure of industrialization, the coinci-

[56] For an overview of Canadian problems with respect to metals, see Wesley L. Gould, "Metals, Oil, and Natural Gas: Some Problems of Canadian-American Co-operation" in David R. Deener (ed.), *Canada-United States Treaty Relations* (Durham: Duke University Press, 1963), pp. 155-65.

[57] Canadian Metal Mining Association, "Submission to the United States Tariff Commission Presented on Behalf of the Lead and Zinc Producing Industry of Canada" (November, 1957), p. 8; reprinted in the *Department of State Bulletin* 42 (1960): 366.

dence of industrialization with the increase in global population suggests that high energy systems play a vital part in sustaining a global population above the three-quarter billion level. Clearly, coal mines and oil wells are more than holes in the ground. Pipelines, which in at least one legal conceptualization are adjuncts to oil refineries, are actually much more than adjuncts or long tubes. They are integral parts of social systems in terms of companies with a measure of *esprit de corps,* industries of grander scope than companies, and regions definable on the globe in terms of cost boundaries, transportation links, and interrelated general purpose communities with identifiable central cores.

Energy systems are essentially regional in nature, although ocean shipment even of refrigerated methane[58] provides extension of sources beyond the land transportation limits of the consuming regions. Thus, the Pacific Northwest subsystem of the North American energy system receives crude oil not only from Canadian sources but also by ship from Venezuela, the Middle East, North Borneo, and Alaska.[59] The mark of the older coal-based energy systems, which changed many of the geographical population distributions that had been set by sail,[60] is upon the newer systems that also make use of petroleum products, natural gas, and electric power. Yet one finds modifications of the pattern imposed by coal and steam, particularly in the American and Canadian West.

Three major international energy systems have come into being: the East European, the West European, and the North American. Each has extensions beyond its continental base for the procurement of fuel and for distribution purposes. Basic stages in the construction of the East European system were consolidation of the Silesian coal mines by the westward movement of the Polish-German border, acceptance by East Ger-

[58] M. Swiss, "Gas at Sea," *Europe and Oil* (November, 1964), 16-17.
[59] *Globe and Mail* (Toronto), May 26, 1961.
[60] Cottrell, *Energy and Society*, pp. 80-81.

many and Czechoslovakia of joint investment in new Polish coal mines, erection of an electricity grid with a central control office in Prague and its connection with the Soviet grid in 1963, and the building of the Druzhba Pipeline.[61]

The Western European system is complicated by the division between the Six and the Seven, by the establishment of three Communities among the Six although with fortunate rather early recognition of the need to rectify the original division, and by a multiplicity of agencies concerned with nuclear energy including OECD's European Nuclear Energy Agency, the European Center for Nuclear Research, and the International Atomic Energy Agency. Additional complications arise from French efforts, among other things, to build a vertically integrated system of production, refining, and distribution and to assure a French market for Saharan crude oil. What reserves of natural gas and petroleum lie under the North Sea remains to be proven, but distribution and priorities systems for natural gas have resulted from the Slochteren discovery in Groningen and the adjoining West German area. Conventional means now produce electricity for export from Switzerland and an Austro-German exchange of surplus summer power from Vorarlberg for thermally-produced German power in the winter peak period.

The North American energy system has several subsystems, particularly that of the Pacific Northwest which receives Peace River gas and Alberta crude oil, to be supplemented by the electricity that will be generated by the Columbia River development. Canadian oil and natural gas enter the Midwest and also the Lake Ontario region of New York. Alberta and Saskatchewan crude oil traverses the United States en route to Sarnia and Port Credit. The pipeline, from which a feeder

[61] Michael Kaser, *Comecon: Integration Problems of the Planned Economies* (London, New York, and Toronto: Oxford University Press, 1965), pp. 70-73; Georg Wedensky, "Achievements of the Soviet Oil and Gas Industries in 1964: Review of the Year," *Europe and Oil* (December, 1964), pp. 12-17.

runs to the Detroit-Toledo area, is now being looped via Chicago. Venezuelan crude reaches eastern Canada over the Montreal-Portland pipeline. And, of course, the eastern regions of the two countries are the beneficiaries of the generation of electric power at Niagara Falls and now along the St. Lawrence. Some natural gas is imported to and exported from Mexico,[62] but Mexican crude oil remains in that country. Clearly the tighter linkages of energy fuel and electric power trade are at the northern border and have been productive to date of relatively effective means of harmonizing the decisions of the Canadian National Energy Board and the Federal Power Commission concerning exports and imports, respectively. Of another color, and one of which Europeans and also the aspirants to a petroleum common market in Latin America[63] should take heed, is the problem of multiple public utilities and resource authorities which in Canada and the United States are found on the provincial and state levels.[64]

The existence of major energy systems that cannot restrain their growth within politically delimited territories but extend to economically determined limits—e.g., Canadian crude oil reaching southward along the West Coast only as far as it can compete with sea-borne crude—is suggestive of something that

[62] Federal Power Commission, Bureau of Natural Gas, *The Gas Supplies of Interstate Natural Gas Pipeline Companies, Calendar Years 1963 and 1964* (Washington, February, 1966), pp. 17-20.

[63] "Common Market is Aim of Latin Americans in ARPEL," *World Oil* 160 (May, 1965): 176, deals with the hopes of the Asistencia Reciproca Petrolera Estatal Latino-Americana, the organization of government oil companies of South America (except Ecuador which lacks a government oil company) and Mexico.

[64] More complete surveys of the three major energy systems in the setting of a systems perspective may be found in Wesley L. Gould, "International Energy Resources and National Values" (Paper presented at the First Plenary Session of Amintaphil, the American Section of the International Association for Philosophy of Law and Social Philosophy, St. Louis, November 28-30, 1966).

may also be derived from John Herz's thesis about the partial supersession of the territorial state. For it is evident that there have come into being regional systems that, as traditional units of the international system, warrant as much consideration and protection as do states. Nations or interconnected sections of nations tend to form a "stateless society," more likely governed by formally separate but actually interrelated boards of directors than by public authorities. To the extent that the welfare of peoples is dependent on their effective functioning, such entities may be more in need of protection than the nations that can disrupt them. But the same passions cannot be generated on behalf of such regions as in support of the nation. The common interest of the segments of transnational regions must be articulated by national voices.

Procedures before the National Energy Board and the Federal Power Commission permit divergent interests, committed to different priorities in the exploitation of various sources of energy, to be heard. Unlike the administrative actions in regard to metals, the proceedings in 1952 in regard to the Montana Power Company's request for Canadian natural gas saw Canada take action designed to assure the Anaconda Copper Mining Company an adequate supply of fuel.[65] Similarly, in more nearly juridical proceedings, in 1960 the National Energy Board permitted an export to the Puget Sound area, in part to enable the El Paso Natural Gas Company to divert other gas to California,[66] while the Alberta Oil and Gas Conservation Board's rejection in 1961 of a proposal for a large-scale movement of natural gas liquids to the United States appears to have been based in part upon the Board's recognition of a need to avoid dislocation of United States production.[67]

[65] Statutes of Alberta, 1951, c. 36; *The Montana Power Company, Opinion No. 223* (February 5, 1952), 11 F.P.C. 1.

[66] National Energy Board, "Report to the Governor in Council," March 21, 1960, section 8, 11.

[67] *Globe and Mail* (Toronto), July 18, 1961.

Much of the terminology in the official reports of these decisions is unavoidably in the traditional formulations pertinent to the political prominence of the territorial state. What is noteworthy is the officials' recognition that there are vital energy systems and social systems, not just dollar-seeking entities, that warrant protection and assistance in the performance of public service. Although lack of formal status leaves transnational regions inarticulate as units, there is unmeasurable significance in these first recognitions that valuable new interaction systems have emerged which need not be defined in terms of either fixed linear boundaries or ethnicity. In terms of both structure and process the fate of these emerging systems in a world beset by a population explosion may be more decisive than the more readily discernable fate of nations. International lawyers, reassessing their subject with the thought that its norms and procedures should have direct relationships with the several facets of international system and subsystem growth, would be remiss if their concern for formally organized public entities were to dull their perception of informal functional systems and the nonlegal data that suggests the desirability of adapting international law to the existence of those systems.

In the several chapters and sections of this book we have made reference to various topics, types of data, and research methods that can render international law a provocative subject for both lawyer and social scientist. It is certainly not a subject of purely technical and thus of secondary interest. If international law has taken on such a character, it is because the lawyer drew too little from other disciplines to present the law in its full vitality, while the social scientist allowed himself to ignore international law either through misconception of its relevance or for other reasons. We hope that we have demonstrated in these chapters and in the annotations to a bibliography which we are currently preparing that the proper multipronged study of international law as it is adapted to and productive of new norms and procedures for a highly interactive and communicative world of diverse cultures as well as a mixture of high energy and low energy societies and regions, can be an examination of the essence of international systems. Tools and concepts, imperfect and requiring improvement and supplementation as research problems are encountered, are at hand for the present and coming generations of scholars. How soon the latter are taught imaginatively and provided with enough stimulating examples in addition to the few presently available will determine just when the discipline of international law can be regarded as freed from the burdens of technicality, textual exegesis, and argumentation.

Subject Index

Index

Index

Index

Index

Index

Index

Index

Index

Index

Index

Index

Author Index

Index

Index

Index

Index

Index